THE ROUGH GUIDE TO

EDINBURGH

Forthcoming titles include

Chicago • Corfu • First-Time Around the World
Grand Canyon • Philippines
Skiing & Snowboarding in North America
South America • The Gambia
Walks In and Around London

Forthcoming reference titles include

Chronicle series: China, England,
France, India • Night Sky

read Rough Guides online

www.roughguides.com

Rough Guide Credits

Text editor: Polly Thomas
Series editor: Mark Ellingham
Production: Rachel Holmes
Cartography: Melissa Baker

Publishing Information

This third edition published July 2002
by Rough Guides Ltd,
62–70 Shorts Gardens, London, WC2H 9AH

Distributed by the Penguin Group:

Penguin Books Ltd, 80 Strand, London WC2R ORL
Penguin Putnam Inc., 375 Hudson Street, New York 10014, USA
Penguin Books Australia Ltd, 487 Maroondah Highway,
PO Box 257, Ringwood, Victoria 3134, Australia
Penguin Books Canada Ltd, 10 Alcorn Avenue,
Toronto, Ontario, Canada M4V 1E4
Penguin Books (NZ) Ltd,
182–190 Wairau Road, Auckland 10, New Zealand

Typeset in Bembo and Helvetica to an original design by Henry Iles.
Printed in Spain by Graphy Cems.

© Donald Reid 2002
368pp, includes index
A catalogue record for this book is available from the British Library.

ISBN 1-85828-887-8

THE ROUGH GUIDE TO

EDINBURGH

by Donald Reid

with additional contributions
by Ellie Buchanan

ROUGH
GUIDES

We set out to do something different when the first Rough Guide was published in 1982. Mark Ellingham, just out of university, was travelling in Greece. He brought along the popular guides of the day, but found they were all lacking in some way. They were either strong on ruins and museums but went on for pages without mentioning a beach or taverna. Or they were so conscious of the need to save money that they lost sight of Greece's cultural and historical significance. Also, none of the books told him anything about Greece's contemporary life – its politics, its culture, its people, and how they lived.

So with no job in prospect, Mark decided to write his own guidebook, one which aimed to provide practical information that was second to none, detailing the best beaches and the hottest clubs and restaurants, while also giving hard-hitting accounts of every sight, both famous and obscure, and providing up-to-the-minute information on contemporary culture. It was a guide that encouraged independent travellers to find the best of Greece, and was a great success, getting shortlisted for the Thomas Cook travel guide award, and encouraging Mark, along with three friends, to expand the series.

The Rough Guide list grew rapidly and the letters flooded in, indicating a much broader readership than had been anticipated, but one which uniformly appreciated the Rough Guide mix of practical detail and humour, irreverence and enthusiasm. Things haven't changed. The same four friends who began the series are still the caretakers of the Rough Guide mission today: to provide the most reliable, up-to-date and entertaining information to independent-minded travellers of all ages, on all budgets.

We now publish more than 150 titles and have offices in London and New York. The travel guides are written and researched by a dedicated team of more than 100 authors, based in Britain, Europe, the USA and Australia. We have also created a unique series of phrasebooks to accompany the travel series, along with an acclaimed series of music guides, and a best-selling pocket guide to the internet and World Wide Web. We also publish comprehensive travel information on our website: www.roughguides.com

Help us update

We've gone to a lot of trouble to ensure that this Rough Guide is as up to date and accurate as possible. However, things do change. All suggestions, comments and corrections are much appreciated, and we'll send a copy of the next edition (or any other Rough Guide if you prefer) for the best letters.

Please mark letters "Rough Guide Edinburgh Update" and send to:

Rough Guides, 62–70 Shorts Gardens, London, WC2H 9AH, or Rough Guides, 4th Floor, 345 Hudson St, New York NY 10014.

Or send an email to mail@roughguides.com
Have your questions answered and tell others about your trip at www.roughguides.atinfopop.com

Acknowledgements

Thanks to Maxine Repath and Melissa Baker for the maps, Rachel Holmes for typesetting, and John Sturges for proofreading.

The author would like to thank Ellie Buchanan for her enthusiastic research towards (and work on) the Festival chapter, Mo for her help with the galleries and museums (amongst other things) and Matt for his insight on the chapter in the Scotland guide and initial help with this edition. The assistance of Historic Scotland and the National Trust for Scotland, Edinburgh & Lothians Tourist Board, as well as Robin Hodge and *The List* magazine, is much appreciated. Particular thanks for getting this edition fighting fit go to the editor, Polly Thomas, and to all those at Rough Guides who have been part of it. Finally, my gratitude to all those friends and colleagues who have contributed hugely to my knowledge and appreciation of Edinburgh, and helped along the way with opinions, suggestions, good meals, coffees and encouragement. Finally, with special thanks to Mo, for all the best days in this city.

Readers' letters

David Clouston, Simon Brooke, Janet M. Gillingham,
Carole Gray, Liz Grumbach, Nils Jensen, Cheryl Johnson,
Alice Lear, Barbara Miller, Chrissie Newson, Donna
Ritenour, Simon Steele, Lisa Stewart, Jane Thompson,
Geoff Wilmott, Dan Wilson.

Cover credits

Main front picture © Francesca Yorke
Front (small image) Princes Street Gardens © Neil Setchfield
Back (top) Whisky sign © Jerry Dennis
Back (lower) Princes Street © Robert Harding

CONTENTS

Listings

Contexts

MAP LIST

Introduction

Perched on a series of extinct volcanoes and rocky crags, **EDINBURGH** enjoys a dramatic natural setting unrivalled by any other major European city. Arrive in the very heart of town – either by day, with an east wind tugging at the flags that seem to fly from every building, or by night, when floodlights float grand architecture above the streets – and you're at once gripped by Edinburgh's romantic historical essence, where ramparts and ridges, turrets and tenements crowd the eye. One native author of genius, Robert Louis Stevenson, declared that "No situation could be more commanding for the head of a kingdom; none better chosen for noble prospects".

In its layout and, many would argue, in its personality too, Edinburgh is divided into its **Old Town** and **New Town**, inscribed together on UNESCO's World Heritage List. The former, perched on the spinal ridge leading down from the majestic cliff-girt Castle, is often dark and mysterious, and still predominantly medieval; the latter, with its graceful Georgian terraces and Grecian architecture, is a planning masterpiece of the Age of Enlightenment, when Edinburgh was Europe's hotbed of intellectual endeavour. The Old Town swirls with gory tales of body-snatchers – crowded with Gothic detailing, its looming medieval housing and historic facades lend a very distinctive appearance and atmosphere – while the New Town, with its douce lawyers and canny bankers, captures the capital's deeply dyed respectability. Being a relatively small city, with a population of under half a million, there are also marked contrasts between the closely packed grandness of Edinburgh's centre and the grim, underprivileged housing estates of the outskirts, as portrayed on the big screen in *Trainspotting* – rarely seen by visitors, but still very much part of the modern city.

A royal capital from its earliest days, Edinburgh's status took a knock when James VI of Scotland left the city for London in 1603 to take up the British throne as James I. Just over a hundred years later, the Scottish parliament also disappeared as Westminster assumed control, and while Edinburgh never lost the style, appearance and trappings of a capital city, its self-importance rang hollow for many. However, the return of the **Scottish Parliament** to Edinburgh in 1999, after nearly three hundred years of rule from London, has lent renewed vigour to the political, commercial and cultural scenes, and Edinburgh is taking the opportunity to prove itself a dynamic, influential and thoroughly modern European capital. The recent opening of the new **National Museum of Scotland**, the redevelopment of **Leith** docklands, the rapid erection of new homes and offices in various parts of the city and the anticipated appearance of the architecturally ambitious Scottish **Parliament building**, due to be unveiled in 2003, are all contributing to this upturn in the city's vitality and spirit.

Above all, Edinburgh is a cultured capital, in part due to its rich literary and artistic connections, but also thanks to the unique creative outpouring of the **Edinburgh Festival**, the largest celebration of the arts in the world. The event draws around a million visitors to the city each August, and generates a carnival atmosphere matched only by the much shorter but even more boisterous celebrations at **Hogmanay**.

Edinburgh also maintains a vibrant **cultural life** throughout the year, with innovative theatre, energetic clubs, live music and heavyweight literary and artistic events. The social life of the city has been equally enlivened in recent years: a number of stylish new Modern Scottish **restaurants**, which use traditional local produce such as venison and salmon to create innovative new dishes, have begun to earn Edinburgh recognition on the culinary map. Long known as a great **drinking** city thanks both to its brewing and distilling traditions and its distinctive *howffs* (old pubs), Edinburgh now boasts a host of stylish bars and a thriving café culture, fuelled mainly by the presence of three universities, plus several colleges, which ensure a youthful presence for most of the year – a welcome corrective to the stuffiness which is often regarded as the city's Achilles heel.

Where to go

The city of Edinburgh spreads over a wide area: suburbs reach north to the shore of the Firth of Forth and south to the hills of Midlothian, and merge into the satellite towns of fertile East Lothian and industrialized West Lothian to the east and west. However, one of the capital's great attractions is that most of the main sights are concentrated in its historic core, and are easily explored on foot – though you do have to be prepared for some punishing inclines and steep flights of stairs.

Right in the heart of the city, it is undeniably **Edinburgh Castle** atop its crag which draws the eye. Still a working castle with a garrison of soldiers and a signal gun fired daily at 1pm, it's a pricey outing – but worth it for the chance to explore the battlements, mug-up on some of the more important moments in Scottish history, and take in some spectacular vistas over the city and its hinterland.

Running west to east from the Castle through the heart of the medieval **Old Town** is Scotland's most famous street, the **Royal Mile**, with its string of impressive and important buildings; however, it's just as rewarding to explore some of the numerous cobbled wynds (narrow lanes) and tightly packed closes which run off the main street. The Royal Mile ends at the **Palace of Holyroodhouse**, still the monarch's Scottish residence; opposite, and in dramatic contrast, is the **new Scottish Parliament**, the city's most important contemporary building. Providing a stunning backdrop to both, and offering a tantalizing sample of Scotland's wild scenic beauty, is **Holyrood Park**, an extensive area of open countryside in the very heart of the city that's dominated by the distinctive profile of **Arthur's Seat**, Edinburgh's highest point.

It's worth heading south of the Royal Mile to see some impressive individual buildings. These include the **Old College** of the University, a late masterpiece of Robert Adam, and the spectacular new **National Museum of Scotland**, a fusion of vernacular and modern styles in honey-coloured sandstone, which contains a wonderfully diverse and well laid-out collection of the nation's treasures, from hordes of Roman silver to items donated by local-boy-made-good Sir Sean Connery.

North of the Royal Mile, across Princes Street Gardens, lies the **New Town**. Its main thoroughfare, **Princes Street**, is dominated by high-street shops but also offers wonderful views of the Old Town skyline, while unexpected vistas of the Firth of Forth open out from the elevated streets to the north. There are many magnificent Neoclassical set pieces here, notably William Henry Playfair's **National Gallery of Scotland**, with its impressive collection of Old Masters and French Impressionist masterpieces; Adam's **Charlotte Square**; and the various Grecian edifices atop **Calton Hill**.

A little beyond the New Town's graceful crescents lie the beautifully laid-out grounds of the **Botanic Garden**, and the **Scottish National Gallery of Modern Art**, the city's most engaging gallery and Britain's oldest specialist collection of twentieth-century painting and sculpture.

Out from the centre, the seedy edge of **Leith**, Edinburgh's medieval port, is softened by a series of great bars, upmarket seafood restaurants and dockland developments, one of which provides a berth for the former royal yacht **Britannia**, a popular attraction for fans of the Royals and Britain's naval heritage. For open outlooks and a breath of fresh air, head on to the old fishing harbour of **Newhaven** or the trim village of **Cramond**, both on the Firth of Forth coast. Many points of interest in Edinburgh's **southern suburbs** are linked to the series of hills which rise here, notably **Craigmillar Castle**, a residence used by Mary, Queen of Scots; and the **Pentlands**, an easily accessible stretch of hills and moorland much appreciated by hikers and mountain bikers.

Edinburgh is well-placed for **day-trips** to other parts of central Scotland. **Glasgow**, Scotland's largest city and home to some stunning art and architecture, is only an hour's travel to the west, while historic **Stirling**, with its superb castle and proximity to the **Highlands**, is a similar distance to the northwest. **St Andrews**, ancient home of the game of golf, takes only a little longer to reach, while anyone keen on Scotland's history would do well to spend a bit of time exploring some spots closer to Edinburgh, including **Linlithgow**, with its soaring, roofless palace, and **East Lothian**, where ruins such as Tantallon Castle are among the country's most dramatic. If you've a car, a trip south into the **Border** region of rolling hills and ruined abbeys offers a taste of an appealing but relatively little-known stretch of open countryside.

When to visit

Edinburgh's **climate** is typically British: clear seasonal divisions ranging from snow in winter to scorching sun in summer, frequently changing weather conditions at any time of year and, overall, just a little bit too much **rain** for anyone's liking. However, Edinburgh's east-coast position ensures that the city suffers less rainfall than western parts of the country, though it is prone to blustery and often bitter **winds** blowing in off the North Sea. Another local phenomenon is the *haar* or **sea mist**, which is wont to roll in from the Firth of Forth and envelop the city after a few warm days in summer. The coldest months are January and February, when the highest daily temperature averages at

	F°		°C		RAINFALL	
	AVERAGE DAILY		AVERAGE DAILY		AVERAGE MONTHLY	
	MAX	MIN	MAX	MIN	IN	MM
Jan	42	34	6	1	2.2	57
Feb	43	34	6	1	1.5	39
March	46	36	8	2	1.5	39
April	51	39	11	4	1.5	39
May	56	43	14	6	2.1	54
June	62	49	17	9	1.9	47
July	65	52	18	11	3.3	83
Aug	64	52	18	11	3.0	77
Sept	60	49	16	9	2.2	57
Oct	54	44	12	7	2.6	65
Nov	48	39	9	4	2.4	62
Dec	44	36	7	2	2.2	57

6°C (42°F) and overnight frosts are common. July is the warmest month, reaching an average high of 18°C (65°F), although **late spring** (May) and **early autumn** (September) are often good times to visit for welcome spells of bright weather and less of the tourist scrum which marks the Royal Mile in high season. With the Festival in full swing, August is a great time to visit Edinburgh – but be prepared for large crowds, scarce accommodation and busy restaurants.

BASICS

BASICS

1

Arrival

I f you're flying into the city, you'll land at Edinburgh International Airport (℡0131/333 1000), seven miles west of the city centre at Turnhouse, close to the start of the M8 motorway to Glasgow. There's just the one terminal, with a small tourist board office in the international arrivals area (daily: April–Oct 6.30am–10.30pm; Nov–March 7.30am–9.30pm); while desks for all the main car rental companies are located by domestic arrivals. Bureaux de Change are located in international arrivals and on the first floor on the way through to departures. From immediately outside the terminal building, regular Airlink shuttle buses (£3.30) connect to Waverley Bridge in the town centre; taxis depart from a rank alongside the bus stop, and charge around £15 for the same journey.

BY TRAIN

Waverley Station (Map 4, K7), right in the centre of town at the eastern end of Princes Street, is the terminus for all mainline **trains**; for **timetable and fare enquiries** call ℡0845/748 4950. The main central exits take you out onto Waverley Bridge, where the Castle appears dramatically ahead of you and the Old Town skyline is to the south, with Princes Street to the north. The northern exit from Waverley leads up a stairway to Princes Street itself, while the southern exit leads to Market Street, the outer fringe of the Old Town. There's a second mainline train stop, **Haymarket Station** (Map 2, F5), just under two miles west on the lines from Waverley to Glasgow, Fife and the Highlands, although this is only really of use if you're staying nearby. The only **left-luggage** facilities are at Waverley Station, adjacent to platform 1 (daily 7am–11pm; from £3.50 per piece).

BY BUS

The main intercity **bus terminal** is located on St Andrew Square (Map 4, I4), a few minutes' walk north from Waverley Station. While a brand new bus station is being built under a shopping mall in the northeast corner of the square (it's due to be operational from late summer 2002), buses arrive and depart from stands on the square itself. A kiosk here displays timetables and sells tickets for a number of the local bus operators, as well as for Citylink and National Express intercity buses. A bank of **left-luggage lockers** is located in the square (£3 for up to 48 hours).

BY CAR

Central Edinburgh in not an easy place to navigate by car, with the medieval layout creating chronic traffic congestion, confusing road systems and poor through routes. A **ring road** (the A720), which can be particularly busy around rush hour, skirts around the southern edge of the city and links the main approaches to Edinburgh from the north and west (the A90 across the Forth Road Bridge, and the M8 motorway from Glasgow respectively) with the main approaches from the south and east (the A7, A68 and A1). If you're staying in Edinburgh, it's a good idea to contact your hotel or guesthouse in advance to find out about parking arrangements nearby – you may find it easiest to leave your car there and use public transport to get into the centre. Otherwise, parking restrictions such as resident-only zones and meter-controlled street parking come into force approximately a mile from Princes Street. Metered parking (tickets are available from grey meters on the pavement) gets more expensive the closer in you go – an average cost is £1/hour. There are a number of large **car parks** in the centre, notably at Castle Terrace immediately to the west of the Castle, the St James Centre at the top of Leith Walk and on New Street beside Waverley railway station. These are often busy and can be expensive (around £1.30 per hour, or £3.40–£4 for four hours).

BY FERRY

Ferries from Zeebrugge in Belgium dock at **Rosyth** on the Firth of Forth, about half an hour northwest of Edinburgh. More details on the daily, year-round service, operated by Superfast Ferries, can be found at ⓦwww.superfast.com; call ⓣ08000/681 676 to book tickets.

Information and maps

Edinburgh's main tourist office is at the top of Princes Mall near the northern entrance to Waverley train station on Princes Street (April & Oct Mon–Sat 9am–6pm, Sun 10am–6pm; May, June & Sept 9am–7pm, Sun 10am–7pm; July & Aug Mon–Sat 9am–8pm, Sun 10am–8pm; Nov–March Mon–Sat 9am–5pm, Sun 10am–4pm; ☎0131/473 3800, ⓦwww.edinburgh.org). Although inevitably flustered at the height of the season, it's efficiently run, with scores of free leaflets and a bank of computers available if you want to search for information on the web (£1 per 20min). For backpacker-related information, head to the Haggis Office at 60 High St (daily 9am–6pm; ☎0131/557 9393, ⓦwww.haggisadventures.com). Although their main function is to run minibus tours of Scotland, staff here are a good source of general information about the backpacker scene around Scotland, and can book hostels and inter-city coaches for you, as well as change money.

The best local events guide is fortnightly **listings** magazine *The List*, which provides coverage of the arts in

EDINBURGH ON THE WEB

ⓦ **www.edinburgh.org** Edinburgh and Lothian tourist board site, with a wealth of local info and an online accommodation booking service.

ⓦ **www.edinburgh.gov.uk** This Edinburgh City Council site gives the lowdown on local services, from transport to kids' facilities, and has lots of links.

ⓦ **www.edinburghfestivals.co.uk** A good gateway into all Edinburgh's major festivals, including the Fringe, Film Festival and Hogmanay.

ⓦ **www.theoracle.co.uk** A useful what's-on site with comprehensive listings and good links.

ⓦ **www.thegen.com** A virtual tour of Edinburgh using moving 360 degree panoramas – fascinating if you've a powerful computer.

ⓦ **www.rampantscotland.com** Excellent links directory, organized by subject, covering all aspects of Scotland.

ⓦ **www.origins.net** A good way to start searching for your long-lost Scottish ancestors, developed in association with the General Register Office of Scotland.

ⓦ **www.edinburgharchitecture.co.uk** Attractive site specializing in the capital's contemporary architecture and design, including six suggested tours, photos and details of the coolest restaurants and hotels.

ⓦ **www.scotchwhisky.net** Intensely flavoured pages packed with everything you could ever want to know about the amber nectar, including where to buy the stuff.

ⓦ **www.ceolas.org** Site specializing in Celtic music, both historical and contemporary, with lots of music to listen to.

ⓦ **www.geo.ed.ac.uk** Produced by the Geography Department of Edinburgh University. Follow the links to "Web Resources" and then to "Gateway to Scotland", which has excellent background information to all things Scottish, and a myriad of links.

INFORMATION AND MAPS

Edinburgh and Glasgow, as well as comprehensive details of forthcoming events; it costs £2.20 and is widely available in newsagents and bookshops The best **maps** of the wider city are Bartholomew's *Streetfinder Colour Atlas* or fold-out *Colour Map* (both £2.99).

Money

The basic unit of currency in Scotland is the pound sterling (£), divided into 100 pence (p). Bank of England banknotes are legal tender in Scotland; in addition, the Bank of Scotland, the Royal Bank of Scotland and the Clydesdale Bank issue their own banknotes. A number of shops and services (but by no means all) will accept payment in euros.

If you want to **change money** from another currency into pounds, the best bets are Post Offices, which will exchange currency commission-free, or the currency exchange bureau in the main tourist office (Mon–Wed 9am–5pm, Thurs–Sat 9am–6pm & Sun 10am–5pm), and beside platform one at Waverley Station (Sept–June

Mon–Sat 7.30am–9pm, Sun 8.30am–9pm; July–Aug Mon–Sat 7am–10pm, Sun 8am–10pm). Otherwise, try Thomas Cook, 28 Frederick St (Mon–Sat 9am–5.30pm). To change money after hours, try one of the upmarket hotels – but expect to pay a hefty commission charge.

You can also exchange money at **banks**; most branches open at 9am or 9.30am, and close between 3.30pm and 5.30pm. All of the main branches (listed on p.304) have **ATM machines**, and there are plenty more scattered around the city. If your card isn't from a UK issuer, check with your home bank to see if you can use it in the UK to withdraw local currency.

Getting around

The best way to navigate Edinburgh's compact centre is on foot. Getting around by car is notoriously problematic: traffic jams are commonplace and finding a parking place is difficult. Buses also suffer in the poor traffic flow, but do offer a fairly comprehensive and reliable service. If you're travelling between the centre and the suburbs, a bus is your best bet, though one or two suburbs to the east and northwest are served by suburban train lines. Taxis are common and useful late at night or when you're in a hurry, while the level of traffic congestion and high number of cycle lanes mean that a bike can be a speedy way of getting around, though the prevalence of hills and cobbled streets means that the ride isn't always smooth.

BUSES

Edinburgh is well served by **buses**, although even locals get confused by the number of companies offering competing services along similar routes. However, most bus stops now have a useful diagram indicating which services pass the stop and which routes they take. **Lothian Buses**, operated by the City Council, provides the most comprehensive service and its maroon double-decker buses are easily recognizable; all services referred to in the Guide are run by them unless otherwise stated. Timetables and passes are available from Lothian ticket centres on Waverley Bridge or 27 Hanover St (enquiry line ☎0131/555 6363), or from the City Council-run Traveline (☎0800/232323) at 2 Cockburn St. A good investment, especially if you're staying far out or want to explore the suburbs, is the £10.50 **pass** allowing a week's unlimited travel on Lothian Buses; you'll need a passport photo. You can also buy a day pass for £2.20 (£1.50 if you buy it after 9.30am, or £4.20 including the airport bus), or, of course, tickets from the driver, for which you'll need exact change – the most common **fare** is 80p.

On a number of busy arterial routes the single-decker buses, run as "City Buses" by **First Edinburgh** (part of the First Bus group; ☎0131/663 9233), have muscled their way onto Lothian Buses' patch, offering a slick service but also creating plenty of confusion as they run their own system

EDINBURGH TOURS BY DAY AND NIGHT

Open-top bus tours are big business in Edinburgh, with three rival companies taking largely similar routes round the main sights. All depart from Waverley Bridge and all allow you to get on and off at leisure, making them a useful means of dotting between the main sights if you're intent on a hard day's sightseeing; day tickets cost around £7. The most entertaining of the three are MacTours, who use a fleet of characterful vintage buses; the brightly coloured Edinburgh Tours use Walkman-style headsets to tell you about the sights rather than a live guide, but tapes are available in seven different languages.

Several companies offer walking tours, including Auld Reekie (☎0131/557 4700) and Mercat (☎0131/557 6464). Most concentrate on the sights and stories to be found on and around the Royal Mile, though they do also offer more specialized excursions, including visits to some of the hidden vaults and closes found underneath the Old Town. These vaults are reputedly haunted, and given the Old Town's spooky atmosphere it's no surprise that evening ghost tours are a popular event, often involving a guide dressed up in elaborate costume and a sidekick primed to scare the group by leaping out from shadowy corners along the way. All the above tours cost around £6 per person and depart regularly from various points along the Royal Mile; however, for camped-up ghoulishness it's worth paying a bit more for the deeply entertaining Witchery Tour (☎0131/225 6745; £7), which leaves from outside the *Witchery Restaurant* on Castlehill. Other specialist outings include the Edinburgh Literary Pub Tour mixing a pub crawl with extracts from local authors acted out along the way(☎ 0131/226 6665; £7); Geowalks offers guided walks up Arthur's Seat in the company of a qualified geologist (☎ 0131/555 5488; £4); while Rebustours do a trip tracing the footsteps of Inspector Rebus (see p.329), hero of Ian Rankin's bestselling detective novels (☎ 0131/557 6464; £6).

GETTING AROUND

of passes (day passes are £1.50, or £2 if travelling before 9.30am; a weekly pass offers unlimited travel for £8). First Edinburgh also run the majority of buses which link the capital with outlying towns and villages; most services depart from and terminate at or near St Andrew Square. A desk in the tourist office on Princes Mall provides information on all local, regional and national buses, including those run by Lothian, First Edinburgh and Citylink.

TAXIS

The city has plenty of **taxi** ranks, and you can also hail black cabs on the street. **Fares** are reasonable – a journey from the city centre to Leith, for example, will cost around £5. The main local cab companies are: Capital Castle Cabs (☎0131/228 2555); Central Radio Taxis (☎0131/229 2468); and City Cabs (☎0131/228 1211).

CARS

It is emphatically *not* a good idea to take a **car** into central Edinburgh: despite the presence of several expensive multistorey car parks, finding somewhere to park involves long and often fruitless searches. Traffic calming has been introduced in several key areas – Princes Street is now one-way for cars and Charlotte Square has adopted a complicated traffic-flow system – and there is a growing network of green-painted bus lanes called "greenways", which must be left clear during rush hours. In addition, Edinburgh's street **parking** restrictions are famously draconian: residents' zone parking areas and double-yellow lines are no-go areas at all times, while cars parked for more than five minutes on single yellow lines or in overdue parking-meter-controlled areas are very likely to be fined £30 by one of the swarms of

CAR RENTAL COMPANIES

Arnold Clark, Lochrin Place ☎ 0131/229 8911.

Avis, 100 Dalry Rd ☎ 0131/337 6363.

Budget, 394 Ferry Rd ☎ 0800/181181.

Europcar, 24 East London St ☎ 0131/557 3456.

Hertz, Waverley Station ☎ 0131/557 5272.

Mitchells, 32 Torphichen St ☎ 0131/229 5384.

Thrifty, 42 Haymarket Terrace ☎ 0131/337 1319.

parking inspectors who patrol day and night. In severe cases, cars can be towed away, with a retrieval fee of £120. Most ticket and parking-meter regulations cease at 6.30pm Monday to Friday, and at 1.30pm on Saturday.

A car becomes a lot more useful if you're planning to visit some of the attractions on the outskirts of the city and beyond, although a number of the principal destinations for day trips out of the city, such as Glasgow, Stirling and North Berwick, are easily reached by train. **Renting a car** is reasonably easy, although it's always worth booking a vehicle as far ahead as possible, particularly for weekend use. Of the companies listed in the box above, local operator Arnold Clark offer very competitive rates, good service and a low insurance excess.

BICYCLES

Edinburgh is a reasonably cycle-friendly city – although hilly – with several **cycle paths**. The local cycling action group, Spokes (☎ 0131/313 2114, ⓦ www.spokes.org.uk), publishes an excellent cycle map of the city (£4.95); it's available from Spokes and from local bookshops and cycle stores. For **bike rental**, try Biketrax, 13 Lochrin Place

GETTING AROUND

(☎0131/228 6333), near Tollcross, or Edinburgh Cycle Hire, 29 Blackfriars St (☎0131/556 5560), just off the Royal Mile; the latter stocks everything from old boneshakers to state-of-the-art mountain bikes, along with accessories such as panniers and child seats. All of these outlets charge around £10 to rent a bike for 4–5 hours, or £15 for 24 hours; locks are included in the price. ID is required, and you'll need to leave a credit card imprint as a deposit.

Newspapers and radio

The principal British daily newspapers are all available in Scotland, many appearing in a special Scottish edition. The *Scotsman* is Edinburgh's quality daily broadsheet with reasonable coverage of national and international news, and is strong on the arts. Its sister paper, the tabloid

Evening News, hits the streets around midday and covers local Edinburgh news, while the sensationalist *Daily Record* is Scotland's most widely read tabloid. On Sundays, the locally produced heavy is the *Scotland on Sunday*, from the same stable as the *Scotsman*, with decent coverage of arts, sport and local and international political round-ups.

Among the local **radio stations**, the best for news, current affairs, sport and arts is BBC Radio Scotland (93.4FM and 810MW). For contemporary music and local gossip, try the main commercial stations Radio Forth (97.3FM), Real Radio (100.3FM) or the dance-based Beat 106 (106.1FM and 105.7FM).

NEWSPAPERS AND RADIO

THE GUIDE

THE GUIDE

Edinburgh Castle

The imposing bulk of **Edinburgh Castle** dominates the skyline of the entire city from atop its volcanic crag. With formidable sheer rockfaces on three sides, it requires no great imaginative feat to comprehend the strategic importance that underpinned the Castle's, and hence Edinburgh's, pre-eminence within Scotland. Would-be attackers, like modern tourists, were forced to approach the Castle from the crag to the east, along which the Royal Mile runs down to Holyrood.

The Castle's disparate styles reflect its many changes in usage, as well as advances in military architecture: the oldest surviving part, **St Margaret's Chapel**, is from the twelfth century, while the most recent additions date back to the 1920s. Nothing remains from its period as a seat of the Scottish court in the reign of Malcolm III (the king who overthrew Macbeth in 1057), and there are very few traces of the fortifications built during the Castle's most turbulent period, the Wars of Independence. Indeed, having been lost to (and subsequently recaptured from) the English on several occasions, the defences were dismantled by the Scots themselves in 1313, and only rebuilt in 1356 when the return of King David II from captivity in England introduced a modicum of political stability. Thereafter, the fortress gradually developed into Scotland's premier castle, with the dual function of fortress and royal palace. It last saw action in 1745, when the Young Pretender's forces, fresh from their victory at Prestonpans, made a half-hearted attempt to storm it, but gave up when cannon fire from the Castle resulted in civilian casualties. Subsequently, advances in weapons technology diminished the Castle's importance, but under the influence of the Romantic movement it came to be seen as a great national monument. A grandiose "improvement" scheme, which would have transformed the Castle into a bloated nineteenth-century vision of the Middle Ages, was considered, but only a few elements of the design, such as the present Gatehouse, were actually built.

Though you can easily take in the views and wander round the Castle yourself, you might like to join one of the somewhat overheated **guided tours** (included in entrance fee), with their talk of war, boiling oil and the roar of the cannon. Alternatively, **audioguides** (£3), with personal headphones and a black box into which you punch different numbers depending on which part of the Castle you're in, are available from a booth just inside the gatehouse. Both the guided tours and audio guides are included in the entrance price.

Edinburgh Castle is open daily (April–Oct 9.30am–6pm; Nov–March 9.30am–5pm; £8); the entrance fee covers all attractions within the Castle confines. Tickets should be purchased from the booth by the Gatehouse, on the Esplanade.

The Esplanade

Map 3, C3.

The Castle is approached via the **Esplanade**, a parade ground laid out in the eighteenth century and enclosed a

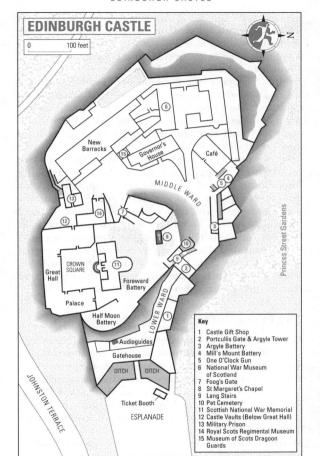

EDINBURGH CASTLE

0   100 feet

N

New Barracks

Governor's House

Café

MIDDLE WARD

Princes Street Gardens

New Barracks

Crown Square

Great Hall

Foreward Battery

Palace

Half Moon Battery

LOWER WARD

Audioguides

Gatehouse

DITCH   DITCH

JOHNSTON TERRACE

Ticket Booth

ESPLANADE

Key
1 Castle Gift Shop
2 Portcullis Gate & Argyle Tower
3 Argyle Battery
4 Mill's Mount Battery
5 One O'Clock Gun
6 National War Museum
   of Scotland
7 Foog's Gate
8 St Margaret's Chapel
9 Lang Stairs
10 Pet Cemetery
11 Scottish National War Memorial
12 Castle Vaults (Below Great Hall)
13 Military Prison
14 Royal Scots Regimental Museum
15 Museum of Scots Dragoon
   Guards

21

hundred years later by ornamental walls, the southern of which commands fine views of the Pentland Hills. For most of the year it acts as a coach park, though in July and August grandstands are erected for the Edinburgh Military Tattoo (see p.296), which takes place every night during August, coinciding with the Edinburgh Festival. A shameless and spectacular pageant of swinging kilts and massed pipe bands, the tattoo makes full use of its dramatic setting. An unfortunate side effect of this is that the skyline is disfigured for virtually the entire summer by the contours of the huge grandstands.

In the northeast corner of the esplanade are two reminders of unhappy times. An Art Nouveau **drinking fountain** on the wall of the Weaving Centre (see p.32) is decorated with reliefs of witches' heads entwined by a snake and marks the spot where some three hundred women deemed to be witches were burned at the stake between 1479 and 1722. Nearby, an equestrian statue of **Field Marshal Earl Haig** recalls the controversial Edinburgh-born commander of the British forces in World War I, whose trench warfare strategy of sending men "over the top" led to previously unimaginable casualties.

The lower defences

At the western end of the Esplanade, the single entrance to the Castle is the **Gatehouse**, a Romantic-style addition from the 1880s, complete with the last drawbridge ever built in Scotland. It was later adorned with appropriately heroic-looking statues of Sir William Wallace and Robert the Bruce. Standing guard by the drawbridge are real-life soldiers, members of the duty regiment in residence at the Castle; while their presence in full dress uniform is always a hit with camera-toting tourists, it's also a reminder that the

Castle is still a working military garrison and the headquarters of the Royal Scots Dragoon Guards.

Rearing up behind is the most distinctive and impressive featureof the Castle's silhouette, the imposing curved curtain wall of the sixteenth-century **Half Moon Battery**, which dominates the only side of the Castle not protected by sheer cliffs and marks the outer limit of the actual defences. Once through the gatehouse, you can pick up an audio guide from the booth immediately opposite; otherwise continue uphill along Lower Ward, passing through the **Portcullis Gate**, a handsome Renaissance gateway marred by the nineteenth-century addition of an upper storey, known as the **Argyle Tower**, complete with anachronistic arrow slits. The tower was named after Archibald, ninth Earl of Argyll, said to have been imprisoned in a room above the Portcullis Gate prior to his execution in 1685.

Beyond this, the wide main path is known as Middle Ward; you'll see the six-gun **Argyle Battery** to the right. This was built in the eighteenth century by Major General Wade, whose network of military roads and bridges still forms an essential part of the transport infrastructure of the Highlands. Further west on **Mill's Mount Battery**, a well-known Edinburgh ritual takes place – the firing of the **One O'clock Gun** (Mon–Sat). Originally designed for the benefit of ships in the Firth of Forth, it serves as an enjoyable spectacle for visitors these days, as well as a useful time signal for city centre office workers. There's an interesting little exhibition about the history of the firing of the gun in a room immediately below Mill's Mount Battery, including various reminiscences of the staff sergeant who has been in charge of the gun since 1978. Known to all as "Tam the Gun", he takes great delight in totting up the number of tourists who approach him to ask what time the One

THE LOWER DEFENCES

O'clock Gun is fired. The first gun to be used as a regular time signal, in 1861, was a huge 64-pound muzzle-loader which required four men to operate; these days, Tam's job is made a bit easier by the fact that a 105mm light gun has recently replaced the 25-pounder which had done service for the last quarter-century. Both batteries offer wonderful panoramic views over Princes Street and the New Town to the coastal towns and hills of Fife across the Forth.

National War Museum of Scotland

In the northwest corner of the Castle, immediately behind the café/restaurant adjacent to the One O'clock Gun, the old hospital buildings are now home to the **National War Museum of Scotland** (free; same hours as Castle), a worthwhile diversion if you're particularly interested in the Castle's military associations. Part of the National Museums of Scotland, it's a recently refurbished exhibition covering the last 400 years of Scottish military history. Scots have been fighting for much longer than that, of course, but the slant of the museum is very definitely towards the soldiers who fought *for* the Union, rather than against it (or against themselves). The rooms are packed with uniforms, medals, paintings of heroic actions and plenty of interesting memorabilia, but the displays veer away from being too triumphalist, reflecting the fears and insecurities of ordinary soldiers, as well as the hardships of life in the services. The curators have shown a similar sensitivity in displaying no favouritism to any one of the many different Scottish regiments, each of which has strong traditions more forcefully paraded in the various regimental museums found in different parts of Scotland – the Royal Scots and the Scots Dragoon Guards, for instance, both have displays in other parts of Edinburgh Castle.

St Margaret's Chapel and around

Uphill from the museum, back on Middle Ward, the **Governor's House** is a 1740s mansion whose harled masonry and crow-stepped gables are archetypal features of vernacular Scottish architecture. It now serves as officers' mess for members of the garrison, while the governor himself lives in the northern side wing. Behind stands the largest single construction in the Castle complex, the **New Barracks**, built in the 1790s in an austere Neoclassical style and still used to accommodate soldiers garrisoned in the Castle. From here a cobbled road snakes round towards the enclosed citadel at the uppermost point of Castle Rock; entered via **Foog's Gate**, it contains the Castle's most important buildings.

Standing at the eastern end of the citadel, twelfth-century **St Margaret's Chapel** is the oldest surviving building in the Castle, and probably in Edinburgh itself. Although once believed to have been built by the saint herself, and mooted as the site of her death in 1093, the chapel's architectural style suggests that it dates from about thirty years later, and was thus probably built by King David I as a memorial to his mother. Used as a powder magazine for three hundred years, this tiny Norman church was eventually rededicated in 1934, after sympathetic restoration. It's plain and austere externally, but the interior preserves an elaborate zigzag archway dividing the nave from the sanctuary.

The battlements in front of the chapel offer the best of all the Castle's panoramic views, and are interrupted by the **Lang Stairs**, which provide an alternative means of access from the Argyle Battery via the side of the Portcullis Gate. Just below the battlements there's a small and immaculately maintained **cemetery**, the last resting place of the soldiers' pets. Continuing eastwards, you skirt the top of the

ST MARGARET'S CHAPEL AND AROUND

Foreward and Half Moon batteries. The latter stands on the site of David's Tower, which was the setting for the infamous Black Dinner in 1440, when the keeper of the Castle, Sir William Crichton (effectively the guardian of the nine-year-old King James II, son of the murdered James I), arranged for a potential rival, the Earl of Douglas, and his younger brother to attend a meal in the tower. After a huge banquet, the visitors were presented with a bull's head – a sign of condemnation to death. They were accused of treason and summarily executed in the Castle courtyard.

Crown Square

Immediately behind Half Moon Battery is the 108-foot Castle Well, which you pass on the way into Crown Square, the highest, most secure and most important section of the entire Castle complex. The buildings around the square include the Royal Palace and banqueting hall used by James IV and his granddaughter, Mary, Queen of Scots. The former is now the secure home of the Honours of Scotland – Scotland's Crown Jewels.

The Palace

The eastern side of Crown Square is occupied by the Palace, a surprisingly unassuming edifice built round an octagonal stair turret, heightened in the nineteenth century to bear the Castle's main flagpole. Begun in the 1430s, the Palace owes its Renaissance appearance to King James IV, though it was remodelled for Mary, Queen of Scots and her husband Henry, Lord Darnley, whose entwined initials (MAH), together with the date 1566, can be seen above one of the doorways. This doorway gives access to a few historic rooms, the most interesting of which is the tiny panelled bedchamber at the extreme southeastern corner, where Mary gave birth to James VI. Along with the rest of the Palace, the room was revamped for James's triumphant homecoming in 1617, though this was to be the last time it served as a royal residence.

The rest of the Palace has recently been refurbished, and there's now a detailed audiovisual presentation on the **Honours of Scotland**, the originals of which are housed in the Crown Room at the very end of the display. Though you might be put off by the slow-moving, claustrophobic queues that shuffle past the displays, the interest in them is justified: these magnificent crown jewels – the only pre-Restoration set in the United Kingdom – serve as one of the most potent images of Scotland's nationhood. They were last used for the Scottish-only coronation of Charles II in 1651, an event which provoked the wrath of Oliver Cromwell, who made exhaustive attempts to have the jewels melted down. Having narrowly escaped his clutches by being smuggled out of the Castle and hidden in a rural church, the jewels later served as symbols of the absent monarch at sittings of the Scottish Parliament before being locked away in a chest following the Union of 1707. For over a century they were out of sight and eventually presumed lost, before being rediscovered in 1818 as a result of a search initiated by Sir Walter Scott.

Of the three pieces comprising the Honours, the oldest is the **sceptre**, which bears statuettes of the Virgin and Child, St James and St Andrew, rounded off by a polished globe of rock crystal: it was given to James IV in 1494 by Pope Alexander VI, and refashioned by Scottish craftsmen for James V. Finer still is the **sword**, a swaggering Italian High Renaissance masterpiece by the silversmith Domenico da Sutri, presented to James IV by Pope Julius II. Both the hilt and the scabbard are engraved with Julius's personal emblem, showing the oak tree and its acorns, the symbols

CROWN SQUARE

THE STONE OF DESTINY

Legend has it that the Stone of Destiny (also called the Stone of Scone) was "Jacob's Pillow", on which Jacob dreamed of the ladder of angels stretching from earth to heaven. Its real history is obscure, but it is known that it was moved from Ireland to Dunadd by missionaries, and thence to Dunstaffnage, from where Kenneth MacAlpine, king of the Dalriada Scots, brought it to the abbey at Scone in 838. It remained there for almost five hundred years and was used as a coronation throne on which all kings of Scotland were crowned.

In 1296, an over-eager Edward I stole what he believed to be the Stone and installed it at Westminster Abbey, where (apart from a brief interlude in 1950 when it was removed in a daring raid by Scottish nationalists and hidden in Arbroath for a couple of months) it remained for seven hundred years. In December 1996, after an elaborate ceremony-laden journey from London, the Stone was finally returned to Scotland, one of many doomed attempts by the Conservative government to convince the Scottish people that the Union was a jolly good thing. Much to the annoyance of the people of Perth and the curators of Scone Palace, and to the general indifference of the Scottish public, the Stone was placed in Edinburgh Castle, where its squat, rather sullen grey appearance makes an odd contrast to the glittering array of jewels and precious metals of the Honours of Scotland.

However, speculation surrounds the authenticity of the Stone, for the original is said to have been intricately carved, while the one seen today is a plain block of sandstone. Many believe that the canny monks at Scone palmed this off on to the English king (some say that it's nothing more sacred than the cover for a medieval septic tank) and that the real Stone of Destiny lies hidden in an underground chamber, its whereabouts a mystery to all but a chosen few.

of the risen Christ, together with dolphins, symbols of the Church. The jewel encrusted **crown**, made for James V by the Scottish goldsmith James Mosman, incorporates the gold circlet worn by Robert the Bruce and is surmounted by an enamelled orb and cross. The glass case containing the Honours has recently been rearranged to create space for a new addition, the **Stone of Destiny** (see box on opposite), a block of rough sandstone little larger than a hefty dictionary, with a rusty iron hoop at either end.

The Great Hall and National War Memorial

The south side of Crown Square is occupied by the **Great Hall**, built during the reign of James IV as a venue for banquets and other ceremonial occasions. Until 1639, the hall was the meeting place of the Scottish Parliament; since then it has served variously as a barracks and a hospital. During this latter period, its hammerbeam roof – the earliest in the city – was hidden from view, but it was restored towards the end of the nineteenth century when the hall was decked out in the full-blown Romantic manner.

In 1755, the Castle church of St Mary on the north side of the square was replaced by a barracks, which in turn was skilfully converted into the quietly reverential **Scottish National War Memorial** in honour of the 150,000 Scots who fell in World War I. This dignified and moving space, designed by Sir Robert Lorimer, incorporates a shrine in which a casket contains a list of the names of all those who died.

The rest of the complex

From Crown Square, you can descend to the **Vaults**, a series of cavernous chambers erected by order of James IV to provide an even surface for the showpiece buildings above. They were later used as a prison for captured foreign nationals, who have bequeathed a rich legacy of graffiti, the most telling being the figure of "Lord Nord" (Lord North, prime minister during the American War of Independence), dangling from a gallows. One of the rooms houses the famous fifteenth-century siege gun, **Mons Meg**, which could fire a 500-pound stone nearly two miles. A seventeenth-century visitor, the London poet, John Taylor, commented: "It is so great within, that it was told me that a child was once gotten there". Mons Meg was used in a number of sieges, but, because of its huge size, could only be transported three miles a day and was soon relegated to ceremonial status. In 1754, it was taken to the Tower of London, where it stayed till Sir Walter Scott persuaded George IV, on the occasion of his 1822 state visit to Scotland, to return it.

Directly opposite the entrance to the Vaults is the **Military Prison**, built in 1842, when the design and function of jails was a major topic of public debate. Although generally used as a military prison, civilian offenders were also confined here during World War I, the most notable being the Marxist John Maclean, who was later to found the Workers' Republican Party. The cells, though designed for solitary confinement, are less forbidding than might be expected.

THE REST OF THE COMPLEX

The Royal Mile

The **Royal Mile**, the name given to the road which travels down along the crest of the ridge linking the Castle with the Palace of Holyroodhouse, was described by Daniel Defoe in 1724 as "the largest, longest and finest street for Buildings and Number of Inhabitants, not in Bretain only, but in the World". Its unique character remains today, with higgledy-piggledy housing, cobbled street and intriguing medieval closes and courtyards. Closely linked to centuries of Scottish history, the Royal Mile remains very much at the heart of Scotland's political life – the new Scottish Parliament is based here, housed temporarily in the Assembly Hall until 2003, when it's scheduled to move to more permanent premises at the Holyrood end of the Royal Mile.

The mile-long street is divided into four separate sections – **Castlehill**, **Lawnmarket**, the **High Street** and the **Canongate**. Branching off from these at right angles are a series of tightly packed closes and steep lanes, entered via archways known as pends. After the construction of the New Town in the 1700s, the tenements on these closes degenerated into notorious slums, but the area has since been transformed, once again becoming a highly desirable place to live. Indeed, the bustle of everyday life is very much part of the atmosphere of the Royal Mile, although it does become a little less pleasant during the summer months when thousands of visitors meander their way along, and the drone of bagpipes being played by buskers at various different locations starts to grate with even the most patriotic of locals. While parts of the street have been marred by too many tacky tourist shops and the odd misjudged new development, it is still one of the most evocative parts of the city, and one that particularly rewards detailed exploration.

CASTLEHILL

Map 3, C8.

The uppermost stretch of the Royal Mile is known as **Castlehill**. Heading downhill from the Castle Esplanade, this is the narrowest section of the Royal Mile, with large old stone buildings looming up on either side. On the northern side of the street, the first building is the former Old Town reservoir, now converted into the **Edinburgh Old Town Weaving Centre** (daily 9am–5.30pm). Very much a commercial enterprise, the complex contains various large shops selling kilts, rugs and other tartan adornments, while noisy looms rhythmically churn the stuff out on the floors below. You can see these up close and try your hand at weaving on a self-guided tour (£4), or dress up in rather ridiculous-looking ancient tartan dress and have your photo snapped (£7).

Rising up behind the Weaving Centre are the red-and-white turrets of **Ramsay Gardens**, surely one of the most picturesque blocks of city-centre flats in the world. The oldest part is the octagonal Goose Pie House, once home of the eighteenth-century poet Allan Ramsay, author of *The Gentle Shepherd* and father of the better-known portrait painter of the same name. During the Jacobite Rebellion of

1745, while Ramsay stayed safely away from the hurly-burly, the house's strategic position near the Castle was utilized by Bonnie Prince Charlie's soldiers for shooting at the Castle sentries. The rest of the block dates from the 1890s and was the brainchild of Patrick Geddes, a pioneer of the modern town planning movement who created these desirable apartments in an attempt to bring the middle classes back to the main streets of the Old Town. Geddes' hope was that "the dingy grey of our cities gain something of the pure azures and flash across its smoky wilderness the gleam of Renaissance hope". In later life, as his Scottish experiment floundered, Geddes went off to pursue his ideals in Grenoble and India. His lasting legacy is the revival of the Old Town, while the student residences he established at nearby Milne's Court are still in use today.

Back on Castlehill, opposite the Weaving Centre, the so-called **Cannonball House** takes its name from the cannonball embedded in its masonry, which according to legend was the result of a poorly targeted shot fired by the Castle garrison at Bonnie Prince Charlie's encampment at Holyrood. The truth, however, is far more prosaic: the ball simply marks the gravitation height of the city's first piped water supply.

Scotch Whisky Heritage Centre

Map 3, C8. Daily: June–Sept 9.30am–6.30pm; Oct–May 10am–5.30pm; tour £6.50; barrel-ride only £4.50.

Just downhill from Cannonball House, the **Scotch Whisky Heritage Centre** gives the lowdown on all aspects of Scotland's national beverage. The full tour starts off with a free dram (a measure) of whisky and then launches into a detailed explanation of how it's made, with a film, a brief lecture and a visit from an entertaining "ghost" who

CASTLEHILL

explains some of the specialized art of blending whisky. The climax is a gimmicky ride in a moving "barrel" through a series of uninspiring historical tableaux, although all in all there's little on offer here which you won't find done rather better on a tour of a real distillery. The centre's **shop**, with its dozens of different brands, will give whisky novices an idea of the sheer range and diversity of the drink.

The Outlook Tower and Assembly Hall

Map 3, C8.

Across the street, the **Outlook Tower** (April–Oct Mon–Fri 9.30am–6pm, Sat & Sun 10am–6pm; Nov–March daily 10am–5pm; £4.25) has been one of Edinburgh's top tourist attractions since 1853, when the original seventeenth-century tenement was equipped with a **camera obscura**. It makes a good introduction to the city: panoramic images are beamed on to a white table in the auditorium, accompanied by a running commentary. For the best views, visit at noon when there are fewer shadows. The viewing balcony is one of Edinburgh's best vantage points, and there are exhibitions on pinhole photography, holography, Victorian photographs of the city, as well as topographic paintings made between 1780 and 1860.

A few doors further on is the **Assembly Hall**, built in 1859 for the breakaway Free Church. Nowadays, however, it is where the annual General Assembly of the Church of Scotland usually meets, though since May 1999 it has been temporarily displaced by the Scottish Parliament, awaiting a more permanent home in Holyrood (see the box opposite). The Hall is nothing to look at from the Royal Mile side; at its northern entrance, on Mound Place, however, stand the twin towers which feature so prominently in the Old Town's skyline.

CASTLEHILL

THE SCOTTISH PARLIAMENT

Modern Scottish politics were defined on September 11 1998, when a referendum saw an overwhelming majority of the Scottish electorate vote to establish a national parliament – the first since the Treaty of Union between England and Scotland in 1707. Following elections to the Parliament the following year, a coalition government was formed by Labour and Liberal Democrat MSPs (Members of the Scottish Parliament). The main opposition party is the Scottish National Party (SNP), which favours complete independence from the UK. Made up of 129 MSPs, the devolved Parliament governs most aspects of Scottish affairs, including education, health and transport, while Westminster retains control over matters such as foreign affairs, defence and macroeconomic policy.

While the Labour/Lib Dem administration has displayed a certain determination in pursuing policies divergent from the Labour government in London, including land reform and the abolition of student tuition fees, it has also been dogged by rows over the cost of its new home at Holyrood (see p.59), as well as the sudden death of much respected First Minister Donald Dewar in 2000 and the resignation of his successor, Henry McLeish, barely a year later.

Until the completion of the Holyrood building in 2003, Parliament meets in the Church of Scotland Assembly Hall on the Lawnmarket. When Parliament is in session, you can watch debates from the large public gallery – free tickets are available from the public entrance in Milne's Court on the Lawnmarket, and from the Scottish Parliament visitor centre on the corner of George IV Bridge and the High Street (☏0131/348 5000, ⓦwww.scottish.parliament.uk). The liveliest debate is First Minister's Questions on Thursday afternoon. If Parliament isn't in session, you can view the empty debating chamber from the public gallery, where stewards are on hand to answer questions.

CASTLEHILL

The Hub

Map 3, C8. Daily 8am–late; ⊤0131/473 2010,
ⓦwww.eif.co.uk/thehub.

The imposing black church building opposite the Assembly
Hall at the foot of Castlehill is **The Hub**; also known as
"Edinburgh's Festival Centre", it's the first permanent home
of the Edinburgh International Festival since the event's
inception in 1947. Although the Festival only takes place
for three weeks every August and early September, The
Hub is open year round, providing performance, rehearsal
and exhibition space, and holding a ticket centre (see p.245)
and a café. The building itself was constructed in 1845 to
designs by James Gillespie Graham and Augustus Pugin,
one of the co-architects of the Houses of Parliament in
London – a connection obvious from the superb neo-
Gothic detailing and the sheer presence of the building,
whose spire is the highest in Edinburgh. It was built as an
Assembly Hall for the Church of Scotland, and became a
parish church when the assembly moved to the United Free
Church hall across the road. On the ground floor level is
the vivid yellow *Hub Café* (see p.199); also worth checking
out is the main hall upstairs, where the original neo-Gothic
woodwork and high-vaulted ceiling are enlivened with a
fabulous fabric design in Rastafarian colours. Permanent
works of art have been incorporated into the centre: lining
the walls of the main stairwell, for example, are over two
hundred delightful foot-high sculptures by Scottish sculptor
Jill Watson, depicting Festival performers and audiences.

LAWNMARKET

Map 3, D8.
Below The Hub, the Royal Mile opens out into the much
broader expanse of **Lawnmarket**, which was once the set-

ting for a linen market, "lawn" being a corruption of "Laon", a town in France where the fabric was made. At its northern end is the entry to **Milne's Court**, whose excellently restored tenements now serve as student residences. Temporarily parked in the courtyard here is a rather incongruous-looking steel-and-glass construction – the public entrance to the Scottish Parliament's debating chamber in the Assembly Hall (open Mon–Fri 10am–noon & 2–4pm; free; see also box on p.35). Immediately beyond, **James Court** was one of Edinburgh's most fashionable addresses before the New Town was built, counting David Hume and James Boswell among its residents.

Gladstone's Land

Map 3, D8. April–Oct Mon–Sat 10am–5pm, Sun 2–5pm; £3.50.
Back on Lawnmarket itself, a taste of life on the Royal Mile in the seventeenth century can be found at **Gladstone's Land**, a magnificent six-storey mansion which takes its name from the merchant Thomas Gledstane [sic], who in 1617 acquired a modest dwelling on the site, and transformed it into the building you see today. The Gledstane family are thought to have occupied the third floor, renting out the rest to merchants in the style of tenement occupation still widespread in the city today. The arcaded ground floor, the only authentic example left of what was once a common feature of Royal Mile houses, has been restored to illustrate its early function as a shopping booth. Several other rooms have been kitted-out in authentic period style to give an impression of the lifestyle of a well-to-do household of the late seventeenth century; the Painted Chamber, with its decorated wooden ceiling and wall friezes, is particularly impressive. Elsewhere, underlining the importance of trade with continental Europe and beyond, the building has Dutch and Chinese porcelain and seventeenth-century

LAWNMARKET

Dutch paintings by Jacob Ruisdael and others. It's also possible to stay here (see p.189–190).

The Writers' Museum

Map 3, D8. Mon–Sat 10am–5pm; also Sun 2–5pm during the Festival; free.

A few paces further on, steps lead down to Lady Stair's Close, where you'll find the **Writers' Museum**. It's situated in **Lady Stair's House**, dating from the 1620s and named after the gorgeous and foul-mouthed eighteenth-century society figure on whose life Walter Scott based his story *My Aunt Margaret's Mirror*. A strange collection which hedges its bets with labels such as "said to be", "reputed to be" or even "similar to", the humdrum miscellany here celebrates Scotland's literary trinity of Scott, Burns and Stevenson. There are assorted locks of hair, walking sticks and a few mementoes of Stevenson's stay in Samoa, plus some oddities such as an enamelled marble apple given by Robert Burns to his wife Jean Armour. Don't miss the painting, *Parliament Square and Public Characters of Edinburgh*, in the Burns Room, which gives a good idea of the layout of the area around St Giles in the eighteenth century. In the courtyard outside, called the **Makars' Court** after the Scots word for a "maker" of poetry or prose, look out for quotations by twelve of Scotland's most famous writers and poets inscribed on paving stones.

Riddle's Court to the Bank of Scotland

On the south side of Lawnmarket, Riddle's Close leads to **Riddle's Court** (Map 3, D9), a typical medieval courtyard where you'll find **MacMorran's Close** and the former home of the Baillie MacMorran, a wealthy merchant who was killed in 1595 while attempting to quell a school riot:

LAWNMARKET

DEACON BRODIE

On the surface, William Brodie – wit, town councillor, cabinetmaker and head of the Incorporation of Wrights and Masons – was an honourable member of late eighteenth-century society. However, like many of his contemporaries he was involved in a variety of more lowly activities, bestowing his custom on cockfights and various drinking clubs where he indulged in a constant round of bingeing, gambling and womanizing. In order to fund these activities, he always carried a piece of putty which he would use to take an impression of any keys left hanging up in houses that he visited. Armed with a copy of the keys cut by a local blacksmith, Brodie then robbed the houses. After the audacious robbery of the Excise Office in Chessel's Court, Canongate, which netted the dismal sum of £16, Brodie disappeared to Holland. One of his accomplices revealed his identity, and he was arrested and brought back to Edinburgh, where he was executed in 1788 on a gallows of his own making. Brodie remained blasé to the end, even writing an absurd will, which he ended with the dedication: "I recommend to all rogues, sharpers, thieves and gamblers, as well in high as in low stations, to take care of theirs by leaving of all wicked practices, and becoming good members of society".

You can visit the popular *Deacon Brodie's Tavern* on the corner of the Lawnmarket and Bank Street and, over a beer, ruminate on the connections between Brodie, Robert Louis Stevenson's similarly themed tale of *Dr Jekyll and Mr Hyde*, and the various split personalities of Edinburgh itself, not least its Old Town and New Town. Rather more unexpectedly, prim Edinburgh teacher Jean Brodie is described by her creator, Muriel Spark, as a direct descendant of the disreputable Deacon.

LAWNMARKET

local boys barricaded themselves into the High School and demanded a week's holiday, and when MacMorran came to sort them out he was shot through the head by one William Sinclair, later to become Sir William Sinclair of Mey. Further down the street, **Brodie's Close** is named after the father of one of Edinburgh's most notorious characters, **Deacon William Brodie** (see box on p.39) – pillar of society by day, burglar by night.

Lawnmarket ends where the Royal Mile reaches a crossroads with George IV Bridge and Bank Street. On the latter stands the grand sandstone **Head Office of the Bank of Scotland** (Map 3, E2), whose Italianate domes and Corinthian pillars stand tall above the Princes Street Gardens. Established in 1695, the Bank of Scotland is the oldest commercial bank in the UK still trading under its original name and statutes. In one of the more colourful episodes in its long history, the bank had to shift over £80,000 in banknotes into the Castle in 1745, to protect them from the army of Bonnie Prince Charlie – regarded, of course, as a threat to the state. The core of the building was designed by Robert Reid and Richard Crichton, pupils of Robert Adam, but its present appearance owes a great deal to David Bryce, who added domes, wings and quadrants in 1862. The banking hall offers a glimpse of the opulent interior and sweeping views out over Princes Street; downstairs, a small **museum** (June–Aug Mon–Fri 10am–4.45pm; free) displays an intriguing collection of scales, coins, primitive cheques and bank notes, including a selection of forgeries dating back to 1716.

INTO THE HIGH STREET: PARLIAMENT SQUARE

Map 3, E9.

The third section of the Royal Mile is known as the **High Street**, and occupies two blocks on either side of the intersection between North Bridge and South Bridge. The heart of the Royal Mile, this is where you might glimpse a bewigged advocate striding across the cobbles, while come the Festival, huge crowds gather to soak up the atmosphere and watch buskers juggle flaming torches from a unicycle or sculpt sets of bagpipes from balloons. Immediately on your right after crossing George IV Bridge and Bank Street, **Parliament Square** (Map 3, E9) is dominated by the High Kirk of St Giles (see p.43) and by the continuous Neoclassical facades of the **Law Courts**. These were originally planned by Robert Adam, one of four brothers in a family of architects (their father William designed Hopetoun House; see p.157), whose work helped give the New Town much of its grace and elegance. Because of a shortage of funds, Adam couldn't be kept on to complete the work, and the present exteriors were built to plans by Robert Reid, the designer of the northern part of New Town, who faithfully quoted from Adam's architectural vocabulary, though without matching his flair. William Stark, a more flamboyant draftsman, designed the **Signet Library** (Map 3, E9), which occupies the west side of the square and has one of the most beautiful interiors in Edinburgh – its sumptuous colonnaded hall a perfect embodiment of the ideals of the Age of Reason. Unfortunately, it can only be seen by prior written application, except on very occasional open days (details available from the tourist office).

Parliament House and around

Facing the southern side of St Giles is **Parliament House** (Map 3, E9), built in the 1630s to house the Scottish Parliament – a role it maintained until the Union, when it passed into the hands of the legal fraternity. Following the Union in 1707, the building became the centre of the

Scottish legal profession – still its function today. The entrance lobby gives access to the impressive **main hall** (Mon–Fri 9am–5pm), the most notable feature of which is the extravagant hammerbeam roof and the delicately carved stone corbels from which it springs – in addition to some vicious grotesques, they include accurate depictions of several castles, including Edinburgh's. In the far corner, a small **exhibition** explains the history of the building and courts, but it's more fun simply to watch the everyday business, with solicitors and bewigged advocates in hushed conferrals, often following the time-honoured tradition of pacing up and down the main hall to prevent their conversation being overheard by anyone sitting on the benches around the walls. Most of the courtrooms have public galleries, and you can sit in on the hearings if you're interested – ask one of the attendants in the lobby to point you in the right direction. Outside, in the square, rears a life-size equestrian statue of King Charles II, wearing the garb of a Roman emperor.

Back on the High Street, set into the pavement beside a bloated memorial to the fifth Duke of Buccleuch, there's a brickwork pattern known as the **Heart of Midlothian**. Immortalized in Scott's novel of the same name, it marks the site of a demolished Tolbooth; you may see passers-by spitting on it for luck. The **Mercat Cross** (Map 3, E8), at the eastern end of St Giles, was once the setting for public executions, as well as rather more joyous events such as the return from France of Mary, Queen of Scots in 1561, when the spouts of the cross were said to have flowed with wine. Little of what remains today is original: the first cross collapsed in 1756, and was only rebuilt in 1885 with financial assistance from William Gladstone. The site is still occasionally used for the reading out of Royal proclamations, such as the dissolution of Parliament.

High Kirk of St Giles

Map 3, E8. April–Sept Mon–Fri 9am–7pm, Sat 9am–5pm, Sun 1–5pm; Oct–March Mon–Sat 9am–5pm, Sun 1–5pm; free.

There's been a church on the site of the **High Kirk of St Giles**, in the middle of Parliament Square, since the ninth century, and though there are surviving sections of a Norman church built in the early twelfth century, the basic structure of the church is a late fifteenth-century design. In the early nineteenth century, St Giles received a much-needed but unsympathetic restoration, covering most of the Gothic exterior with a smooth stone coating that gives it a certain Georgian dignity while sacrificing its medieval character almost completely. The only part not to receive this treatment is the late fifteenth-century tower, whose resplendent crown spire is formed by eight flying buttresses.

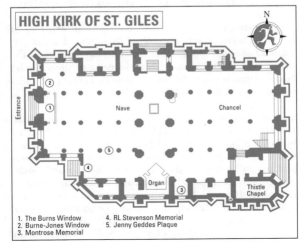

HIGH KIRK OF ST. GILES

N

Entrance

Nave

Chancel

Organ

Thistle Chapel

1. The Burns Window
2. Burne-Jones Window
3. Montrose Memorial
4. RL Stevenson Memorial
5. Jenny Geddes Plaque

St Giles is almost invariably referred to as a cathedral, although it was only the seat of a bishop on two brief and unhappy occasions in the seventeenth century – once when Charles I tried to force episcopalian government on the Scots Kirk, and again immediately after the Restoration of Charles II in 1660. However, St Giles is better known as a bastion of Scottish Presbyterianism, particularly because it was from here that **John Knox** (see box on p.50) launched and directed the Scottish Reformation. According to one of Edinburgh's best-known legends, the attempt in 1637 to introduce the English prayer book, and thus episcopal government, so incensed a humble stallholder named Jenny Geddes that she hurled her stool at the preacher, uttering the immortal words: "Out, out, does the false loon dare say Mass at my lugg [ear]?", thus prompting the rest of the congregation to chase the offending clergyman out of the building. A tablet in the north aisle marks the spot from where Jenny let rip.

In contrast to the restored exterior, the **interior** of St Giles has retained much more of its medieval character. Especially notable are the four massive piers supporting the tower, which date back, at least in part, to the church's Norman predecessor. In the nineteenth century, St Giles was adorned with a whole series of funerary monuments in order to give it the character of a national pantheon on the lines of Westminster Abbey. Several Pre-Raphaelite stained glass windows were also installed; the best of these, designed by Edward Burne-Jones and William Morris and showing Old Testament prophets and the Israelites crossing the River Jordan, can be seen on the facade wall of the **north aisle**. Alongside is the great **west window**, which was dedicated to Robbie Burns in 1985, causing enormous controversy – as a hardened drinker and womanizer, the national bard was far from being an upholder of accepted Presbyterian values. Look out also for an elegant bronze relief of **Robert Louis**

ROBERT LOUIS STEVENSON

Born in Edinburgh, Robert Louis Stevenson (1850–94) was a sickly youngster, his solitary childhood dominated by his governess, who told him tales from Calvinist folklore. In 1875, Stevenson abandoned a career in law and decided to channel his energies into literature.

While a student, Stevenson had made his mark as an essayist, and in his lifetime he published over 100 essays. Other early successes were two travelogues, An Inland Voyage and Travels with a Donkey in the Cevennes, kaleidoscopic jottings based on journeys in France in 1878–79. It was there that Stevenson met Fanny Osbourne, an American, who was estranged from her husband and had two children in tow. His voyage to join her in San Francisco formed the basis for his most important factual work, The Amateur Emigrant, a vivid firsthand account of the great nineteenth-century European migration to the United States.

Having married the now-divorced Fanny, Stevenson began an elusive search for an agreeable climate which took the couple to Switzerland, the French Riviera and the Scottish Highlands. It was around this time that he began writing novels, achieving immediate acclaim in 1881 for Treasure Island, a highly moralistic adventure yarn that began as an entertainment for his stepson. Published in 1886, his most famous short story, Dr Jekyll and Mr Hyde, was an allegory of Edinburgh's Old Town dual personality of prosperity and squalor, and an analysis of its Calvinistic preoccupations with guilt and damnation. The same year saw the publication of the historical romance, Kidnapped.

In 1887, Stevenson left Britain for good and eventually settled in Samoa. Scotland continued to be his main inspiration, however: he wrote Catriona as a sequel to Kidnapped, and was at work on two more novels with Scottish settings at the time of his sudden death from a brain haemorrhage in 1894. He was buried on the top of Mount Vaea overlooking the Pacific Ocean.

INTO THE HIGH STREET: PARLIAMENT SQUARE

Stevenson on the south side of the church by the American artist, Augustus St Gaudens. The original design had the author reclining on a bed smoking a cigarette; it was altered so that he now lies on a chaise longue, pen in hand, a pose deemed rather more respectful of the Presbyterian work ethic. On the other side of the organ is a memorial to the **Marquis of Montrose**, leader of the forces of Charles I in Scotland, who was captured, executed and dismembered in 1650.

At the southeastern corner of the church, the **Thistle Chapel** was built by Sir Robert Lorimer in 1911 as the private chapel of the sixteen knights of the Most Noble Order of the Thistle. Self-consciously derivative of St George's Chapel in Windsor, it's an exquisite piece of craftsmanship, with an elaborate ribbed vault, huge drooping bosses and extravagantly ornate stalls.

UPPER HIGH STREET

Map 3, E8.

The first main building on the northern side of the High Street is the **High Court of Justiciary**, Scotland's highest criminal court, outside which stands a statue of the philosopher David Hume, one of Edinburgh's greatest sons, looking decidedly wan and chilly dressed in nothing but a Roman toga. A little further on, opposite the Mercat Cross, the U-shaped **City Chambers** were designed by John Adam, brother of Robert, as the Royal Exchange. Local traders never warmed to the new premises, however, preferring to remain outdoors on the street, so the town council established its headquarters there instead. Extraordinarily, the rear of the building has twelve storeys to accommodate the sharp drop onto Cockburn Street

Beneath the City Chambers lies **Mary King's Close**. Built in the early sixteenth century, it was closed off for many years after the devastation of the 1645 plague, before being entirely covered up by the chambers in 1753. During World War II, parts of the close were brought back into public use as an air-raid shelter, and today brief tours of this rather spooky "lost city" are run regularly throughout the day by Mercat Tours (see p.11) – booking is strongly recommended as numbers are restricted. A little further down the High Street is **Anchor Close**, site of the printing works of William Smellie, who published the first ever edition of the *Encyclopedia Britannica* there in 1768.

LOWER HIGH STREET

Map 3, F8–G8.

At the junction of the south side of the High Street and South Bridge stands the **Tron Kirk**, the longstanding focal point for Hogmanay revellers until today's organized events shifted the crowds to other parts of the city. Built in the 1630s to house the congregation evicted from St Giles when the latter became the seat of a bishop, the church has a less than happy history: the south aisle was removed in the late eighteenth century in order to make room for the South Bridge, and the original spire was destroyed in the Great Fire of 1824. The Tron remained in use as a church until 1952 and was then closed for forty years before reopening as the **Old Town Information Centre** (Easter–May Thurs–Mon 10am–1pm & 2–5pm, June–Sept daily 10am–7pm).

Excavations within the church have revealed sections of an old close, **Marlin's Wynd**. The cobbled steps and the traces of old foundations on the wynd, which formerly contained bookshops and markets, are highly evocative of Edinburgh's past, making this an essential stop on the Royal Mile. In the same building, the **Edinburgh Old Town Renewal Trust** presents a series of informative displays on the history of the Old Town.

Beyond the intersection of North Bridge and South Bridge, there are fewer impressive buildings, though you can find plenty of historic titbits if you're willing to seek them out. Back on the northern side of the High Street, for example, nestles **Paisley Close**. Above its entrance is a bust of a youth with the inscription "Heave awa' chaps, I'm no' dead yet", the words uttered in 1861 by a boy trapped by rubble following the collapse of a tenement in the close, and who was subsequently dug out by rescue workers.

In **Chalmer's Close**, just to the east, **Trinity Apse** serves as a poignant reminder of the fifteenth-century Holy Trinity Collegiate Church. Formerly one of Edinburgh's most outstanding buildings, it was demolished in 1848 to make way for an extension to Waverley train station. The stones were carefully numbered and stored on Calton Hill so that the church could be reassembled at a later date, but many were pilfered before sufficient funds became available, and only enough remained to reconstruct the apse on this site. This now houses a **Brass Rubbing Centre** (Mon–Sat 10am–5pm, plus Sun noon–5pm during the Festival only; last rubbing sold 1hr before closing; free), where you can rub your own impressions from Pictish crosses and medieval brasses (from £1.20 per rubbing).

On the other side of the High Street, the **Museum of Childhood** (Mon–Sat 10am–5pm; Sun noon–5pm during the Festival only; free), was founded by an eccentric local councillor who disliked children. Although he claimed that the museum was a serious social archive for adults, it has always attracted swarms of kids, who delight in the dolls' house, teddy bears, marionettes and other toys. The founder's quirky sense of humour comes over on some of the captions for exhibits, and even more so in his unendearing wish to have a memorial window in honour of King Herod placed at the museum's entrance.

John Knox's House

Map 3, G8. Mon–Sat 10am–5pm, plus Sun noon–5pm in July & Aug; £2.25.

Diagonally opposite the Museum of Childhood is the much-photographed **John Knox's House**, a three-storeyed building with distinctive wooden balconies projecting out into the High Street. With its outside stairway, biblical motto and sundial adorned with a statue of Moses, it gives a good impression of how the Royal Mile must have once looked. Thought to have been built around the beginning of the sixteenth century, the house was partially destroyed by English soldiers in 1544, and has since been restored many times. Although Knox is thought to have stayed here between 1560 and 1572, the link may stem solely from a period at the end of the eighteenth century when the house was known as "Knox the Booksellers". What's known is that James Mosman, royal goldsmith to Mary, Queen of Scots, did reside in the house: the initials IM and MA (Mosman and his wife Mariota Arres) are still visible on the outer west wall of the building.

John Knox's House, on the "knuckle" of the High Street, adjoins the Netherbow Arts Centre, a busy theatre venue during the Festival. Throughout the rest of the year it hosts art and photography exhibitions (free) and has a swiss-themed café.

The rather bare **interior**, with its labyrinthine layout – typical of Old Town houses – contains a sparse **museum** displaying explanatory material on Knox's life and career, including early editions of works by him (such as the inimitably titled *Answer to a Great Number of Blasphemous Cavillations*) and other notable contemporaries. In recognition of the building's connection with James Mosman, a

JOHN KNOX

The Protestant reformer John Knox was born around 1510 in East Lothian. Ordained to the priesthood in 1540, Knox became a private tutor, in league with Scotland's first significant Protestant leader, George Wishart. After Wishart was burned at the stake for heresy in 1546, Knox became involved with the group who carried out the revenge murder of Cardinal David Beaton, subsequently taking over his castle in St Andrews. The following year, this was captured by the French; Knox was carted off to work as a galley slave and freed in 1548 by the English.

When the Catholic Mary Tudor acceded to the English throne in 1553, Knox fled to Geneva, where he was quickly won over to Calvin's radical version of Protestantism. It was here that he wrote his most infamous treatise, attacking the three Catholic women then ruling Scotland, England and France.

When Knox was allowed to return to Scotland in 1555, he took over as spiritual leader of the Reformation. He championed an alliance with Protestant Elizabeth I, which proved crucial to the establishment of Protestantism as the official religion of Scotland in 1560: the deployment of English troops against the French garrison in Edinburgh dealt a fatal blow to Franco–Spanish hopes of re-establishing Catholicism in both Scotland and England. Although the following year saw the accession of Catholic Mary, Queen of Scots, to the Scottish throne, apparently Knox was able to retain the upper hand in his high-profile disputes with her.

Before his death in 1572, Knox began mapping out the organization of the Scots Kirk, sweeping away all vestiges of episcopacy and giving laymen a more prominent role. He also proposed a nationwide education system, to be compulsory for the very young, and free for the poor. His final legacy was the posthumously published *History of the Reformation of Religion in the Realm of Scotland*, a justification of his life's work.

mock-up of a goldsmith's workroom has been installed on the first floor. On the second floor, there are fireplaces with attractive, albeit somewhat haphazardly positioned, Dutch tiles, wood-panelled walls and painted ceilings, which together create a passable replica of a sixteenth-century townhouse.

THE CANONGATE

For over seven hundred years, the district through which the **Canongate** runs was a burgh in its own right, officially separate from the capital; between the two was the Netherbow Port, one of six original gateways into the city, located on the High Street near the present-day Netherbow Arts Centre. A notorious slum area even into the 1960s, the Canongate has been the subject of some of the most ambitious **restoration** programmes in the Old Town, though the lack of harmony between the buildings renovated in different decades can be seen fairly clearly. For such a central district, it's interesting to note that most of the buildings here are residential, and by no means are they all bijou apartments. The development of the Canongate is ongoing, particularly at its lower end around the site of the new Parliament building. Along this stretch, it's worth poking around the eclectic array of small **shops**, which range from a gallery of historic maps and sea charts to genuine bagpipe makers.

Upper Canongate

Near the top of the Canongate, a good example of the restoration work can be seen at **Chessel's Court** (Map 3, H9), a mid-eighteenth-century development with fanciful Rococo chimneys. It was formerly the site of the Excise Office, scene of the robbery that led to the arrest and execution of Deacon Brodie (see p.39). Over the road the **Morocco Land** (Map 3, H9) is a reasonably faithful reproduction of an old tenement, incorporating the original bust of a Moor from which its name derives.

Dominated by a turreted steeple and an odd external box clock, the late sixteenth-century **Canongate Tolbooth** (Map 3, I8), a little further down the north side of the street, has served both as the headquarters of the burgh administration and as a prison, and now houses **The People's Story** (Mon–Sat 10am–5pm, plus Sun 2–5pm during the Festival only; free), a lively museum devoted to the everyday life and work of Edinburgh people down the centuries, with sounds and tableaux on various aspects of city living – including a typical Edinburgh pub.

Next door, **Canongate Kirk** (Map 3, I8) was built in the 1680s to house the congregation expelled from Holyrood Abbey when the latter was commandeered by James VII (James II in England) to serve as the chapel for the Order of the Thistle. It's a curiously archaic design, still Renaissance in outline, and built to a cruciform plan wholly at odds with the ideals and requirements of Protestant worship. Its churchyard, one of the city's most exclusive **cemeteries**, commands a superb view across to Calton Hill. Among those buried here are Adam Smith, the eighteenth-century political thinker who first developed the principles of the free-market economy, Mrs Agnes McLehose (better known as Robert Burns' "Clarinda") and Robert Fergusson, regarded by some as Edinburgh's greatest poet, despite his death at the age of 24; his headstone was donated by Burns, a fervent admirer, who also wrote the inscription.

Lower Canongate

Opposite the church, the **Museum of Edinburgh** (Mon–Sat 10am–5pm; plus Sun 2–5pm during the Festival only; free) is based in Huntly House (Map 3, I8). Constructed in the late sixteenth century, the building was bought in 1647 by the Incorporation of Hammermen, who converted it into flats; it was then restored in 1927 to serve as a local history museum. Exhibits include a quirky array of old shop signs, some dating back to the eighteenth century, as well as displays on indigenous industries such as glass, silver, pottery and clockmaking, and on the dubious military career of Field Marshall Earl Haig. Also on view is the original version of the National Covenant of 1638; modern science has failed to resolve whether or not some of the signatories signed with their own blood, as tradition has it.

Among the intriguing series of closes and entries on this stretch of the Canongate, **Dunbar's Close** (Map 3, J7), on the north side of the street, has a beautiful seventeenth-century walled garden tucked in behind the tenements. Opposite this is the entry to Crichton's Close, through which you'll find the **Scottish Poetry Library** (Mon–Fri noon–6pm, Sat noon–4pm; free), a small island of modern architectural eloquence amid a sea of monstrous construction work and large-scale developments. The eastern side of the building is made from a section of an old city wall, while the rest is an attractive, thoroughly contemporary design using brick, wood, glass, Caithness stone and blue tiles. The library, which moved here in 1999 from older premises further up the Royal Mile, contains Scotland's most comprehensive collection of native poetry. Visitors are free to read the books, periodicals and leaflets, or listen to recordings of poetry in English, Scots and Gaelic. Readings and events are organized throughout the year.

At the very foot of the street, the entrance to the residential **Whitehorse Close** (Map 3, J8) was once the site of the inn from where stagecoaches began the journey to London. Stridently quaint, it drips with the characteristic features of Scottish vernacular architecture: crow-stepped gables, dormer windows, overhanging upper storeys and curving outside stairways.

Holyrood and Arthur's Seat

At the foot of the Canongate section of the Royal Mile lies Holyrood, Edinburgh's historic royal quarter and the site of the seventeenth-century Palace of Holyroodhouse, where the monarch stays when visiting the city. The whole flavour of the area is being transformed, however, with the erection of the new Scottish Parliament immediately opposite the palace, and the accompanying ranks of hotels, offices and tourist attractions that are being built nearby. Due to be completed in 2003, the new Parliament will be without doubt the largest and most important piece of contemporary architecture in Scotland, a national symbol tying together both the modern in a historic location, and its urban situation with the rural aspect of Holyrood Park sweeping off to one side.

Holyrood's origins go back to the twelfth century, and are described in a fifteenth-century manuscript which is still kept in the palace: the story goes that King David I, son of Malcolm III and St Margaret, went out hunting one day and was suddenly confronted by a stag who threw him from his horse and seemed ready to gore him. In desperation, the king tried to protect himself by grasping its antlers, but instead found himself holding a crucifix, whereupon the animal ran off. In a dream that night, he heard a voice commanding him to "make a house for Canons devoted to the Cross"; he duly obeyed and founded an **abbey** in 1128, which he named Holyrood ("rood" being an alternative name for a cross). A more likely story, however, is that David, the most pious of all Scotland's monarchs, simply acquired a supposed relic of the True Cross and decided to build a suitable home for it.

Holyrood soon became a favoured **royal residence**, its situation in a secluded valley making it far more agreeable than the draughty Castle. At first, monarchs lodged in the monastic guesthouse, to which a wing for the exclusive use of the court was added during the reign of James II. This was transformed into a full-blown palace for James IV, which in turn was replaced by a much larger building for Charles II, although he never actually lived there. Indeed, it was something of a white elephant until Queen Victoria started making regular trips to her northern kingdom, a custom that has been maintained by her successors.

Just beyond the palace grounds lies the marvellous **Holyrood Park**, a large area of semi-wild parkland and peaceful lochs, dominated by **Arthur's Seat**, an extinct volcano which affords stupendous views from its summit. Easily reached on foot through the park is the attractive village of **Duddingston**, home to a twelfth-century parish church and the house in which Bonnie Prince Charlie is reputed to have spent the night before the battle of Prestonpans.

THE PRECINCTS OF THE PALACE

Map 3, K8.

On the north side of **Abbey Strand**, which forms a sort of processional way linking Canongate with Holyrood, stands

Abbey Lairds, a four-storey sixteenth-century mansion which once served as a home for aristocratic debtors and is now occupied by royal flunkies during the summer seat of the court. Here, Historic Scotland have a small information centre and bookshop promoting the properties they look after around Scotland (daily: April–Oct 9.30am–6pm; Nov–March 9.30am–5pm).

Legend has it that Mary, Queen of Scots used to bathe in sweet white wine in the curious little turreted structure nearby known as **Queen Mary's Bath House**; it's more likely, however, that it was either a summer pavilion or a dovecote. Its architecture is mirrored in the **Croft an Righ**, a picturesque L-shaped house in a quiet, generally overlooked corner beside the eastern wall of the complex. Near here, at the eastern edge of the palace grounds, is the area known as **St Anne's Yards**, formerly a place where debtors who had sought the sanctuary of the Abbey could live, free from the threat of arrest. Over time it became a busy community, with over a hundred residents in the early nineteenth century.

THE PALACE OF HOLYROODHOUSE

Map 3, L8. Daily: April–Oct 9.30am–6pm; Nov–March 9.30am–4.30pm; £6.50.

In its present form, the **Palace of Holyroodhouse** is largely a seventeenth-century creation. However, the tower house of the old palace was skilfully incorporated to form the northwestern block, with a virtual mirror image of it erected as a counterbalance at the other end. The three-storey **courtyard** is an early exercise in Palladian style, exhibiting a punctilious knowledge of the rules of classical architecture to create a sense of absolute harmony and unity. It's important to remember that Holyroodhouse is still a working palace, and because of this, **public access**

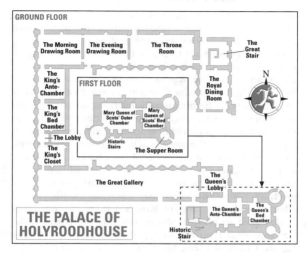

varies throughout the year. Between November and March, the only way to see the palace is as part of an hour-long **guided tour**; at other times of the year, visitors are free to move at their own pace. The buildings are closed to the public during state functions, including the period of General Assembly of the Church of Scotland, which lasts for a fortnight in the middle of May, and the annual royal visit, which usually takes place in the last two weeks of June and the first in July.

Inside, the **State Apartments** are decked out with oak panelling, tapestries, portraits and decorative paintings, all overshadowed by magnificent white stucco **ceilings**. In the Morning Drawing Room, portraits of Bonnie Prince Charlie and George IV, loser and winner, hang side by side. The most eyecatching chamber, however, is the **Great Gallery**, which takes up the entire first floor of the northern wing. During the 1745 sojourn of the Young Pretender, this was the setting for a lively banquet, evoked in detail in Scott's novel *Waverley*, and it's still used for big ceremonial occasions. On the walls of the gallery hang 89 portraits commissioned from the seventeenth-century Dutch artist Jacob de Wet to illustrate the royal lineage of Scotland from its mythical origins in the fourth century BC; the result is unintentionally hilarious, as it's clear that the artist's imagination was taxed to bursting point by the need to paint so many different faces without having an inkling as to what the subjects actually looked like. Legend has it that he trawled the streets of the Old Town for sitters to provide faces for the early obscure figures, and a frequently recurring feature in many of the portraits is a prominent nose, not dissimilar from that of his patron, Charles II. In the adjacent **King's Closet**, de Wet's *The Finding of Moses* provides a biblical link to the portraits, the Scottish royal family claiming descent from Scota, the Egyptian pharaoh's daughter who discovered Moses in the bulrushes.

The oldest parts of the palace, the **Historical Apartments** date back to the sixteenth century, and are mainly of note for their associations with Mary, Queen of Scots and in particular for the brutal murder, organized by her husband, Lord Darnley (see box on p.82), of her private secretary, David Rizzio, who was stabbed 56 times and dragged from the small closet, through the **Queen's Bedchamber**, and into the **Outer Chamber**. Until a few years ago, visitors were shown apparently indelible blood-stains on the floor of the last, but these are now admitted to be fakes and have been covered up. A display cabinet in the same room shows some pieces of **needlework** woven by the deposed queen while in English captivity; another case has an outstanding **miniature portrait** of her by the French court painter, François Clouet.

HOLYROOD ABBEY

Map 3, L8.

In the grounds of the palace lie the wonderfully evocative ruins of **Holyrood Abbey**. Of King David's original Norman church, the only surviving fragment is a doorway in the far southeastern corner. Most of the remainder dates from a late twelfth- and early thirteenth-century rebuilding in the Early Gothic style.

If the weather is clement, it's well worth taking a wander around the paths and lawns which surround the skeletal walls of the abbey. The surviving parts of the **west front**, including one of the twin towers and the elaborately carved entrance portal, show how resplendent the building must once have been. Unfortunately, it was all but destroyed during the Reformation. Charles I attempted to restore some semblance of unity by ordering the erection of the great east window and a new stone roof, but the latter collapsed in 1768, causing grievous damage to the rest of the structure. By this time, the Canongate congregation had another place of worship, and schemes to rebuild the abbey were abandoned.

THE SCOTTISH PARLIAMENT SITE

Map 3, J8.

Immediately opposite Abbey Strand, the massive construction site between the Royal Mile and Holyrood Road is where the new **Scottish Parliament** is being built. For decades, campaigners for home rule for Scotland envisaged the Old Royal High School building on Calton Hill (see p.107) as the place where the long-awaited Scottish Parliament would sit. In the run-up to the devolution referendum, however, the Scottish Office unexpectedly announced that the school was too small to accommodate the proposed Parliament and its offices, and various alternative sites were suggested, including the empty docklands at Leith. Eventually a disused brewery at the foot of the Royal Mile was identified as the ideal location, and a competition to design the building was won by Catalan architect **Enric Miralles**, in association with Edinburgh-based architects RMJM. Their concept centres on a series of petal-shaped buildings which have been compared (both favourably and unfavourably) to upturned boats. Miralles died in 2000, causing a few ripples of uncertainty as to whether the famously whimsical designer had in fact set down his final vision. The structure will cost something upward of £250 million, and is due to be ready in 2003, until which time the Parliament is sitting in the Church of Scotland Assembly Hall on the Mound.

For more on the setting up and composition of the Scottish Parliament, see the box on p.35.

While the building is being completed, a temporary **visitor centre** (daily 10am–4pm; free) has been established on the southeast corner of the site, between the palace and Dynamic Earth, where you can view plans, models and computer images of the proposed structure.

OUR DYNAMIC EARTH

Map 3, L2. April–Oct daily 10am–6pm; Nov–March Wed–Sat 10am–5pm; £7.95.

Although the largest, the new Parliament building is by no means the only newcomer to this historic area. On the Holyrood Road side of the construction site, a pincushion of white metal struts shelters **Our Dynamic Earth**, a hi-tech attraction about the natural world aimed mainly at families. Although James Hutton, the Edinburgh-born

"Father of Geology", lived nearby in the eighteenth century, there are few specific links to Edinburgh or Scotland. You're taken in a "time machine" elevator to a room where the creation of the universe, 15 billion years ago, is described using wide-screen video graphics, eerie music and a deep-throated commentary. Subsequent galleries describe the formation of the earth and continents with crashing sound effects and a shaking floor, while the calmer grandeur of glaciers and oceans is explored through magnificent large-screen landscape footage. The "Casualties and Survivors" gallery describes the history of life on earth, from primordial swamps to life-size models of some of the odd creatures who once inhabited the earth, while, further on, the polar regions – complete with a real iceberg – and tropical jungles are imaginatively recreated, with interactive computer screens and special effects at every turn. Outside, the dramatic **amphitheatre**, which incorporates the steps leading up to the entrance, makes for a great venue for outdoor theatre and music performances – notably during the Festival.

HOLYROOD PARK

Map 5.

A natural wilderness in the very heart of the modern city, **Holyrood Park** – or Queen's Park – is unquestionably one of Edinburgh's main assets, as locals (though relatively few tourists) readily appreciate. Packed into an area no more than five miles in diameter is an amazing variety of landscapes – hills, crags, moorland, marshes, glens, lochs and fields – representing something of a microcosm of Scotland's scenery. The highest point is the summit of Arthur's Seat, situated in the southern part of the Park, though its lofty dominance means that the park as a whole is often referred to simply as "Arthur's Seat".

HOLYROOD PARK

WALKS IN HOLYROOD PARK

The obvious target for a decent walk in Holyrood Park is to the summit of Arthur's Seat, the highest point in the city. The easiest route is from the car park beside Dunsapie Loch. Less arduous than it looks, the climb takes about twenty minutes, starting off gently at first and then becoming steeper towards the summit. You can also start at Duddingston, from where a long flight of stairs and a steep path link up to the Dunsapie starting point.

A longer but more satisfying approach begins at the entrance to the park beside the Palace of Holyroodhouse: cross over to the south side of Queen's Drive, then take the path which passes St Margaret's Well, heading towards St Margaret's Loch and St Anthony's Chapel. Before reaching the chapel follow the path as it curves southwards into the flat glen called Dry Dam. From here it's a steady climb up the north face of Arthur's Seat to the top. The walk takes about one and a half hours altogether.

An enjoyable alternative to Arthur's Seat is a walk is along the Radical Road pathway, which runs along the base of the Salisbury Crags (a series of 400ft-high basalt rock formations) and offers an inspiring outlook over the city. You can join the path at either the Holyrood or Newington end, and there's an easy return along the grassy verge beside the Queen's Drive. A wilder and lonelier option is to traverse the top of the crags, though of course it's inadvisable to get too close to the edge, as the ground can be slippery and the rock unstable in places.

To learn more about the formation and geology of Arthur's Seat, join one of Geowalk's guided walks (£4), which are led by a qualified geologist. Frequency depends on demand (as well as the weather) – to find out more, call ℡0131/555 5488. The Holyrood Park Rangers also organize walks on a Wednesday afternoon, departing at 2pm from the Park HQ near Holyroodhouse.

HOLYROOD PARK

The wide open green spaces of the park make it a popular spot for joggers and cyclists, and you can often see rock climbers making their way up the cliffs of Salisbury Crags. A single tarred road, the **Queen's Drive**, circles the park, enabling many of its features to be seen by car, though you really need to stroll around to appreciate it fully. In a small stone-built gate lodge at the entrance to the park from Holyrood Road, the **Holyrood Park Ranger Service** has a small information point (Map 5, B3; Mon–Thurs 10am–4pm, Fri 10am–3.30pm), where you can pick up a map of suggested walking routes or find out about ranger-led walks which depart from the lodge at 2pm on Wednesdays.

Note that sometime in 2002, the ranger service will move to a brand new Park HQ in the area behind the Palace of Holyroodhouse.

From the Palace gates, following Queen's Drive in a clockwise direction, a ten minute walk takes you to **St Margaret's Loch** (Map 5, D2), a nineteenth-century man-made pond above which stand the scanty ruins of **St Anthony's Chapel** (Map 5, D3), another fine vantage point. From here, the road's loop is one-way only, ascending to **Dunsapie Loch** (Map 5, F5), again an artificial stretch of water, which makes an excellent foil to the eponymous crag behind, and a common starting point for the walk to the summit of Arthur's Seat.

Arthur's Seat

Map 5, D6.

A majestic extinct volcano rising 823ft above sea level, **Arthur's Seat** is Edinburgh's single most prominent landmark, resembling a huge crouched lion when seen from the

HOLYROOD PARK

63

west. There's no satisfactory story to explain the name: there's certainly little reason to associate it with the British king of the Holy Grail legends. One possibility is that it derives from the Gaelic phrase *Ard-na-Said*, meaning "Height of Arrows", from the days in the early twelfth century when the area was used as a hunting ground.

There are several ways up to the summit, the quickest of which is from Dunsapie Loch (see box on p.62). The views from the top are all you'd expect, covering the entire city and much of the Firth of Forth; on a clear day, you can even see the southernmost mountains of the Highlands. The composer Felix Mendelssohn climbed Arthur's Seat in July 1829, noting: "It is beautiful here! In the evening a cool breeze is wafted from the sea, and then all objects appear clearly and sharply defined against the gray sky; the lights from the windows glitter brilliantly".

DUDDINGSTON

Continuing along Queen's Drive around Arthur's Seat takes you to a roundabout. The turnoff here leads to another roundabout; taking the first exit, you pass beneath **Samson's Ribs** (Map 5, D7), a group of basalt pillars strikingly reminiscent of the Hebridean island of Staffa, and come to **Duddingston Loch** (Map 5, F7), the only natural stretch of water in the park, now a bird sanctuary where you can see ducks, swans, greylag geese and occasionally one or two less common water birds such as herons and grebes. You can walk easily along parts of the shore, though it takes a bit more determination (and decent footwear) to get all the way round the often muddy circular path. Above the loch, just outside the park boundary, perches **Duddingston Kirk** (Map 5, F7). Dating back in part to the twelfth century, the church is the focus of one of the most unspoilt old villages in Edinburgh. In the gateway of the church are a *loupin-on-stane*, a platform for mounting a horse, and *jougs*, an iron collar and chain set into the wall and formerly used for humiliating offenders. According to tradition, Bonnie Prince Charlie stayed in **no. 8 Duddingston Causeway**, a plain-looking house built in 1721, on the night before his victory at the battle of Prestonpans in 1745. Duddingston can be reached on foot through Holyrood Park; after a drink in the excellent *Sheep Heid Inn* (see p.235), which serves decent bar meals and also has a traditional skittle alley, take bus #42/46 from Duddingston Road West in either direction to get back to the city centre.

DUDDINGSTON

South of the Royal Mile

Before the elevated viaducts of George IV Bridge and Southbridge were built, the main thoroughfare immediately to the south of the Royal Mile was Cowgate, originally used for bringing cattle to market. Linked to the Holyrood area by its eastern extension, Holyrood Road, Cowgate today is a gloomy street even in daylight, hemmed in by tall buildings, and, with the exceptions of St Cecilia's Hall and the Magdalen Chapel, holding little in the way of sights. At night, however, though a little seedy, it's one of the city's prime spots for nightclubs. The western end of the street leads to the wide open space of Grassmarket, at the very foot of the Castle's intimidating southern crags; for centuries, it was the venue for livestock sales, and also the scene of executions and other grisly goings-on, such as the activities of the body-snatchers Burke and Hare. Further west lies the city's theatre district, centred on Lothian Road and Grindlay Street.

To the south of Grassmarket stand **Greyfriars Kirk**, whose spooky courtyard is linked to legends both sentimental and sinister, and, facing it, the distinguished modern sandstone edifice of the **National Museum of Scotland**, the new sanctum of the nation's most treasured artefacts. This, together with the adjoining **Royal Museum of Scotland**, which houses an amazing miscellany of displays and objects from around the world, make up Scotland's most impressive and engaging large-scale museum, well worth half a day or more to explore properly. Just beyond the museum lies the **University of Edinburgh**; the scattered campus – a mix of impressive older buildings and fairly ghastly tower blocks – dominates this part of town as far as the **Southside** area and the stretch of parkland known as the **Meadows**.

COWGATE

Among Edinburgh's oldest surviving streets, **Cowgate** was formerly one of the city's most prestigious addresses. However, with the construction of Southbridge and George IV Bridge to provide a link between the Old and New towns, Cowgate was all but entombed below street level. The water supply for the Old Town was diverted to serve the new residences, resulting in severe shortage in the lower parts of the old city, which led to sporadic outbreaks of cholera in the 1840s. Hans Christian Andersen, who visited Edinburgh around this time, wrote, "poverty and misery seem to peep out of the open hatches which normally serve as windows". In the last decade or so, however, Cowgate has experienced something of a revival, with various nightclubs and Festival venues establishing themselves. Few tourists venture here, though, and the contrast with the neighbouring Royal Mile remains stark.

St Cecilia's Hall

Map 3, H3. Wed & Sat 2–5pm; during the Edinburgh Festival Mon–Sat 10.30am–12.30pm; £1.

Standing at the corner of Cowgate and Niddry Street, **St Cecilia's Hall** is Scotland's oldest purpose-built concert hall. Established for the Musical Society of Edinburgh in 1763, the hall thrived until the emergence of the New Town attracted concert-goers away from the area. After a spell as a Masonic Lodge, St Cecilia's was purchased by Edinburgh University in 1966 and restored to its original function.

Concerts are only rarely held in St Cecilia's Hall these days – for contact details, see the listing on p.239.

Externally, the building looks unexciting: the original entrance on Niddry Street is blackened with grime, and the new one created in the 1960s resembles a public toilet. The interior, however, is a beautiful shallow-domed structure, which has been restored and extended to house the **Russell Collection** of antique keyboard instruments, comprising a variety of virginals, spinets, clavichords and harpsichords, most of which are in working order – as staff will happily demonstrate. At present, the collection is very low-key, but there are plans to upgrade it with the help of funding from the Lottery over the next few years.

Magdalen Chapel

Map 3, E4. Mon–Fri 9.30am–4pm; free.

Towards the western end of Cowgate, almost immediately beneath George IV Bridge, **Magdalen Chapel** was built between 1541 and 1544 with money bequeathed by prominent citizen Michael MacQueen. Nondescript in the extreme from the outside, it's an intriguing discovery if you've a particular interest in church architecture or Scottish religious history, housing the only pre-Reformation stained glass in Scotland to have survived *in situ*. It was also the likely setting for the first ever General Assembly of the Church

COWGATE

of Scotland in 1560. In the 1620s, the Incorporation of Hammermen added a handsome tower and steeple, and later transformed the chapel into their guildhall; the building also saw service as a mortuary for the bodies of Covenanters hanged in the Grassmarket (see box on p.72), and was also used to display mechanical curiosities in the eighteenth century. The sixteenth-century **stained glass** takes the form of a set of four brilliantly coloured heraldic roundels on the south wall; look out for the lower left-hand roundel, depicting the arms of the MacQueen family, which contains the heads of several savages.

GRASSMARKET

Map 3, D4–C4.

At its western end, Cowgate opens out into a much wider, partly cobbled area called the **Grassmarket**, used as the city's cattle market from 1477 to 1911. Though it's surrounded by tall tenements, you still get an unexpected view up to the precipitous crags of the Castle, and come springtime, it's sunny enough for the cafés here to put tables and chairs along the pavement on the quieter, tree-lined side of street. The Grassmarket has, however, played an important role in the murkier aspects of Edinburgh's past. The public gallows were located here, and it was the scene of numerous riots and other disturbances down the centuries. It was to here, in 1736, that Captain Porteous was dragged from the Tolbooth and lynched by a mob upset that he escaped punishment for killing nine citizens when, "inflamed with wine and jealousy", according to one contemporary account, he ordered the town guard to shoot into a potentially restless crowd watching a public execution. The notorious duo William Burke and William Hare had their lair in a now-vanished close just off the western end of the Grassmarket: they would lure victims here, murder them and then sell

GRASSMARKET AND VICTORIA STREET SHOPS

The Grassmarket and Victoria Street hold some of the most idiosyncratic and colourful shops in Edinburgh. Near the eastern end of Grassmarket (called, confusingly, the "West Bow"), look out for Armstrongs, which stocks secondhand clothes, from full tartan regalia to seventies fashions, and The Cooks Bookshop, owned by Clarissa Dickson Wright of TV programme *Two Fat Ladies*' fame, selling new and secondhand books on all matters culinary. Heading up cobbled Victoria Street, take a look into Robert Cresser at no. 40, a gloomy, timeless emporium dedicated to selling brushes of all kinds, shapes and sizes. Opposite this is the *Bow Bar*, one of Edinburgh's finest traditional pubs, with wooden panelling and charming old mirrors, while a little further up, back on the Castle side, stands Iain Mellis's superbly pungent cheesemongery, whose wooden shelves are piled high with an incredible selection of mainly British cheeses. The tall building across the street from this, Byzantium, harbours various shops and booths selling jewellery and antiques.

their bodies to the eminent physician Robert Knox. Eventually, Hare betrayed his partner, who was duly executed in 1829, and Knox's career was finished off as a result. Today, the Grassmarket still feels seamy, though the cluster of busy bars and restaurants along its northern side are evidence of a serious attempt to clean up its image.

- -

With a collection of pubs along its length, the Grassmarket is one of the most popular drinking spots in the city, particularly amongst students. In summer, cafés and restaurants have space to lay out alfresco tables and chairs.

- -

GRASSMARKET

At the northeastern corner of the Grassmarket stand five old tenements of the old **West Bow**, which formerly zigzagged up to the Royal Mile. The rest of this was replaced in the 1840s by curving **Victoria Street**, an unusual two-tier thoroughfare with arcaded shops below and a pedestrian terrace above. This sweeps up to George IV Bridge and the **National Library of Scotland** (Map 3, E3), which holds a rich collection of illuminated manuscripts, early printed books and historical documents as well as the letters and papers of prominent Scottish literary figures. These are displayed in regularly changing thematic exhibitions (usually Mon–Sat 10am–5pm, Sun 2–5pm; free).

GREYFRIARS AND AROUND

Map 3, E5.

The **statue of Greyfriars Bobby** at the southwestern corner of George IV Bridge must rank as Edinburgh's most sentimental tourist attraction. Bobby was a Skye terrier acquired as a working dog by a police constable named John Gray; when Gray died in 1858, Bobby began a vigil at his grave, which he maintained until he died fourteen years later. In the process, he became an Edinburgh celebrity, fed and cared for by locals who gave him a special collar (now in the Museum of Edinburgh; see p.52) to prevent him from being impounded as a stray. His statue was modelled from life, and erected soon after his death; thanks to a spate of cloying books and tear-jerking movies, his story has since gained international renown.

The grave Bobby mourned over is in the **Greyfriars Kirkyard**, entered through the gateway behind the statue. Many famous figures are buried here, including the poet and bestseller **Allan Ramsay Senior**, and designer of the

New Town **James Craig**. Among the clutter of grandiose seventeenth- and eighteenth-century funerary monuments, the most striking mausoleum belongs (perhaps not surprisingly) to the Adam family of architects. Greyfriars Kirkyard is most closely associated, however, with the long struggle to establish **Presbyterianism** in Scotland: in 1638, it was the setting for the signing of the National Covenant, while in 1679, some 1200 **Covenanters** (see box below) were imprisoned in the enclosure at the southwestern end of the yard. Set against the northern wall is the **Martyrs' Monument**, erected in 1706, with an inscription added in 1771, part of which reads:

THE COVENANTERS

When Charles I, inspired by his belief in the divine right of kings, sought to impose a new *Book of Common Prayer* and episcopacy on the Scottish people in 1637, reaction was strong. Fuelled by anger at such high-handed interference, a number of leading figures in Scotland drew up a National Covenant, calling for "a glorious marriage of the kingdom and God" through the maintenance of Presbyterian church structures. In an undemocratic age, ordinary citizens showed their support for the Covenant by signing it; over 5000 people lined up to do so at Greyfriars Kirkyard, and some 300,000 across Scotland subsequently added their names. In November 1638, the General Assembly of the Church of Scotland denounced Charles's Episcopalian reforms, and the Covenanters readied themselves for civil war against royalist forces. With the outbreak of the Civil War in England, they forged links with the English opposition to Charles through the Solemn League and Covenant of 1643.

Following the execution of Charles I in 1649, Charles II's

"Here lies interr'd the dust of those who stood,
'Gainst perjury, resisting unto blood".

An example of a **mort safe** – a lockable iron structure designed to deter grave-robbers – can be seen beside the path running along the south side of the church. After the founding of Edinburgh University, a shortage of bodies to use for dissection led to **grave-robbing**, and as early as 1711, more than one hundred years before the heyday of Burke and Hare, the Royal College of Surgeons reported: "Of late there has been a violation of sepulchres in the Greyfriars Churchyard by some who most unchristianly have been stealing, or at least attempting to carry away, the

acquiescence to the Covenant persuaded the Scots to back their monarch. This set them against Oliver Cromwell, who sent an army north, defeated the Scottish forces, and subdued large parts of Scotland, capturing Edinburgh Castle along the way.

After the restoration of the monarchy in 1660, Charles II reneged on his signing of the Covenant and sought to reintroduce episcopacy. Weakened by defeats in the Civil War, resistance within Scotland tended to be more passive this time, largely isolating those still supporting the Covenant, who were forced to hold their conventicles (prayer meetings) outdoors and resorted to a series of unsuccessful armed uprisings such as the battle of Bothwell Bridge in 1679. The Episcopal church was, however, never accepted in Scotland and by the 1680s Presbyterianism, albeit in a more moderate form than that advocated by the Covenanters, was accepted as the foundation of the Church of Scotland. Covenanter resistance weakened after this point with only a hard core, known as the Cameronians, surviving into the eighteenth century.

bodies of the dead out of their graves".

The graveyard rather overshadows **Greyfriars Kirk** itself; completed in 1620, it was the first church built in Edinburgh after the Reformation. It's a real oddball in both layout and design, having a nave and aisles but no chancel, and adopting the anachronistic architectural language of the friary that preceded it, complete with medieval-looking windows, arches and buttresses.

At the western end of Greyfriars Kirkyard is one of the most significant surviving portions of the **Flodden Wall**, the city fortifications erected in the wake of Scotland's disastrous military defeat of 1513. When open, the gateway beyond offers a shortcut to **George Heriot's School** (Map 3, D5), otherwise approached from Lauriston Place to the south. Founded as a home for poor boys by "Jinglin Geordie" Heriot, James VI's goldsmith, it is now one of Edinburgh's most prestigious fee-paying schools; although you can't go inside, you can wander round the quadrangle, whose array of towers, turrets, chimneys, carved doorways and traceried windows is one of the finest achievements of the Scottish Renaissance.

THE NATIONAL MUSEUM OF SCOTLAND

Map 3, E5. Mon & Weds–Sat 10am–5pm, Tues 10am–8pm, Sun noon–5pm; free. Ⓦwww.nms.ac.uk/mos.

Immediately opposite the statue of Greyfriars Bobby, on the south side of Chambers Street, stands the striking honey-coloured sandstone building of the **National Museum of Scotland**. Opened in 1998 to deserved acclaim, both for its elegant design and for its respectful but imaginative treatment of the nation's treasures, this is undoubtedly Scotland's premier museum. The fresh, open atmosphere of the building is combined with terrific features: specially commissioned art works; the

Discovery Centre, specifically aimed at 5–14-year-olds (for more on this, see "Kids' Edinburgh", p.263); the **exhibIT** computer bank with databases of the museum's collections; and the **Tower Restaurant**, a sleek, stylish venue with fabulous views which is also open in the evenings (see p.204).

The lack of a figurehead national museum had been keenly felt in Scotland for decades, but it wasn't until the late 1980s that funding was made available, with construction beginning in 1996. Designed by architects Benson and Forsyth, it was built principally from sandstone quarried near Elgin in northeast Scotland. The most striking feature of the exterior is the cylindrical entrance tower, which breaks up the building's angular, modern lines and echoes the shape of Edinburgh Castle's Half Moon Battery. Tall windows reveal glimpses of the interior, an effect continued inside, where unexpected views of the floors above and below, as well as out onto the street, emphasize the interconnectedness of the layers of Scotland's history.

The main entrance to the museum is at the base of the tower, although it is also possible to enter through the adjoining Royal Museum of Scotland (see p.79). The information desk in **Hawthornden Court**, the central atrium, is a useful orientation point. On this level you'll also find the museum shop, the sound-guide desk and access to the Royal Museum's café. The glossy **brochure** on sale (£4.99) is more a photographic souvenir than a guidebook, but free **guided tours** on different themes take place throughout the day, and audio headsets (free) give detailed information on artefacts and displays.

Beginnings and early people

To get to the first section, "**Beginnings**", take the lift or stairs from Hawthornden Court down to Level 0. Here,

Scotland's story before the arrival of man is recounted with audiovisual displays, artistic re-creations and a selection of rocks and fossils, including some Lewisian gneiss, the oldest rock in Europe, and "Lizzie" (*Westlothiana lizziae*), the oldest known fossil reptile in the world.

The second section, "**Early People**", also on Level 0, covers the period from the arrival of the first people to the end of the first millennium AD. This, in many ways, is the most engrossing section of the entire museum, an eloquent testament to the remarkable craftsmanship, artistry and practicality of Scotland's early people. The best way to approach this section is from the doors of the main lift, where you are confronted by eight giant bronze figures in the distinctive post-industrial style of Edinburgh-born sculptor **Sir Eduardo Paolozzi**. Small display compartments containing artefacts such as necklaces and bracelets are incorporated into the bronze figures. The innovative use of contemporary art is continued with installations by the environmental artist **Andy Goldsworthy**, who shapes natural materials into sinuously beautiful geometrical patterns. Look out for *Hearth*, created from pieces of wood found on the construction site of the new museum, and *Enclosure*, four curved walls of slate roof tiles, and four separate panels of cracked clay set into the walls of the museum. Among the artefacts on display, highlights include the **Trappain treasure** hoard, around 44lb of silver plates, cutlery and goblets found buried in East Lothian; the **Cramond Lioness**, a sculpture from a Roman tombstone found recently in the Firth of Forth (see p.124); and the beautifully detailed gold, silver and amber **Hunterston brooch**, dating from around 700 AD.

The Kingdom of the Scots

The "**Kingdom of the Scots**" on Level 1 covers the period between Scotland's development as a single independent nation and the union with England in 1707. Standing at the entrance to the section in Hawthornden Court is the **Dupplin Cross**, a symbol of the different peoples who united under king Kenneth MacAlpin to form a single kingdom in 843. Many famous Scots are represented here, including Robert the Bruce, Mary, Queen of Scots and her son James VI, under whom the crowns of Scotland and England became united in 1603. Star exhibits include the **Monymusk reliquary**, an intricately decorated box said to have carried the remains of St Columba; the **Lewis chessmen**, exquisitely idiosyncratic twelfth-century pieces carved from walrus ivory; and the "**Maiden**", an early form of the guillotine. The section on the church is of interest not only for the craftsmanship of some of the objects, most notably the silver gilt **St Fillan's crozier**, but also because just outside the window you can glimpse Greyfriars Kirkyard, where the National Covenant – the document which demanded a Presbyterian rather than Episcopalian form of worship in Scotland and provoked numerous battles in the sixteenth and seventeenth centuries – was signed in 1638 (see p.72–73).

In the National Museum, the upmarket *Tower Restaurant* serves light meals through the day; alternatively, head through to the Royal Museum, where a café serving cakes, coffee and light snacks is located in the impressive main hall.

Also on this floor, the often overlooked heritage and society of the **Gaels**, the people who populated most of northern and western Scotland, is covered in "Na Gaidheil", with displays of beautifully patterned Highland brooches; claymores and dirks, the Highlander's fighting weapons; and an exquisite clarsach, or harp, dating from around 1500.

THE NATIONAL MUSEUM OF SCOTLAND

Scotland Transformed

Level 3 shows exhibits under the theme "**Scotland Transformed**", covering the century or so following the Union of Parliaments in 1707. This was the period which saw the last of the Highland uprisings under Bonnie Prince Charlie (whose silver travelling canteen is on display), yet also witnessed the expansion of trade links with the Americas and developments in industries such as weaving, and iron and steel production. Dominating the floor is a reconstructed steam-driven **Newcomen engine**, which was still being used to pump water from a coal mine in Ayrshire in 1901. In contrast, alongside it stands part of a thatched, cruck-frame house of the 1720s, of a type in which many Scots still lived during this time.

Industry and Empire

The next stage of the country's development, "**Industry and Empire**", is covered by exhibits on levels 4 and 5. Following the early innovations of steam and mechanical engineering, Scotland went on to pioneer many aspects of heavy engineering, with ship and locomotive production to the fore. As a result, there's a stolid functionality to many of the exhibits here, including the heaviest in the museum, the steam locomotive *Ellesmere*, which has the honour of being the first object installed in the new building – it had to be lowered into place before the upper storeys could be completed. This era was particularly productive and enterprising for Scotland, and other fields are covered alongside industrial progress, including domestic life, leisure activities and the development of art, design and architecture. It has been claimed that Scotland's greatest export was its people, and in recognition of this the displays reflect the influence of Scots outside Scotland, both as a result of emigration, and through such luminaries as James Watt, Charles Rennie Mackintosh (see p.136) and Robert Louis Stevenson (see p.45).

The Twentieth Century Gallery

For the **Twentieth Century Gallery** on Level 6, a range of Scots, from schoolchildren to celebrities, were asked to pick a single object to represent the twentieth century. Choices are intriguing, controversial and unexpected, from computers to football strips, cans of Irn Bru to a black Saab convertible. Tony Blair, who went to Fettes school in Edinburgh, chose a Fender Stratocaster guitar, and former Edinburgh "milkie" Sir Sean Connery a milk bottle. The obvious challenge is implicitly made: what would you choose, and why? Other features worth taking in here include a small **cinema** showing black-and-white documentary films about life in Scotland in the 1930s, and the often-overlooked but delightful **roof garden**, accessed by a lift. Up here, sweeping views open out to the Firth of Forth, the Pentland Hills, and across to the Castle and Royal Mile skyline.

THE ROYAL MUSEUM OF SCOTLAND

Map 3, F5. Mon–Sat 10am–5pm, Tues 10am–8pm, Sun noon–5pm; free.

Interlinked with the National Museum, though also with its own entrance, is the **Royal Museum of Scotland**, a dignified Venetian-style palace with a cast-iron interior, built in 1866 and extended in 1914. Intended as Scotland's answer to the museum complex in London's South Kensington, the Royal Museum contains an extraordinarily eclectic range of exhibits, from exotic stuffed animals to colonial loot. The neat slogan used to describe the different roles of the sister museums is that the National Museum shows Scotland to the world, and the Royal Museum shows the world to Scotland.

The **sculpture** in the lofty entrance hall begins with a superb Assyrian relief from the royal palace at Nimrud, and ranges via classical Greece, Rome and Nubia to buddhas from Japan and Burma and a totem pole from British Columbia. Also on the ground floor are the **Power Collections**, which include a double-action beam engine designed by James Watt in 1786, a section of the Inchkeith lighthouse and the control desk from Hunterston A nuclear reactor.

Upstairs, there's a fine array of Egyptian **mummies**, ceramics from ancient Greece to the present day, costumes, jewellery, natural-history displays and a splendid selection of European **decorative art**, ranging from early medieval liturgical objects via Limoges enamels and sixteenth-century German woodcarving to stunning **French silverware** made during the reign of Louis XIV. Finally, on the **top floor**, you'll come to a distinguished collection of historic scientific instruments, a small selection of arms and armour, plus sections on geology, ethnology and Oriental arts. The Asian selection includes the **Ivy Wu Gallery**, which displays and interprets the arts of China, Korea and Japan; look out for a splendid sixteenth-century Chinese throne and Buddhist art from each of the three nations.

THE UNIVERSITY AND AROUND

Immediately alongside the Royal Museum on Chambers Street is the earliest surviving part of the **University of Edinburgh** (Map 3, G4; ⓦwww.ed.ac.uk). Variously referred to as Old College or Old Quad, it houses only a few University departments nowadays; the main campus colonizes the streets and squares to the south. Founded in 1582 by James VI (later James I of England), the university is now the largest in Scotland, with over 13,000 students, and enjoys a high standing in Britain as a whole with particularly strong reputations in areas such as medicine and cutting-edge technology. However, due to the fact that the various faculties and buildings are scattered around this area, and that students live in many different parts of Edinburgh, the university plays a less prominent role in city life than in many university towns.

The Old College, the entrance to which faces onto South Bridge, was designed and begun by Robert Adam. However, money became tight after the Napoleonic Wars, and it was completed after Adam's death (in a considerably modified form) by William Playfair (1789–1857), one of Edinburgh's greatest architects. Playfair built just one of Adam's two quadrangles (the dome, topped by a golden "Youth", was not added until 1879), and his magnificent Neoclassical Upper Library is now mostly used for ceremonial occasions. The only way to see the library is as part of a general Old College tour, which take place at 1pm on the last Friday of every month (free), departing from the Edinburgh University Centre at 7–11 Nicolson St (bookings are recommended; call ☎0131/650 2252). The one part of the Old Quad open to the public on a regular basis is the small **Talbot Rice Art Gallery** (Tues–Sat 10am–5pm; free), which displays, in rather lacklustre fashion, some of the University's large art and bronze collection, including a number of twentieth-century works by Scots artists Joan Eardley and William McTaggart. The best part of the gallery, worth navigating the complex entrance route to find, are the rooms given over to touring and temporary avant garde exhibitions, mounted here on a regular basis – in particular, the show held during the Festival is normally worth catching.

A little further up South Bridge (on its southern extension, Nicolson Street) is the glass-fronted **Festival Theatre** (Map 3, G5; see p.244), a refurbished music hall which

DARNLEY'S MURDER

In January 1567, the husband of Mary, Queen of Scots Lord Darnley, suffering from smallpox (or perhaps syphilis), was brought to a church known as Kirk o'Field, close to what is now the quadrangle of Old College, in order to ensure that he did not infect his infant son later James I and VI) in Holyrood. On the night of February 9, the building was destroyed by a huge explosion and the body of Darnley was found in the grounds outside. There were no signs of his body having been in an explosion: examination showed that he had been strangled. Mary, Queen of Scots, who had visited her husband on the evening in question and was later seen walking up Blackfriars Wynd, is generally considered to have been implicated in the murder. These allegations have never been proved, but what is known is that Mary was by then involved with the Earl of Bothwell, who was almost certainly responsible for the deed. After his arrest and suspiciously speedy acquittal, Bothwell abducted Mary on her way from Stirling to Linlithgow, divorced his own wife and married the queen on May 15, 1567. Within a month Mary had surrendered to the enraged nobles of Scotland: Bothwell fled to Orkney and then Norway, where he died in captivity eleven years later.

opened in 1994, giving the city a long-awaited venue for presenting opera and dance on a large scale. Opposite this is the stately facade of **Surgeons' Hall** (Map 3, H5), a handsome Ionic temple built by Playfair as the headquarters of the Royal College of Surgeons. Most of it is accessible to the public one day a year only, but the exception is the **museum** (Mon–Fri 2–4pm; free), entered from 9 Hill Square, which has intriguing, if somewhat specialist exhibits on the history of medicine, including a book bound with the skin of body-snatcher William Hare.

LOTHIAN ROAD AND AROUND

Map 2, G7.

The area immediately **west** and **southwest** of the Old Town was formerly known as **Portsburgh**, a theoretically separate burgh outside the city walls that was nonetheless a virtual fiefdom of Edinburgh. Since the 1880s and the construction of the **Royal Lyceum Theatre** on Grindlay Street, the area has gradually developed into something of a theatre district, with the Usher Hall, Traverse Theatre and Filmhouse cinema, along with a collection of good restaurants and bars, all within a few hundred yards of each other. Running north-south through the area is the wide **Lothian Road**, which together with perpendicular Morrison Street has seen a good deal of construction in recent years, most prominently the Edinburgh Conference Centre and various large financial headquarters. The **Museum of Fire** (Map 3, B6; by appointment only; ℡0131/228 2401; free) on Lauriston Place next to the Edinburgh College of Art, records the history of the oldest municipal fire brigade in Britain, formed in 1824. It contains a small collection of well-preserved manual, horse-drawn and motorized fire appliances – fascinating for shiny-red-engine fans of all ages.

Lothian Road meets Lauriston Place at **Tollcross** – marked by a clock in the middle of a busy crossroads, this area is lively at night and holds intimate art-house cinema The Cameo. Beyond Tollcross, the open parkland areas of the **Meadows** and **Bruntsfield Links** mark the transition to Edinburgh's genteel Victorian villa suburbs. The streets closest to the meadows in the suburbs of **Newington**, **Marchmont** and **Brunstfield** are dominated by students' flats; further south again is **Morningside**, whose prim-and-proper outlook was immortalized in Muriel Spark's *The Prime of Miss Jean Brodie*, and remains a favourite target for ridicule.

The New Town

Edinburgh's **New Town**, itself well over two hundred years old, covers a very rough semi-circle of about half-a-mile in radius, with its base along Princes Street, which runs east-west. The area stands in total contrast to the Old Town: the layout is symmetrical, the streets broad and straight, and most of the buildings are Neoclassical. The entire area, right down to the names of its streets, is something of a celebration of the Union, which was then generally regarded as a proud development in Scotland's history. Though originally intended as a residential quarter, the New Town today is the bustling hub of the city's professional, commercial and business life, dominated by shops, banks and offices.

The area chiefly owes its existence to the vision of **George Drummond**, who made schemes for the expansion of the city soon after becoming Lord Provost in 1725. Work began on the draining of the Nor' Loch below the Castle in 1759, a job that was to take some sixty years. The North Bridge, linking the Old Town with the top of Leith Walk (the main thoroughfare to Leith), was built between 1763 and 1772. In 1766, a public competition was launched for a plan for the New Town, and the next year the design submitted by a 20-year-old architect, **James Craig**, was chosen. Its gridiron pattern was perfectly matched to the site: the central **George Street**, flanked by showpiece squares, was laid out along the main ridge, with the parallel **Princes Street** and **Queen Street** on either side below, and two smaller streets, Thistle Street and Rose Street in between the three major thoroughfares. These smaller streets were for coach houses, artisans' dwellings and shops. Princes and Queen streets were built up on one side only, so as not to block the spectacular views of the Old Town and Fife. Architects were accordingly afforded a wonderful opportunity to play with vistas and spatial relationships, particularly well exploited by Robert Adam, who contributed extensively to the later phases of the project. The "First New Town", as the area covered by Craig's plan came to be known, received a whole series of **extensions** in the first few decades of the nineteenth century, all in harmony with the Neoclassical style; these extended the New Town north towards the former village of **Stockbridge**, west towards the **Dean Village** and east to **Calton**.

In many ways, the layout of the New Town is its own most remarkable sight, an extraordinary grouping of squares, circuses, terraces, crescents and parks, with a few set pieces such as **Register House** on Princes Street, the north frontage of **Charlotte Square** at the western end of George Street and the assemblage of curiosities on and around **Calton Hill**. It also contains an assortment of Victorian additions, notably the **Scott Monument** (near Waverley Station off Princes Street), as well as three of the city's most important public collections – the **National Gallery of Scotland** at the foot of the Mound halfway along Princes Street, the **Scottish National Portrait Gallery** just off St Andrew Square on Queen Street, and the **Scottish National Gallery of Modern Art**, a mile or so out from the centre on the far bank of the Water of Leith. This waterway, the source of power for mills from the late eighteenth century onwards, has a number of inter-

THE NEW TOWN

esting communities along its course, including **Dean Village** and **Stockbridge**, near which is the 28-hectare **Royal Botanic Garden**, an oasis of calm in an otherwise busy city. Three miles west of the centre the natural world is also on view at **Edinburgh Zoo**, which spreads over the slopes of Corstorphine Hill.

PRINCES STREET

Although only allocated a subsidiary role in James Craig's original plan of the New Town, **Princes Street** (Map 4, L5–C8) had developed into Edinburgh's principal thoroughfare by the middle of the nineteenth century, a role it has retained ever since. It's principally known as a shopping street, though in fact much of its character results from the sunken **Princes Street Gardens** on the south side of the street, which allow unobstructed and magnificent **views** across to the Castle and the Old Town. Indeed, without the views Princes Street would lose much of its appeal: its northern side, dominated for the most part by ugly department stores, is almost always crowded with shoppers, and few of the original eighteenth-century buildings remain.

The gardens are pleasantly laid out with trees and colourful flowerbeds, and offer ample space to relax or picnic during the summer. Formed from the area once filled by the Nor' Loch, they are divided into East and West sections on either side of the **Mound** (Map 4, H7–H8), a steep hill running between Princes Street and the Old Town, which was formed, as its name suggests, from heaps of earth and other waste dumped here when the New Town was being built. Most of the principal places of interest along Princes Street are found either in or adjacent to the gardens, including **Waverley railway station**, the distinctive Gothic **monument to Walter Scott**, and, at the foot of the Mound, the two grand, Grecian-temple-style buildings which house the collection of the **National Gallery of Scotland**.

Waverley Station and around

Princes Street's rise to prominence was ensured by the coming of the **railway**, which follows a parallel course to the south. The tracks are well concealed, running through West Princes Street Gardens under the Castle, and spreading out as they come into **Waverley Station** (Map 4, K7) near the eastern end of Princes Street. Indeed, the rumble and tooting of the trains, while nothing like as dramatic as the hiss and chug of the old steam locomotives, still adds to the blend of modern-day bustle and centuries-old history right at the heart of Edinburgh.

Immediately between Waverley Station and Princes Street is **Princes Mall** (Map 4, K6), a reasonably sensitive modern redevelopment, with an open-air piazza on its street-level roof that's a favourite haunt of street-theatre groups and other performing artists during the Festival. Also located on the piazza is Edinburgh's Tourist Information Office (see p.6). Towering above this is *The Balmoral* (see p.179), one of the most luxurious hotels in the city. Formerly the **North British Hotel**, and still popularly known as the "NB", its name was changed in the 1980s in a gesture of political correctness by new owners: North Britain was an alternative name for Scotland throughout the eighteenth and nineteenth centuries, and is regarded by Scots as an affront. Originally built by the owners of the North British Railway for travellers arriving at Waverley Station, *The Balmoral* maintains its association with the railway, and the timepiece on its bulky clocktower is always kept two minutes fast in order to encourage passengers to hurry to catch their trains.

PRINCES STREET

Register House and around

Diagonally opposite the *Balmoral*, Princes Street's most distinguished building is **Register House** (Map 4, K5; Mon–Fri 10am–4pm; free), framing the perspective down North Bridge and providing a good visual link between the Old and New towns. Register House was designed in the 1770s by Robert Adam to hold records such as birth, marriage and death certificates, a function it has maintained ever since. It's a mine of information if you're interested in researching your Scottish ancestry, and small exhibitions of historic documents are often mounted as well. The exterior is a model of restrained Neoclassicism; the interior, centred on a glorious Roman rotunda, has a dome lavishly decorated with plasterwork and antique-style medallions. Unfortunately, the majesty of the building was marred when the **St James Centre** (Map 4, L4) was constructed to the rear, a grey, angular behemoth of a shopping arcade, woefully out of keeping with the elegant Georgian buildings around it and now regarded as the city's worst ever planning blunder.

The Scott Monument

Map 4, I6.

Set in the northeastern corner of East Princes Street Gardens just to the west of Waverley Station, facing Princes Street's grand Victorian shopping emporium Jenners (see p.271), the 200ft-high **Scott Monument** is the largest memorial in the world to be erected to a writer. Built with donations from the public in memory of Sir Walter Scott within a few years of his death, its magisterial, if somewhat incongruous, Gothic spire-like design is the single work of George Kemp, a local artist and craftsman; while it was still under construction, he stumbled into a canal one foggy evening and drowned. The architecture is closely modelled on Scott's beloved Melrose Abbey (see p.168) – his country mansion, Abbotsford, was nearby – while the rich sculptural decoration shows sixteen Scottish writers and 64 characters from the *Waverley* novels. Underneath the archway stands a **statue** of Scott with his deerhound Maida, carved from a thirty-ton block of Carrara marble. If the weather is clear and you don't mind trudging up the narrow internal spiral staircase, it's worth paying the admission price for some inspiring – if heady – vistas of the city below and the hills and firths beyond.

Each December and January, as part of an annual winter festival, East Princes Street Gardens play host to a giant ferris wheel, outdoor skating rink and stalls selling Christmas gifts.

The National Gallery of Scotland

Map 4, H8. Mon–Sat 10am–5pm, Sun noon–5pm; free, entrance charge for some temporary exhibitions

Standing between the east and west sections of Princes Street Gardens are two grand sandstone buildings; nearest to Princes Street, Playfair's **Royal Scottish Academy** (Map 4, H7), is the more elaborate of the two, a Grecian-style Doric temple topped with a statue of Queen Victoria and four sphinxes. Having fallen into a bad state of repair, it's now closed until at least the summer of 2003 while undergoing renovation as part of the £26-million Playfair Project, due for full completion in 2005; eventually, it will be used as an extension of the the **National Gallery of Scotland**, the building immediately to the rear of the Royal Scottish Academy. Another of Playfair's constructions, the National Gallery is a plainer, much less dated yet

SIR WALTER SCOTT

Alongside Robert Burns and Robert Louis Stevenson, Sir Walter Scott (1771–1832) is part of Edinburgh's triumvirate of great literary figures, and of the three it is Scott who can claim to have had the most profound influence on English literature in general.

Born in a house on College Wynd (now Guthrie Street) to a solidly bourgeois family, Scott contracted polio as a child and was sent to recuperate at his grandfather's farm in the Borders, where his imagination was fired by tales of local history and legends. He returned to Edinburgh in 1779 to be educated at the High School, and then Edinburgh University where he studied law, qualifying as an advocate in 1792. His real interests remained elsewhere, however, and throughout the 1790s he transcribed hundreds of old Border ballads, publishing a three-volume collection entitled *Minstrelsy of the Scottish Borders* in 1802. An instant success, *Minstrelsy* was followed by Scott's own narrative poems *Lay of the Last Minstrel*, *Marmion* and *The Lady of the Lake*.

In 1797, Scott and his wife Charlotte moved to 39 North Castle St in Edinburgh's New Town, and he divided his time between Edinburgh and his border seat at Abbotsford. Despite the popularity of his early work, and the fact that he had two prestigious paid jobs – one as the Sheriff-Depute of Selkirkshire, the other as clerk to the Court of Session in Edinburgh – Scott's finances remained shaky. From 1813, he was writing to pay the bills and thumped out a veritable flood of historical novels using his extensive knowledge of Scottish history and folklore. His best works came in the space of the next ten years, beginning with *Waverley* (1814), a runaway success despite the fact that it was published anonymously. This was followed with more novels "by the author of *Waverley*", including *Guy Mannering* (1815), *Rob Roy* and *The Heart of Midlothian* (both 1818), *Ivanhoe* (1819) and *Kenilworth* (1821). By this time Scott was *the* pre-eminent public figure in Edinburgh and Scottish life, organizing the successful search for the Honours of Scotland – which were discovered in Edinburgh Castle in 1818, the same year he was created a baronet – and co-ordinating the tartan-draped visit of George IV to Edinburgh in 1822. This event, seen as a watershed between the turbulent years of the Jacobite rebellions and Scotland's embrace of the more worldly vision of the United Kingdom, crowned Scott's romantic refashioning of his country's landscape and history, a vision which has endured as the prominent popular image of Scotland to this day. Only a few years later, however, a publishing venture Scott was involved in crashed, leaving him with huge debts which he vowed to pay off by writing. He buried himself in his craft, producing a succession of weighty tomes; of these, only *Tales of a Grandfather*, another reworking of Scottish legends, stands out, but in six years he earned over £50,000 for his creditors. Inevitably, however, his health suffered and his last years were plagued by illness. He died at Abbotsford in 1832 and was buried within the ruins of Dryburgh Abbey.

Although even his best-known works seem ponderous and heavy by today's standards, his undoubted lyricism and colourful, romantic plots can prove delightful if you've the patience to tackle them. Beyond that, however, his lasting importance is in his essential invention of the historical novel, a formula whose instant appeal and sustained hold over the bestselling lists of the day has been matched by very few authors since.

equally grand edifice built in the 1840s which now houses Scotland's premier collection of pre-twentieth-century European art. Though by no means as vast as national collections found elsewhere in Europe, the gallery benefits not just from a clutch of exquisite Old Masters and Impressionist works, but also from the fact that its manageable size ensures that it won't take you hours to stroll round; the collection is imaginatively displayed, and there's a pleasantly unrushed atmosphere. Elsewhere in the city, the Scottish National Portrait Gallery (see p.100), the Scottish National Gallery of Modern Art (p.112) and its neighbour the Dean Gallery (p.114), display other parts of the collection. A free bus service (Mon–Sat 11am–5pm, Sun 12–5pm) connects all four buildings.

The ongoing Playfair Project means that the National Gallery of Scotland will be using a temporary entrance at its southern (Old Town) end for all of 2002. However, this will be clearly signposted and the layout within will remain largely the same.

The innovative and often controversial influence of the National Galleries' flamboyant director, Timothy Clifford, is immediately apparent on the **ground floor**, where the rooms have been restored to their 1840s appearance, with the pictures hung closely together on claret-coloured walls, and are intermingled with sculptures and *objets d'art* to produce a deliberately cluttered effect. As a result some lesser works, which would otherwise languish in the vaults, are displayed a good 15ft up. Two small, late nineteenth-century works in Room XII – one anonymous, the other by A.E. Moffat – show the gallery as it was in the nineteenth century, with paintings stacked up even higher than at present.

Though individual works are frequently rearranged, the layout is broadly chronological, starting in the upper rooms above the entrance and continuing clockwise around the ground floor. The upper part of the rear extension is devoted to smaller panels of the eighteenth and nineteenth centuries, while the basement contains the majority of the Scottish collection. The gallery has a programme of temporary exhibitions, which may mean that some of the paintings described below will not be on display. There are no guided tours; instead, **audioguides** (£2), available in five languages, provide commentaries on the more important works. Free leaflets showing the floor plan are available.

Early Italian, Netherlandish and German works

From the gallery's main entrance, you pass through a lobby area and a set of doors; from here, the ground-floor galleries lead off to left and right; head upstairs to begin a chronological tour in **Room A1**. Here, among the gallery's most valuable treasures, are the *Trinity Panels*, the remaining parts of the only surviving pre-Reformation altarpiece. Painted by **Hugo van der Goes** in the mid-fifteenth century, they were commissioned for the Holy Trinity Collegiate Church (which was demolished to make way for Waverley Station) by its provost Edward Bonkil, who appears in the company of organ-playing angels in the finest and best preserved of the four panels. On the reverse sides are portraits of James III, his son (the future James IV) and Queen Margaret of Denmark. Their feebly characterized heads, which stand in jarring contrast to the superlative figures of the patron saints accompanying them, were modelled from life by an unknown local painter after the altar had been shipped to Edinburgh. The panels are turned every half hour.

Of the later Netherlandish works elsewhere on this upper floor, **Gerard David** is represented by the touchingly anecdotal *Three Legends of St Nicholas*, while the *Portrait of a Man* by **Quentin Massys** is an excellent early example of northern European assimilation of the forms and techniques of the Italian Renaissance. Many of his German contemporaries developed their own variations on this style, among them **Lucas Cranach**, whose splendidly erotic *Venus and Cupid* is sometimes on view. Along with the *Trinity Panels*, the other outstanding highlight of Room A1 is **Botticelli**'s superb *The Virgin Adoring the Sleeping Christ Child*, which has been carefully restored and now positively glows with colour and light.

The Italian Renaissance

The main ground-floor rooms are best approached in a clockwise direction from the entrance. There's more Italian art in **Room I**, including three graceful works by **Raphael**, particularly *The Bridgewater Madonna* and the tondo of *The Holy Family with a Palm Tree*, the latter another example of the striking luminosity that restoration can reveal.

Of the four mythological scenes by **Titian**, the sensuous *Three Ages of Man*, an allegory of childhood, adulthood and old age, is one of the most accomplished compositions of his early period. The companion pair of *Diana and Acteon* and *Diana and Calisto*, painted for Philip II of Spain, show the almost impressionistic freedom of his late style. **Bassano**'s truly regal *Adoration of the Kings*, a dramatic altarpiece of *The Deposition of Christ* by **Tintoretto**, and several other works by **Veronese**, complete a fine Venetian collection.

Seventeenth-century southern European works

Moving through to **Room IV**, look out for **El Greco**'s *An Allegory (Fábula)*, painted during his early years in Italy – an intriguing departure from his usual religious themes, which depicts two figures and a monkey staring into a glowing torch. Indigenous Spanish art is represented by **Velázquez**'s

An Old Woman Cooking Eggs, an astonishingly assured work for a lad of nineteen, and by **Zurbaran**'s *The Immaculate Conception*, part of his ambitious decorative scheme for the Carthusian monastery in Jerez. Look out also for the two small copper panels by the short-lived but enormously influential Rome-based German painter **Adam Elsheimer**; *The Stoning of St Stephen* is a tour de force of technical precision.

The series of *The Seven Sacraments* by **Poussin** are displayed in their own small room off Room IV, whose floor and central octagonal seat repeat some of the motifs in the paintings. Based on the artist's extensive research into biblical times, the series marks the first attempt to portray scenes from the life of Jesus and the early Christians in an authentic manner, rather than one overlaid by artistic conventions. The result is profoundly touching, with a myriad of imaginative and subtle detailing right down to eyelashes and fingernails. In **Room IV**, Poussin's younger contemporary **Claude**, who also left France to live in Rome, is represented by his largest canvas, *Landscape with Apollo and the Muse*, which radiates his characteristically idealized vision of Classical antiquity.

Seventeenth-century Flemish and Dutch works

Moving through to rooms **VI** and **IX**, **Rubens**' *The Feast of Herod* is an archetypal example of his grand manner, in which the gory subject matter is overshadowed by the lively depiction of the delights of the table; the painting's rich colours have been revived by recent restoration. Like all his large works, it was executed with extensive studio assistance, whereas the three small *modellos*, including the highly finished *Adoration of the Shepherds*, are all from his own hand. The trio of large upright canvases by **van Dyck** date from his early Genoese period; of these, *The Lomellini Family* shows his mastery in creating a definitive dynastic

PRINCES STREET

●

95

image. Among the four canvases by **Rembrandt** is a poignant *Self Portrait Aged 51*, and the ripely suggestive *Woman in Bed*, which probably represents the biblical figure of Sarah on her wedding night, waiting for her husband Tobias to put the devil to flight. *Christ in the House of Martha and Mary* is the largest and probably the earliest of the thirty or so surviving paintings by **Vermeer**; as the only one with a religious subject, it inspired a notorious series of forgeries by Han van Meegeren. There are two portraits by **Hals**, while his *Verdonck* stands in animated contrast to Rembrandt's self portrait. There's also an excellent cross-section of the specialist Dutch painters of the age, including the strangely haunting *Interior of the Church of St Bavo in Haarlem* by **Pieter Saenredam**.

European works of the eighteenth and nineteenth centuries

The stairwell between rooms VI and XI holds some of the gallery's best-known paintings. Of the large-scale eighteenth-century works, **Tiepolo**'s *The Finding of Moses*, a gloriously bravura fantasy (the Pharaoh's daughter and her attendants appear in sixteenth-century garb) stands out; despite its enormous size, it has lost a large portion from the right-hand side. By way of contrast, the gems of the French section are the smaller panels, in particular **Watteau**'s *Fêtes Vénitiennes*, an effervescent Rococo idyll, and **Chardin**'s *Vase of Flowers*, a copybook example of still-life painting.

There's also a superb group of early Impressionist works such as Jean Bastien **Lepage**'s beautifully innocent *Pas Meche*, and Camille **Pissarro**'s *Kitchen Garden L'Hermitage*. Impressionist masters are also well represented; there's a collection of sketches, painting and bronzes by **Degas**, including the influential *Portrait of Diego Marteli*, as well as **Monet**'s *Haystacks (Snow)* and **Renoir**'s *Woman Nursing Child*. Representing the post-Impressionists are three outstanding examples of **Gauguin**'s work, including *Vision After the Sermon*, set in Brittany; **Van Gogh**'s *Olive Trees*; and **Cézanne**'s *The Big Trees* – a clear forerunner of modern abstraction.

English and American paintings

The western side of the gallery (rooms **X**, **XI** and **XII**) holds the relatively small but impressive collection of English works. **Hogarth**'s *Sarah Malcolm*, painted in Newgate Prison the day the murderess was executed, once belonged to Horace Walpole, who also commissioned **Reynolds**' *The Ladies Waldegrave*, a group portrait of his three great-nieces. **Gainsborough**'s *The Honourable Mrs Graham* is one of his most memorable society portraits, while **Constable** himself described *Dedham Vale* as being "perhaps my best".

The National Gallery owns a wonderful array of watercolours by Turner, faithfully displayed in the basement (Room B2) each January, when damaging sunlight is at its weakest. At other times of the year, you can enjoy two of his fine Roman views displayed in one of the darker galleries (usually Room XI).

More unexpected than the scarcity of English works is the presence of some exceptional American canvases, among them **Benjamin West**'s Romantic fantasy, *King Alexander III Rescued from a Stag* and **John Singer Sargent**'s virtuoso *Lady Agnew of Lochnaw*. Room XII is also the designated spot for one of the gallery's most recent major purchases, **Canova**'s 1817 statue *The Three Graces* – saved for the nation at the last minute from the hands of the J. Paul Getty Museum in California. However, as part of the purchase agreement, it's on loan to the Victoria and Albert Museum in London until 2006.

PRINCES STREET

Scottish art

Displayed in the rear basement area and reached through rooms VI and VII, the gallery's Scottish collection covers the entire gamut of Scottish painting from seventeenth-century portraiture to the Arts and Crafts movement, but on balance it's something of an anticlimax. There are, however, some important works displayed within a broad European context: painted in Rome, **Gavin Hamilton**'s *Achilles Mourning the Death of Patroclus*, for example, is an unquestionably arresting image. **Allan Ramsay**, who became court painter to George III, is represented by his *Portrait of a Lady*, once thought to be of Flora MacDonald, Bonnie Prince Charlie's much romanticized rescuer.

A number of the gallery's larger Scottish canvases are given the space they deserve in the **ground floor rooms**, including **Sir Henry Raeburn**'s large portraits, the swaggering masculinity of *Sir John Sinclair* in Highland dress is a fine example of technical mastery. Raeburn was equally assured when working on a small scale, as shown in one of the gallery's most popular pictures, *The Rev Robert Walker Skating on Duddingston Loch*.

Other Scottish painters represented include the versatile **Sir David Wilkie**, whose huge historical painting, *Sir David Baird Discovering the Body of Sultan Tippo Saib*, is in marked contrast to his genre scenes such as *Penny Wedding* (displayed in the basement). **Alexander Nasmyth**'s tendency to gild the lily can be seen in his *View of Tantallon Castle and the Bass Rock*, where the dramatic scenery is spiced up by the inclusion of a shipwreck.

- -
Between George Street and Princes Street is Rose Street,
a pedestrianized lane with a number of off-beat shops
and traditional pubs – a visit to each of the latter was
once considered the city's ultimate pub crawl.
- -

PRINCES STREET

THE WEST END OF PRINCES STREET

At the western end of West Princes Street Gardens is the **graveyard of St Cuthbert's Church** (Map 4, C9). Author of the classic account of drug addiction, *Confessions of an English Opium Eater* (published in 1821), Thomas de Quincey (1785–1859) spent the last thirty years of his life in Edinburgh and is buried here. Nearby, another of the city's grand former railway hotels, the *Caledonian* (see p.179) overlooks the point where Princes Street meets Lothian Road, a junction known to locals as the **West End** (Map 4, B8). North and west of here, the western extension to the New Town was the last part to be built (between 1822 and 1850), and the Victorian additions deviate from the surrounding overriding Neoclassicism. One notable example is the city's principal Episcopal church, **St Mary's Cathedral** (Map 2, G5) – not to be confused with the less ornate St Mary's Catholic Cathedral at the eastern end of the New Town beside the St James Centre. The last major work of Sir George Gilbert Scott, the Episcopal cathedral was built in imitation of the Early English Gothic style. Otherwise, close proximity to the city centre has ensured that the area is now mostly taken up with offices, as well as being home to a decent clutch of bars and restaurants.

GEORGE STREET AND AROUND

Running parallel to and north of Princes Street, **George Street** (Map 4, I5–B7) was originally designed to be the centrepiece of the First New Town, joining the two grand **squares** of St Andrew and Adam-designed Charlotte. Once the site of the city's most august financial institutions, George Street has become a marginally higher-brow version of Princes Street in the last decade: the big-money deals are now done in designer-label shops, and refitted banks sell most of their liquid assets in pint glasses.

At the eastern end of George Street lies **St Andrew Square** (Map 4, I5); slap in the middle is a tall pillar topped with a statue of Lord Melville, Pitt the Younger's Navy Treasurer, while the eastern side is enhanced by a handsome eighteenth-century town mansion, designed by Sir William Chambers and headquarters of the Royal Bank of Scotland since 1825.

The Scottish National Portrait Gallery

Map 4, I3. Mon–Sat 10am–5pm, Sun 2–5pm; free.

Just to the north of the St Andrew Square, facing Queen Street (which runs parallel to George Street), the **Scottish National Portrait Gallery** is the most underrated of Edinburgh's large museums and galleries. The building is itself a fascinating period piece, its red-sandstone exterior, modelled on the Doge's Palace in Venice, encrusted with statues of famous Scots – a theme taken up in the soaring marble entrance hall, which has a mosaic-like frieze procession of great figures from Scotland's past executed by **William Hole**. You can check these out by standing in the entrance hall and craning your neck or going up to the balcony and peering over the rail. A little easier to contemplate are Hole's huge and equally detailed murals of stirring episodes from the nation's history, which adorn the walls behind the balcony. Temporary exhibitions are displayed in the galleries on the ground floor, which is where you'll also find the gallery shop and a pleasant **café** (which closes 30min before the gallery), serving coffees, teas, cakes and wholesome lunchtime meals.

The Permanent Collection

The **permanent collection** is located on the two upper floors. In contrast to the more global outlook of its sister

National Galleries (see pp. 89, 100 & 112), the Portrait Gallery devotes itself to images of famous Scots – a definition stretched to include anyone with the slightest Scottish connection – and is dominated by native artists. Taken as a whole, the gallery offers an engaging procession through Scottish history, with familiar images of famous Scots such as Bonnie Prince Charlie, Mary, Queen of Scots and Robert Burns, though apart from matter-of-fact labels indicating artist and subject, there isn't much provided in the way of historical background, and you'll get much more from the place if you're already familiar with the basics of Scottish history and culture.

On the gallery's second (top) floor are three interlinked rooms covering a sweep of six centuries from Independence in the early fourteenth century to the end of the Victorian era. Kings and queens dominate the early works; thereafter many portraits are included for their sheer quality of expression as much as the importance of their subject: an excellent seventeenth-century study of Charles Seton, second Earl of Dunfermline, is attributed to **van Dyck**; look out also for **John Michael Wright**'s tartan-clad Lord Mungo Murray, who died in the disastrous attempt to establish a Scottish colony in Panama.

Eighteenth-century highlights include portraits of the philosopher-historian David Hume by **Allan Ramsay**, and the bard Robert Burns by his friend **Alexander Nasmyth**, plus a varied group by **Raeburn**: subjects include Sir Walter Scott, the fiddler Niel Gow and the artist himself. The gallery owns two portraits of Bonnie Prince Charlie (not always on display at the same time): one, by **Antonio David**, showing him as an aristocratic, rosy-cheeked twelve-year-old; the other, by **Maurice-Quentin de la Tour**, depicts him as an older, dashing warrior in armour, and was originally purchased by the prince himself. Thomas **Gainsborough**'s portrait of *John, 4th Duke of*

Argyll depicts the man who "pacified" the Highlands after the Jacobite rebellion – though an enemy to many, he was feted by the establishment. The star portrait from the nineteenth century is that of physician **Sir Alexander Morison**, made by his patient, the lunatic painter **Richard Dadd**.

Twentieth-century portraits claim as much room on the first floor as six centuries on the floor above, recognising the relative familiarity of the subjects as well as a much broader range of artistic style. Here you'll find **David Mach**'s clever photomontages of sporting stars Stephen Hendry and Alex Ferguson, a larger-than-life bright red bust of socialist Jimmy Reid by **Kenny Hunter**, and many other royals, inventors, politicians, tycoons and celebrities. Visitors to the café can enjoy the company of Sean Connery, captured by acclaimed Scottish artist **John Bellany**.

Charlotte Square

Map 4, B7.

At the western end of George Street, **Charlotte Square** was designed by Robert Adam in 1791, a year before his death. For the most part, the architect's plans were faithfully implemented, an exception being the domed and porticoed church of St George, which was simplified on grounds of expense. The church's interior was gutted in the 1960s and refurbished as **West Register House** (Map 4, A7), a kind of annexe to Register House at the opposite end of Princes Street; in addition to its role as a record office, it also it also stages small, fairly worthy documentary exhibitions (Mon–Fri 10am–4.45pm; free).

Once the most exclusive quarter of the city, Charlotte Square maintained its prestige when the New Town began to change to commercial use, attracting the offices of the city's most important law firms. By the 1980s, however, it was becoming more and more difficult for the expanding companies to fit into the available space, and for a period in the 1990s the square was eerily empty. However, the wheel has turned again and the **north side** is once more Edinburgh's premier address; the Scottish cabinet meet at number six, the official residence of the First Minister of the Scottish Parliament.

The Georgian House

Map 4, B6. March–Oct Mon–Sat 10am–5pm, Sun 2–5pm; £5.

Restored by the National Trust for Scotland (NTS), the lower floors of neighbouring 7 Charlotte Square are open to the public under the name of the **Georgian House**, whose contents give a good idea of what the interior must have looked like during the period of the first owner, the head of the clan Lamont. The rooms are decked out in period furniture, including a working barrel organ which plays a selection of Scottish airs, and are hung with fine paintings, including portraits by Ramsay and Raeburn, seventeenth-century Dutch cabinet pictures, and a beautiful *Marriage of the Virgin* by El Greco's teacher, the Italian miniaturist Giulio Clovio. In the basement are the original wine cellar, lined with roughly made bins, and a kitchen complete with an open fire for roasting and a separate oven for baking; video reconstructions of life below and above stairs are shown in a nearby room.

National Trust for Scotland headquarters
Map 4, B7.

The NTS' love affair with Charlotte Square is continued on the south side, most of which is taken up with the their main Scottish **headquarters**. Over the past few years, the buildings have been superbly restored to something approaching their Georgian grandeur, and it's well worth stepping through the entrance of number 28 to peer at the sumptuous interior. One floor up, a small **gallery** (Mon–Sat 10am–5pm, Sun noon–5pm; free) shows a varied collection of twentieth-century Scottish art. The highlights are a number of attractive works by the Scottish Colourists (see p.113), such as Samuel Peploe's *Still Life with Roses and Mirror*, with its angular boldness and rich pink- and ivory-colouring. Two adjoining rooms offer an introduction to the Trust in general, with a video showing highlights of their properties around Scotland. Downstairs, there's a **shop** selling National Trust books and souvenirs, as well as a very pleasant **café**. Authentically decked out with severe Georgian family portraits, the same room is used to serve up rather grand "Taste of Scotland" meals in the evenings (see p.207).

NORTHERN NEW TOWN

Begun in 1801, the **Northern New Town** was the earliest extension to the First New Town; today, it roughly covers the area north of Queen Street, between India Street (Map 4, C2–C3) to the west and Broughton Street to the east (Map 4, L2), and stretches as far as Fettes Row to the north (just off the area of our Map 4). The Northern New Town has survived in far better shape than its predecessor: with the exception of Dundas Street, almost all of it is intact, and the area has managed to preserve its predominantly residential character.

Work began on the western end of the New Town, north of Charlotte Square and west of George Street, in 1822. Instead of the straight lines of the earlier sections, there were now the gracious curves of Randolph Crescent, Ainslie Place and the magnificent twelve-sided **Moray Place** (Map 4, A4), designed by the vainglorious James Gillespie Graham, who described himself, with no authority to do so, as "architect in Scotland to the Prince Regent".

Today the houses are used both as offices and grand residential homes – simply strolling around these streets gives you a very clear idea of the refined dignity these Georgian terraces were able to lend Edinburgh's professional classes.

Mansfield Place Church

Map 2, H4.
One of the Northern New Town's most intriguing buildings is the neo-Norman **Mansfield Place Church**, on the corner of Broughton and East London streets, designed in the late nineteenth century for the strange, and now defunct, Catholic Apostolic sect. Having lain redundant and neglected for three decades, it has suddenly acquired cult status, its preservation the current obsession of local conservation groups. The chief reason for this is its cycle of **murals**, made in the late nineteenth century by the Dublin-born **Phoebe Anna Traquair**, a leading light in the Scottish Arts and Crafts movement. Traquair laboured for eight years on this decorative scheme, which has all the freshness and luminosity of a medieval manuscript, yet it was almost lost due to leaks and rot in the fabric of the building. Mansfield Place Church's future was secured, and the precious murals saved, however, when it was acquired by a trust in 1998. The building is currently undergoing major refurbishment, with the basement being turned into offices for Scottish voluntary groups, and the upper level beside the murals being transformed into a large performance and exhibition space.

CALTON

Map 2, I4.
Of the various extensions to the New Town, the most intriguing is **Calton**, which branches out from the eastern

end of Princes Street and encircles the volcanic Calton Hill. For years the centre of a thriving **gay** scene (see p.253), it's an area of extraordinary showpiece architecture, dating from the time of the Napoleonic Wars or just after and intended as an ostentatious celebration of the British victory. While the predominantly Grecian architecture led to Calton being regarded as a "Georgian Acropolis", it is, in fact, more of a shrine to local heroes.

Waterloo Place forms a ceremonial way from Princes Street to Calton Hill, crossing the impressively engineered Regent Bridge (built by lighthouse engineer Robert Stevenson, grandfather of Robert Louis Stevenson). On the southern side of Waterloo Place lies the sombre and overgrown **Old Calton Burial Ground**, in which you can see Robert Adam's plain, cylindrical memorial to David Hume, and a monument, complete with a statue of Abraham Lincoln, to the Scots who died in the American Civil War. Hard up against the cemetery's eastern wall, perched above a sheer rockface, stands a picturesque castellated building which many visitors arriving at Waverley Station below mistake for Edinburgh Castle itself. In fact, it's the only surviving part of **Calton Jail**, formerly Edinburgh's main prison, built in 1791 and extended in 1817 when the Tolbooth jail on the High Street was taken down. Public executions took place on the prison roof until the 1860s, watched by crowds which gathered on Calton Hill. There's no public access these days. Next door is the massive **St Andrew's House**, built in the 1930s to house civil servants.

Further on, set majestically in a confined site below Calton Hill, is one of Edinburgh's greatest buildings, the Grecian **Old Royal High School**, designed by Thomas Hamilton and modelled on the Temple of Theseus in Athens, with Doric columns dominating the central portico and matching colonnaded wings. The High School – alma mater to, among others, Robert Adam, Walter Scott and Alexander Graham Bell – started life as an adjunct to Holyrood Abbey; in 1578 it was given its own building just down the hill from where the present Old College of the University stands (see p.80). In 1829, it moved into the splendid building on Calton Hill, and moved yet again in 1968 to new premises west of the city. For many years, it was assumed that the Old Royal High School building would be the site of Scotland's new parliament, but less than a year before the first elections it was announced that the venue was too small for the parliament envisaged, and that a brand-new building would be commissioned (see p.59). Now unwanted as a debating chamber, its future use is uncertain. Thomas Hamilton also built the **Robert Burns Monument**, a circular Corinthian temple, just across the road, modelled on the Monument to Lysicrates in Athens.

On the night of April 30 each year, Calton Hill is the setting for the Beltane Fire Festival (see p.299), a pagan Celtic ritual celebrating the arrival of spring.

Calton Hill

The upper part of **Calton Hill** is reached via a long flight of stairs from Waterloo Place, opposite the western end of St Andrew's House. Robert Louis Stevenson reckoned that Calton Hill was the best place to view Edinburgh, "since you can see the castle, which you lose from the castle, and Arthur's Seat, which you cannot see from Arthur's Seat". If the panoramas from ground level are spectacular enough, those from the top of the **Nelson Monument** (April–Sept Mon 1–6pm, Tues–Sat 10am–6pm; Oct–March Mon–Sat

CALTON

10am–3pm; £2, or £4 joint ticket with Scott Monument), on the right as you come to the top of the stairs, are even better. Begun just two years after Nelson's death, this is one of Edinburgh's oddest buildings, resembling a gigantic spyglass. Each day at 1pm, a white ball drops down a mast at the top of the monument; together with the one o'clock gun fired from the Castle battlements, these were a daily check for the mariners of Leith who needed accurate chronometers to ensure reliable navigation at sea.

Alongside stands the **National Monument**, begun in 1822 by Playfair to plans by the English architect Charles Cockerell. It was intended to be a replica of the Parthenon, but funds ran out with only twelve columns completed. Subsequent schemes to finish the monument similarly foundered, earning it the nickname "Edinburgh's Disgrace". On the opposite side of the hill, the grandeur of Playfair's classical **Monument to Dugald Stewart** seems totally disproportionate to the stature of the man it commemorates: a now-forgotten professor of philosophy at the University.

Playfair also built the adjacent **City Observatory** for his uncle, the mathematician and astronomer John Playfair, whom he honoured in the cenotaph outside. Because of pollution and the advent of street lighting, which impaired views of the stars, the observatory proper had to be relocated to Blackford Hill, in the south of the city, before the end of the century, though the equipment here continues to be used by students. At the opposite end of the complex is the **Old Observatory**, one of the few surviving buildings by James Craig, designer of the New Town. New schemes for the development of Calton Hill, either grandiose or foolish (or both), are proposed on a regular basis: with the possibility of cash from the Lottery Fund, one of these may some day be carried out.

ALONG THE WATER OF LEITH

The northern extent of the New Town is reached at the **Water of Leith**, a small but significant river which flows for eight miles from the Pentland Hills through the western and northern parts of the city and empties into the Firth of Forth at Leith (see p.118). Unlike most other large cities in Britain, Edinburgh was not built on the banks of a major river, preferring to keep to its defensive location around the Castle Rock and using Leith as its trading port. However, the Water of Leith had a strong enough flow to turn water turbines, and this, combined with its proximity to the Old Town of Edinburgh, meant that mills and other light industries grew up along its banks in places such as **Dean Village** and **Canonmills**. Fording points and bridges were also important, with villages such as **Stockbridge** well established by the time Edinburgh spread northwards in the early nineteenth century, eventually to envelop these communities. Around this time, the large estates on the northern bank of the river were used to lay out the city's **Botanic Garden**, still one of Edinburgh's most attractive spaces, as well as attractive large houses and institutions, such as those which now house the **Scottish National Gallery of Modern Art** and the **Dean Gallery**. The Water of Leith has a **walkway** running much of its length, the most interesting stretch of which links the attractions listed below. Note, however, that this is unlit and therefore not a place to venture after dark.

The Royal Botanic Garden

Map 2, G3. Daily: March & Sept 9.30am–6pm; April–Aug 9.30am–7pm; Oct & Feb 9.30am–5pm; Nov–Jan 9.30am–4pm; free. On the northern side of the Water of Leith, with entrances on Inverleith Row and Arboretum Place, lies the seventy-acre site of the **Royal Botanic Garden**, particularly renowned for its rhododendrons, which blaze out in a glorious patchwork of colours in April and May. In the heart of the grounds, a group of hothouses designated the **Glasshouse Experience** (daily: March–Oct 10am–5pm; Nov–Feb 10am–3.30pm; free, but donation requested) displays orchids, giant Amazonian water lilies, and a 200-year-old West Indian palm tree, the latter planted in the elegant 1850s glass-topped Palm House. Many of the most exotic specimens were brought to Edinburgh by the aptly named George Forrest, who made seven expeditions to southwestern China between 1904 and 1932. There is also a major new **Chinese-style garden**, featuring a pavilion, waterfall and the biggest collection of Chinese wild plants outside China. At the highest point of the gardens sits **Inverleith House**, built in 1774, formerly an annexe to the Gallery of Modern Art, and now used for exhibitions. **Guided tours** of the garden (£2) leave from the West Gate on Arboretum Place at 11am and 2pm April to September.

The *Terrace Café* at the Royal Botanic Garden offers stunning views of the Old Town skyline (see p.213).

Stockbridge and Dean Village

Straddling both sides of the Water of Leith just to the south of the Botanic Garden, the old Edinburgh village of **Stockbridge** (Map 2, G4) has retained a distinctive identity in spite of its absorption into the Georgian face of the New Town, and is particularly renowned for its antique **shops** and "alternative" outlets. The residential upper streets on the northwestern side of the river were developed by Sir Henry Raeburn, who named the finest of them **Ann Street**. After Charlotte Square, Ann Street is the most prestigious address in Edinburgh – former residents include writers Thomas De Quincey and J.M. Ballantyne. Alone among New Town residences, the street's houses each have front gardens. Lower down, fringing the river between Stockbridge and Canonmills, are neat rows of two-storey terraces known as the "Stockbridge Colonies". Built in 1861 to house artisans – look out for the trade symbols engraved onto some of the gable ends along Glenogle Road – the Colonies are today something of a bohemian enclave, inhabited by a number of artists.

In Stockbridge, look out for the row of quirky shops and friendly restaurants along St Stephen Street.

From Stockbridge, a riverside path leads southwest to Dean Village, passing en route **St Bernard's Well**, a pump room covered by a mock-Roman temple. Commissioned in 1788 by Lord Gardenstone to draw mineral waters from the Water of Leith, it has been recently restored, although the mosaics in the pump room where the (fairly foul) water from the mineral spring is drawn are only occasionally on view (contact Water of Leith Conservation Trust on ☎0131/445 7367 for details). The path and river pass underneath the soaring four-arched **Dean Bridge**, a feat of 1830s engineering by Thomas Telford, before entering **Dean Village** (Map 2, G4), an old milling community that's one of central Edinburgh's most picturesque, yet oddest, corners. Its tight cobbled lanes and closes are surrounded by an assorted jumble of mews terraces and brick-built mill buildings rising up from the often gloomy valley floor, the atmosphere of terminal decay arrested by the conversion of some of the mills into chic flats.

ALONG THE WATER OF LEITH

GETTING TO THE MODERN ART AND DEAN GALLERIES

One of the most pleasant ways of getting to the Modern Art and Dean galleries is along the Water of Leith walkway. The walkway starts at the village of Balerno, west of the city at the foot of the Pentland Hills, and follows the River Leith to its mouth at the port of Leith. Two useful places to pick up the central section of the walkway are at Canonmills (Map 2, H3), near the eastern gate of the Royal Botanic Garden, or Stockbridge, at the end of Saunders Street (Map 2, G4); from either starting point follow the river upstream, leaving the walkway either at the *Hilton Hotel*, on the right-hand side shortly after you go under Belford Bridge, or at the marked path a few hundred metres further on, which leads directly to the rear of the Modern Art gallery.

Alternatively, a free bus runs on the hour (Mon–Sat 10am–5pm, Sun noon–5pm) from outside the National Gallery on the Mound, stopping at the National Portrait Gallery on the way. The only regular public transport running along Belford Road is bus #13, which leaves from the western end of George Street.

The Scottish National Gallery of Modern Art

Map 2, F5. Mon–Sat 10am–5pm, Sun noon–5pm; free.

Set in spacious wooded grounds just beyond the northwestern fringe of the New Town, about ten minutes' walk from either the cathedral or Dean Village, the **Scottish National Gallery of Modern Art**, on Belford Road, was established as the first collection in Britain devoted solely to twentieth-century painting and sculpture. The grounds serve as a sculpture park, featuring works by Jacob Epstein,

Henry Moore and Barbara Hepworth, while inside, the display space is divided between temporary loan exhibitions and selections from the gallery's own holdings; the latter are arranged thematically, but are almost constantly moved around. What you get to see at any particular time is therefore a matter of chance, though the most important works are nearly always on view. The establishment of the complementary Dean Gallery across the road (see p.114) has widened the scope of the displays, and linked exhibitions are a common feature. Both galleries have excellent **cafés**; if it's a sunny day, head for the one at the Gallery of Modern Art, which has a pleasant outdoor terrace.

French painters are particularly well represented, beginning with early twentieth-century work such as **Bonnard**'s *Lane at Vernonnet* and **Vuillard**'s jewel-like *Two Seamstresses*. There are a few examples of the Fauves, notably **Matisse**'s *The Painting Session* and **Derain**'s dazzlingly brilliant *Still Life*, as well as a fine group of late canvases by **Leger**, notably *The Constructors*. Among some striking examples of German Expressionism are **Kirchner**'s *Japanese Theatre*, **Feininger**'s *Gelmeroda III*, and a wonderfully soulful wooden sculpture of a woman by **Barlach** entitled *The Terrible Year, 1937*. Cubism is given high-profile representation by **Picasso**'s *Soles* and **Braque**'s *Candlestick*.

Of works by Americans, **Roy Lichtenstein**'s *In the Car* is a fine example of his Pop Art style, while **Duane Hanson**'s fibreglass *Tourists* is typically unflinching. English artists on show include **Sickert**, **Nicholson**, **Spencer**, **Freud**, **Hockney** and **Hirst** but, as you'd expect, slightly more space is allocated to Scottish artists. Of particular note are the Colourists – **S.J. Peploe, J.D. Fergusson, Francis Cadell** and **George Leslie Hunter** – whose works are attracting fancy prices on the art market, as well as evergrowing posthumous critical acclaim. Although they didn't form a recognizable school, they all worked in France and displayed considerable French influence in their warm, bright palettes. Also worth exploring is the vivid realism of the more recent Edinburgh School, whose members include **Anne Redpath**, **Sir Robin Philipson** and **William Gillies**, and the distinctive styles of contemporary Scots such as **John Bellany**, a portraitist of striking originality, and the poet-artist-gardener **Ian Hamilton Finlay**. There are also works by **Steven Campbell**, **Ken Currie** and **Peter Howson**, a group of artists based in Glasgow whose work, noted for its figurative, almost comic-strip style and aggressive social comment, came to international attention in the 1980s and 90s.

The Dean Gallery

Map 2, F5. Mon–Sat 10am–5pm, Sun noon–5pm; free.

Opposite the Modern Art Gallery on the other side of Belford Road is the latest addition to the National Galleries of Scotland, the **Dean Gallery**, housed in an equally impressive Neoclassical building completed in 1833. The interior of the gallery, built as an orphanage and later an education centre, has been dramatically refurbished specifically to make room for the work of Edinburgh-born sculptor **Sir Eduardo Paolozzi**, which was partly assembled from a bequest by Gabrielle Keiller (of the marmalade family), and partly from a gift of the artist himself, which included some 3000 sculptures, 3000 books and 2000 prints and drawings.

Visitors are given an awesome introduction to Paolozzi's work by the huge *Vulcan*, a half-man, half-machine which squeezes into the Great Hall immediately opposite the main entrance. No less persuasive of Paolozzi's dynamic creative talents are the rooms to the right of the main entrance, where his London studio has been expertly recreated right down to the clutter of half-finished casts, toys and empty pots of glue. Hidden amongst this chaos is a large part of his bequest, with incomplete models piled four or five deep on the floor and designs stacked randomly on shelves. In the adjoining room a selection of his sculptures and drawings are exhibited in a more traditional manner.

Also on the ground floor is the **Roland Penrose Gallery**, which houses an impressive collection of Dada and Surrealist art; Penrose was a close friend and patron of many of the movements' leading figures. **Marcel Duchamp**, **Max Ernst** and **Man Ray** are all represented in the gallery; look out also for **Dali**'s *The Signal of Anguish* and **Magritte**'s *Magic Mirror*, along with work by **Miró** and **Giacometti** – all hung on crowded walls with an assortment of artefacts and ethnic souvenirs gathered by Penrose and his artist companions while travelling. The adjoining **Gabrielle Keiller Library** contains a unique collection of surrealist literature, manuscripts and correspondence, and there's a wonderful pen-and-ink caricature of Picasso by **De Chirico**, as well as a series of **Picasso**'s own cartoons satirizing General Franco.

The rooms upstairs are normally given over to special **touring exhibitions**, which usually carry an entrance charge.

EDINBURGH ZOO

Map 2, C5. Daily: April–Sept 9am–6pm; Oct & March 9am–5pm; Nov–Feb 9am–4.30pm; £7.

A couple of miles west of the galleries, **Edinburgh Zoo** is set on an eighty-acre site on the slopes of Corstorphine Hill, and is home to over one thousand animals, including a number of endangered species such as white rhinos, red pandas, pygmy hippos and poison-arrow frogs. A spacious and well-run place with a good record of protecting and breeding rare animals, it is principally a family-oriented attraction, and as a consequence most of the attractions are laid out to appeal to and inform children. Making the most of the space offered by Corstorphine Hill, the **African Plains Experience** has a walkway leading you out over the animals to viewing platforms, while other engaging new additions include the **Magic Forest**, showcasing smaller primates, and an educational **Evolution Maze**, themed on Darwin's theories, where your progress can be cut off suddenly by a water fountain. However, the zoo's chief claim to fame is its crowd of **penguins** (the largest number in captivity anywhere in the world), a legacy of Leith's whaling trade in the South Atlantic. Visitors flock in for the **penguin parade**, which takes place daily at 2.15pm from April to September, and on sunny March and October days: the birds gather in a long line and take a waddle through the zoo's grounds in the company of their ranger.

Buses #2, #26, #31, #36, #69, #85 and #86 leave for the Zoo from Princes Street.

Out from the centre

As the panoramas from some of the city's elevated spots indicate, there's a lot more to Edinburgh than its historic core. Best known and most intriguing of the suburbs is Leith, the port of Edinburgh, situated a mile and a half from the east end of Princes Street down the wide boulevard of Leith Walk. Leith's transformation in the last twenty years from run-down docklands to the city's trendiest quarter has been dramatic. While low-quality housing, prostitutes on the streets and undeveloped wastelands give some parts of Leith a seedy edge straight out of the movie *Trainspotting*, elsewhere you'll find some of the most fashionable apartments and restaurants in the city. Most recently, the area has seen large dockland developments such as Terance Conran's shopping and cinema complex, Ocean Terminal, which has the former Royal Yacht Britannia moored alongside. On either side of Leith, the Firth of Forth coastline holds the suburbs of Newhaven to the west, which originated in the fifteenth century as a fishing village, and Portobello to the east, a faded Victorian seaside resort whose main appeal is its beach – the closest to the city centre. Also on the shoreline of the Firth, but to the northwest of Edinburgh, are the more placid charms of the old Roman village of Cramond, and country mansions Lauriston Castle and Dalmeny House.

South of the city lies a wide band of well-heeled residential suburbs, interspersed with large out-of-town shopping centres and the occasional sprawling, depressed housing estate, one of which, Craigmillar, lies near medieval **Craigmillar Castle** – one of Mary, Queen of Scots' favoured residences. There's a rural aspect to this part of the city, with various hills, parks and, on Edinburgh's southern edge, the **Pentland Hills** range, which offer ten square miles of Highlandesque scenery and some excellent walks and mountain-bike routes.

Getting there

The majority of Edinburgh's suburbs are well served by a comprehensive **bus** network, mostly radiating from St Andrew Square (Map 4, J4) or Princes Street (Map 4, K5–C8) in the city centre. There is an extensive network of off-road **cycle paths** which link the centre with most of the suburbs mentioned in this chapter, including Leith, the Pentlands and Cramond. The handy *Edinburgh Cycle Map* is available at most local bicycle and book shops, and costs £3.

LEITH AND AROUND

Until the early twentieth century, **LEITH** (Map 6) was a separate entity from Edinburgh. As Scotland's major east coast port, it played a key role in the nation's history: monarchs, armies and the lifeblood of continental trade arrived via its harbour. It even served as the seat of government in the seventeenth century, and finally became a burgh in its own right in 1833. In 1920, however, Leith's physical proximity and the perceived advantages of municipal government saw it incorporated into the capital. In the decades that followed, the area went into seemingly terminal decline: the population dropped dramatically, and much of its centre was ripped out, to be replaced by grim housing estates.

The 1980s, however, saw an astonishing turnaround. Against all the odds, a couple of waterfront bistros proved enormously successful; competitors followed apace, and today the port boasts what's arguably the best concentration of good restaurants (particularly seafood) in Edinburgh. The surviving historic monuments have been spruced-up, and a host of housing developments built or restored. The renaissance of the dockland area in particular has also seen the arrival of a vast new building housing civil servants from the Scottish Executive, as has the huge **Ocean Terminal** complex and the adjacent former **Royal Yacht Britannia**.

**For reviews of Leith's best seafood bistros
and other restaurants, see p.220.**

Leith is a brisk twenty-minute walk from the city centre down Leith Walk; alternatively, take one of the many buses (such as #7, #10, #12 and #14) that follow the same route.

Around the port

While you're most likely to come to Leith for the bars and restaurants, there's much in the area itself that warrants exploration; though the shipbuilding yards have gone, it remains an active port with an appealing, rough-edged character. Most of the showpiece Neoclassical buildings lie on or near **The Shore** (Map 6, G4–H3), the tenement-lined road running alongside the final stretch of the Water of Leith, just before it disgorges into the Firth of Forth. Nearby, buildings of note include the former **Town Hall** (Map 6, H5), on the parallel Constitution Street, now the headquarters of the local constabulary and immortalized in the tongue twister, "The Leith police dismisseth us". Other buildings worth a look are the Classical **Trinity House** on Kirkgate (Map 6, G5), built in 1816; and the massive **Customs House** (Map 6, G3) on the corner of Commercial Street and The Shore. To the west, set back from The Shore, is **Lamb's House** (Map 6, H4), a seventeenth-century mansion comparable to Gladstone's Land in the Old Town (see p.37). Built as the home of the prosperous merchant Andro Lamb, it currently functions as a day centre for old people.

Just east of the police station lies **Leith Links** (Map 6, I6), an area of predominantly flat parkland. Documentary evidence suggests that the Links was a golf course in the fifteenth century, giving rise to Leith's claim to be the birthplace of the sport. Certainly golf's first written rules were drawn up here in 1744, ten years before they were formalized in St Andrews.

Britannia

Map 6, F1. Daily: April–Sept 9.30am–4.30pm; Oct–March 10am–3.30pm; £7.75. Ⓦwww.royalyachtbritannia.co.uk.

A little to the west of The Shore, moored alongside **Ocean Terminal**, a huge shopping and entertainment centre designed by Terence Conran, is one of the world's most famous ships, the **Royal Yacht Britannia**. Launched in 1953 at John Brown's Shipyard on Clydeside, the *Britannia* was used by the royal family for 44 years for state visits, diplomatic functions and royal holidays. The yacht came to Leith following her decommission in 1997, but many members of the royal family felt that scuttling would have been a more dignified end. As it is, coachloads of visitors draw up and swarm over the once hallowed decks by day, while by night, the function suites where kings and presidents were formerly entertained are now rented out as prestigious hospitality venues.

Visitor numbers on *Britannia* are restricted, so it's always worth booking ahead; call ☎0131/555 5566 to ensure there's space for you at an appropriate time slot.

Visits to *Britannia* begin in a purpose-built **visitor centre**, located inside Ocean Terminal, where you can see a reconstructed sergeants' mess and the royal barge, the small motor launch that used to ferry the Queen to and from the ship. There are also displays of royal holiday snaps and video clips of *Britannia*'s most famous moments, which included the evacuation of Aden in 1986 and the British handover of Hong Kong in 1997. On leaving the visitor centre, you're given an audio handset and allowed to roam around the yacht. You can visit the **bridge**, the **admiral's quarters**, the **officers' mess** and most of the **state apartments**, including the state dining and drawing rooms, as well as the cabins used by the Queen and the Duke of Edinburgh, viewed through a glass partition. The yacht has been largely kept as she was when she was in service, with a well-preserved 1950s dowdiness, which the audio guide loyally attributes to the Queen's good taste and frugality in the lean postwar years. Certainly the atmosphere is a far cry from the opulent splendour which many expect, but it's by no means warm and homely. Interestingly, however, *Britannia* was the one place where the Queen said she could truly relax.

Among the quirkier aspects of *Britannia*'s history, you learn that a full Marine Band was always part of the three-hundred-strong crew; hand signals were used by the sailors to communicate orders, as shouting was forbidden; and a special solid mahogany rail was built onto the royal bridge to allow the Queen to stand on deck as *Britannia* came into port, without fear of a gust of wind lifting the royal skirt.

To get to Ocean Terminal, catch **bus #22** from the east

LEITH AND AROUND

end of Princes Street or the top of Leith Walk; alternatively hop on one of the Mac Tours (daily; £6.50) or Guide Friday (April–Sept daily, Oct–March Sat & Sun only; £3.50) **tour buses** which leave from Waverley Bridge (Map 4, J7).

Newhaven

Map 6, B2.

Immediately to the west of Leith (and reachable by a fifteen minute walk along Commercial Street/Lindsay Road) lies the village of **NEWHAVEN**, built by James IV at the start of the sixteenth century as an alternative shipbuilding centre to Leith: his massive warship, the *Great Michael*, capable of carrying 120 gunners, 300 mariners and 1000 troops and said to have used up all the trees in Fife, was built here. Newhaven has also been a ferry station and an important fishing centre, landing some six million oysters a year at the height of its success in the 1860s. Today, the simple old stone harbour still has a pleasantly salty feel despite the erection of new buildings nearby. Among various modern developments, the old fish market remains, housing *Harry Ramsden's* fish and chip café, a couple of fish merchants and the small **Newhaven Heritage Museum** (Map 6, B1; daily noon–5pm; free), a fascinating collection of costumes and other memorabilia that's staffed by enthusiastic members of local fishing families.

From the harbour itself, the high-speed inflatable boats of **Seafari Adventures** (summer only; ☏0131/331 5000, ⓦwww.seafari.co.uk) whizz out to the Forth Islands and South Queensferry (see p.154) on trips to view puffins and other birds, the occasional porpoise and lots of seals as well as a spectacular sight of the Forth bridges.

From the centre of Edinburgh, the most direct **bus** route

to Newhaven is the #11 from Princes Street or the top of Leith Walk; services #7, #10 and #16, also from Princes Street, go via Leith.

Portobello

Map 2, L4–M4.

Among Edinburgh's least expected assets is its sandy **beach**, most of which falls within **PORTOBELLO**, about three miles east of the centre of town. Founded in 1739 on wasteland between Leith and Musselburgh, the area was named after the naval victory of Puerto Bello in Panama. In Victorian times and even in the early part of this century, Portobello was a busy resort, known as "Brighton of the North"; today, a sunny summer's day still sees it drawing the crowds, though only dogs and paddling toddlers tend to brave the chilly North Sea water. In spite of a few tacky amusement arcades and a half-hearted funfair, Portobello retains a certain faded charm, and a walk along the promenade is a pleasure at any time of the year.

The streets running down to the beach hold an interesting mishmash of Georgian and Victorian houses. The odd-looking **Tower** (Map 2, M4) near the western end of the promenade was built in 1785 as a summer house, using stones from assorted demolished medieval houses, including, so tradition has it, the Mercat Cross, the old buildings of Edinburgh University and even parts of St Andrews Cathedral. Nearby, at 4 Bridge Street, a plaque marks the birthplace of music-hall giant **Sir Harry Lauder** (1870–1950), responsible for famously sentimental songs such as *Roamin' in the Gloamin'* and *I Love a Lassie*.

Portobello is easily reached from the city centre by **buses** #15 or #46 from St Andrew Square and #15, #26, or First Edinburgh #86 from Princes Street.

LEITH AND AROUND

CRAMOND AND LAURISTON CASTLE

Tucked in beside the River Almond, where it empties into the Firth of Forth some three miles northeast of the city centre and five miles west along the coastline from Leith, **CRAMOND** (Map 2, B2) is one of the city's most atmospheric – and poshest – old villages. At its heart is a narrow row of step-gabled, whitewashed houses perched on the slope rising up from the banks of the Almond, with various alleys and sets of steps joining a riverbank pathway to the single narrow road leading to the shore. By the car park at the end of this road, look out for boards explaining the still-visible foundations of a Roman fort here, while nearby, there's also a tower house, as well as a seventeenth-century church, inn and mansion. The Romans, who seem to have had little to do with the fortified crag where Edinburgh Castle now is, clearly made use of Cramond as a harbour: in addition to the remains of the fort, a wonderful Roman sculpture of a lioness devouring a man was discovered in the river in 1996. It's thought that it was simply thrown into the river after the Romans departed, and it's now on display in the National Museum of Scotland on Chambers Street (see p.74).

Cramond village is pleasant enough to wander through, though that won't take you long. It's worth venturing a bit further afield, though, as there are a number of interesting short **walks** in the area: across the causeway at low tide to uninhabited (except for seabirds) **Cramond Island** (Map 2, B1); eastwards along the seafront – with sweeping views out to sea – towards the gasometers of **Granton** (Map 2, F2); a couple of miles along the River Almond past former mills and their adjoining cottages towards the sixteenth-century **Old Cramond Brig** (the first permanent crossing point over the river you come to heading upstream); and, after a short ferry crossing from Cramond village over the

Almond, through the Dalmeny estate to **Dalmeny House** (Map 1, D2; see p.126). Apart from the last one, which is just a little longer, these walks should take around an hour each for the round trip back to Cramond.

Buses #40 and #41 run to Cramond from Hanover Street (Map 4, G6) or the west end of George Street (Map 4, F6).

After a walk along the shore at Cramond, the *Cramond Inn* (see p.235 for a review) is a fine spot for real ale and good pub grub.

Lauriston Castle

Map 2, C3. 40min obligatory guided tours leave every hour: April–Oct Mon–Thurs & Sat–Sun 11am–1pm & 2–5pm; last tour at 4.20pm; Nov–March Sat & Sun 2–4pm only; call ahead to confirm tour times on ☏0131/336 2060; £4.50.

Roughly five miles west of the city centre and a mile east of Cramond, the country mansion of **Lauriston Castle**, stands in its own parkland overlooking the Firth of Forth. Though it doesn't rank as one of the country's most glamorous stately homes, the original sixteenth-century tower house lends the neo-Jacobean structure historic authenticity, and its unusual interior makes for a quirky glimpse of life in a well-to-do family at the start of the twentieth century. In 1902 it became the retirement home of a prosperous local cabinet-maker, who decked out the interior with his private collection of furniture and antiques, including Flemish tapestries and ornaments made of Blue John from Derbyshire. He also added a number of domestic features, ranging from central heating and secondary glazing to an en-suite Edwardian bathroom, incorporating a flushing toilet and a splendidly sturdy bath-cum-shower. On the death of the last private owners in 1926, Lauriston Castle was gifted to the nation and the interior has been left untouched.

The castle is set in large well-kept **grounds** (daily 9am–dusk; free), which afford wonderful views down to the Firth of Forth and across to Fife, and hold some immaculately-kept croquet lawns where Edinburgh Croquet Club play (members only).

The best way to reach the castle by **bus** from the city centre is to catch #41 from George Street (Map 4, F6) to Quality Street and Main Street in Davidsons Mains (Map 2, C3) and walk the half-mile along Cramond Road South to the castle gates.

DALMENY

Map 1, D2.

In 1975, Edinburgh's boundaries were extended to include a number of towns and villages which were formerly part of West Lothian. Among them was **DALMENY**, two miles west of Cramond, which can be reached directly from the city centre (St Andrew Square) by bus (First Edinburgh #43) or train from Waverley or Haymarket stations to Dalmeny Station, half a mile from the centre of the village in the direction of South Queensferry. Another option is to walk the coastal path from Cramond (see p.124), which passes through the estate of **Dalmeny House** (July & Aug Mon, Tues & Sun noon–5.30pm; £4), the seat of the earls of Rosebery. Built in 1815 by the English architect William Wilkins, it was the first stately home in Scotland to be built in Tudor Gothic Revival style, and features a picturesque turreted roofline, fan vaulting and hammerbeam ceilings. Although open to the public only for a very limited period every summer, the extravagant interior and engaging collection of treasures are among the most interesting in the country. The family **portraits** include one by Raeburn of the fourth earl, who commissioned the house, and one by Millais of the fifth earl, the Earl of Rosebery, a former British prime minister. There are also likenesses of other famous society figures by Reynolds, Gainsborough and Lawrence. Among the **furnishings** are a set of tapestries made from cartoons by Goya, and the Rothschild Collection of eighteenth-century French furniture and *objets d'art*. There's also a fascinating collection of objects associated with Napoleon Bonaparte – including some of the items he used during his exile in St Helena. These were amassed by the fifth earl, who wrote a biography of the emperor.

Dalmeny House is a mile and a half from the centre of the **village**, a quiet community built around a spacious green. Its focal point is the mid-twelfth-century **St Cuthbert's Kirk**, a wonderful Norman church that has remained more or less intact. Although very weather-beaten, the south doorway is particularly notable for its illustrations of strange beasts. More vividly grotesque carvings can be seen inside on the chancel corbels and arch.

CRAIGMILLAR CASTLE

Map 2, L7. April–Sept daily 9.30am–6.30pm; Oct–March Mon–Wed & Sat 9.30am–4.30pm, Thurs 9.30am–noon, Fri & Sun 2–4.30pm; £2. **Craigmillar Castle**, where the murder of Lord Darnley, second husband of Mary, Queen of Scots was plotted, lies in a green belt five miles southeast of the city centre. It's one of the best-preserved medieval fortresses in Scotland, and before Queen Victoria set her heart on Balmoral, she considered using it as her royal castle north of the border – a possibility which seems odd now given its proximity to the ugly council-house estate of Craigmillar, one of Edinburgh's most deprived districts.

The oldest part of the castle is the L-shaped **tower**

house, which dates back to the early 1400s: it remains substantially intact, and the great hall, with its resplendent late Gothic chimneypiece, is in good enough shape to be rented out for functions. A few decades after Craigmillar's completion, the tower house was surrounded by a quadrangular wall with cylindrical corner towers pierced by some of the earliest surviving gunholes in Britain. The west range was remodelled as an aristocratic mansion in the mid-seventeenth century, but its owners abandoned the place a hundred years later, leaving it to picturesque decay.

To get to the castle, take **bus** #30, #33 or First Edinburgh #86, or any bus heading for Hawick or Jedburgh, from Princes Street or North Bridge (both Map 4, L6) to the district called Little France. From here the castle is a ten-minute walk along Craigmillar Castle Road.

THE SOUTHERN HILLS

The suburbs to the south of Edinburgh's centre are marked by a series of **hills**, mostly built up on their lower slopes only, which offer good, not overly demanding, walking opportunities, with plenty of sweeping panoramic views. The **Royal Observatory** (Map 2, H7; Mon–Sat 10am–5pm, Sun noon–5pm; £3.50) stands at the top of Blackford Hill, just a short walk south of Morningside along Cluny Gardens, or accessible by buses #24 from the west end of Princes Street (Map 4, C8) or Lothian Road (Map 4, B9), and #41 from Hanover Street (Map 4, H6) and the Mound (Map 4, H7). Though mostly given over to scientific research, there's a small visitor centre here which seeks to explain the mysteries of the solar system by means of various hands-on exhibits and CD-Roms, and you also get to see the observatory's two main telescopes.

At the foot of the hill, the bird sanctuary of Blackford Pond is the starting point for one of the many trails running through the **Hermitage of Braid** nature reserve (Map 2, H6–7), a lovely shady area along the course of the Braid Burn. The castellated eighteenth-century mansion along the burn, after which the reserve is named, now serves as a visitor centre (Mon–Fri 1–4pm, Sun noon–5pm) which has a handful of displays on local plant and animal life. Immediately to the south are the **Braid Hills** (Map 2, H8), most of whose area is occupied by two golf courses, which are closed on alternate Sundays in order to allow access for walkers.

Further south again are the looming **Pentland Hills** (Map 1, C5), or the Pentlands, a chain some eighteen miles long and five wide, which rise to 1898ft (579m) and are often powdered with snow in winter. The Pentlands offer the most extensive **hill-walking** within easy reach of Edinburgh, with well-managed paths and tracks crisscrossing the range; these are also used by the city's keen **mountain bikers** to get off-road and uphill. The best map of the region is the Ordnance Survey Landranger **map** no. 66.

A good starting point for walks or bike rides is **FLOTTERSTONE** (Map 1, D4), ten miles south of the city centre on the A702, and served by First Edinburgh bus #101 or MacEwan's Coach #100, which leave from Princes Street (Map 4, G7) or Lothian Road (Map 4, B9). Flotterstone is an old staging post on the route south: there's been an inn here since the seventeenth century, and the present *Flotterstone Inn* is a good spot for a drink or a pub meal after your exertions. Numerous walks, from gentle strolls along well-marked paths to a ten-mile traverse of the hills and moors, are outlined in a pamphlet available from Flotterstone Regional Park Information Centre (daily: May–Sept 9am–7pm; Oct–April 9am–5pm), just past the *Flotterstone Inn*. One suggested walk is described in the box on p.131.

An alternative entry point to the Pentland Hills is **SWANSTON** (Map 1, D4), a tiny, unspoiled and highly exclusive hamlet of whitewashed thatched roof dwellings that's separated from the rest of the city by almost a mile of farmland. **Robert Louis Stevenson** (see box on p.45) spent his boyhood summers in Swanston Cottage, immortalized in his novel *St Ives*. There's a car park by the village, or you can catch **buses** #4 or #17 from Princes Street, and #27 from Hanover Street (Map 4, H6) or The Mound (Map 4, H7) in the city centre to Oxgangs Road, from where you walk to the hamlet along Swanston Road. A path leads uphill from the car park, and links into the network of well-defined trails and paths which cover most of the Pentlands range.

You can also get a taste of the Pentlands scenery from the dry-ski slopes at **Hillend country park** (Map 1, D4), at the northeastern end of the Pentlands range, a mile or so east of Swanston. From the car park by the ski centre, take the path up the right-hand side of the dry ski slopes, turning left shortly after crossing a stile to reach a viewpoint with outstanding views over Edinburgh and Fife. An easier way into the range is to take the **chair-lift** from the ski centre (open to non-skiers Mon–Fri 1–9pm, Sat & Sun 10am–7pm; £1.40). The **dry ski slope** (April—Oct Mon–Fri 9.30am–9pm, Sat & Sun 9.30am–5pm, Nov–March Mon-Sat 9.30am–9pm, Sun 9.30am–7pm) has two sections, a main slope and a nursery, and access to them is by the hour (£6.60 for the first hour, £2.70 thereafter on the main slope; £4.10/£2 on the nursery slop). Ski or snowboard hire and instruction are available separately. The minimum age for the slopes is six.

Bus #4 runs from Princes Street to the ski centre, as well as the hourly First Edinburgh #315 from St Andrew Square. From Princes Street both First Edinburgh #101 and MacEwans Coach #100 services go past the ski centre and carry on to Flotterstone.

HIKING AND BIKING IN THE PENTLANDS

The following suggested round-trip hike in the Pentlands is moderately tough, lasts around four hours and takes in hills, reservoirs and moorland. From the car park beside the ranger centre at Flotterstone (see p.129) a pleasant side road leads up to Glencorse Reservoir. The road swings round it, then goes through a tight pass and on to Loganlee Reservoir, where a path leads on from the west end of the reservoir, through a short pass called Green Cleugh, to come out on the far side of the Pentland range, where the large expanse of Thriepmuir Reservoir stretches out in front of you. Cross the bridge over a "neck" in the reservoir; the path heads inland for a while, but take the first right to return to the reservoir and then follow it to Harlaw Reservoir beyond. At the far end of Harlaw Reservoir is another small ranger centre; from here, take the path to your right over flat moorland and through the pass between Bell's Hill and Harbour Hill. The path runs down a burn to rejoin Glencorse Reservoir.

It is possible to mountain bike along the same route, though for a more testing circuit, start from the car park at Nine Mile Burn, six miles south of Flotterstone. There's a long, steep uphill start along a rough, often muddy path to the top of Cap Law on the main Pentland ridge. Carry on across the plateau and then down the back of Hare Hill to Thriepmuir Reservoir, crossing the bridge over the "neck". Head along the tarred road for half a mile, turning left at the T-junction onto the Old Road, which after some distance becomes a jeep track; continue along this track till you get to a signpost at Listonshields. Turn left here in the direction of North Esk Reservoir, and immediately after passing the reservoir, take the left-hand path which crosses the river and climbs briefly over the shoulder of Spittal Hill. You then have an exhilarating downhill run past Spittal farm back to your starting point.

THE SOUTHERN HILLS

Day-trips from Edinburgh

Relatively short distances and good transport links make many parts of south and central Scotland feasible day-trips from Edinburgh. Less than an hour's travel west of Edinburgh is Glasgow, the largest city in Scotland and long a rival to the capital in terms of prestige, influence and importance. The many contrasts between the two cities are, in their own way, a compelling reason to pay a visit to Glasgow, where decades of industrial decline have given way to a reawakened appreciation of the city's stunning Victorian and early twentieth-century design and architecture. One of the most important legacies of this period are the unique and flamboyant buildings designed by Art Nouveau visionary Charles Rennie Mackintosh. Other attractions include a wealth of museums and art galleries, including the diverse Burrell Collection, the city's medieval cathedral, and, for those making an evening as well as a day of their visit, there's an opportunity to tap into Glasgow's hip and vibrant nightlife scene.

Less than an hour northwest of Edinburgh, the essential day-trip for those interested in the main events in Scottish history is to **Stirling**, with its fine castle and battle sites. North of here, it's possible to get a taste of the spectacular landscapes of the **Highlands** in areas such as the **Trossachs** and around **Pitlochry**, both eminently reachable in a day. The rolling hills of the **Borders** region south of the capital, and the North Sea coastline of **East Lothian** offer some equally attractive countryside dotted with historic castles and ruined abbeys. A little closer to Edinburgh, in **Midlothian**, is the intriguing Rosslyn Chapel, while in **West Lothian**, the ruined royal palace at **Linlithgow** and the imposing iron geometry of the Forth Rail Bridge are two of Scotland's grandest spectacles. **St Andrews**, home to Scotland's oldest university and perched on the east coast thirty miles northeast of Edinburgh, takes a little longer to get to, but is just about compulsory for anyone with an affection for the game of golf.

   Transport links from Edinburgh to Glasgow, Stirling, Linlithgow and parts of East Lothian by both train and bus are regular and efficient; services further afield, including those to St Andrews and the Borders, tend to be slightly less so, though both can be reached by at least one form of public transport.

GLASGOW

Map 7.

GLASGOW is separated from Edinburgh by a mere forty miles and can be reached by train in under an hour, but for two cities so geographically close, the contrasts could hardly be more marked. Edinburgh is well-heeled establishment, Glasgow is industrial grit; Edinburgh has professions, Glasgow workers; Edinburgh is tweedy, Glasgow trendy; Edinburgh is rugby, Glasgow football.

   Although Glasgow doesn't have the same dramatic visual impact as Edinburgh, a bit of time spent familiarizing your-

GLASGOW

self with the idiosyncratic, creative vibe found in its grand municipal buildings as well as its hyper-cool "style-bars" is invariably repaid. In a day you should easily be able to take in the area known as **Merchant City**, home of Glasgow's prosperous traders in the eighteenth-century, as well as the nearby medieval **Cathedral**. Visitors interested in finding out more about the city's outstanding Victorian and early twentieth-century architecture will find plenty of excellent examples, many of them the work of the world-famous designer **Charles Rennie Mackintosh**, who took Glasgow's architecture to the forefront of early twentieth-century design.

A more laid-back side of Glasgow can be found in its **West End**, the student quarter, which is studded with a series of excellent art galleries and museums. The city's most impressive museum is the **Burrell Collection**; though further out of town, it's well worth the time spent getting there, not just for the eclectic treasures gathered under its roof but also its unexpected parkland setting.

With regular trains running back to Edinburgh as late as 11.30pm, you could consider sampling some of Glasgow's **nightlife**, consistently sparkier and more cutting-edge than Edinburgh's, or taking in some of the city's innovative and high-quality theatre and live music.

Arrival and information

Trains to Glasgow (every fifteen minutes through the day, and half-hourly in the evening and at weekends) run from Edinburgh's Waverley and Haymarket stations, and pull into **Queen Street Station** (Map 7, K5), on the corner of George Square, right at the heart of the city. A ten-minute walk away is **Central Station** (Map 7, I6), the main terminus for trains to the south. **Buses** also run regularly, departing from Edinburgh's St Andrew Square and arriving at Glasgow's **Buchanan Street bus station** (Map 7, K5), just to the north of Queen Street Station.

The city's efficient **tourist information office** is at 11 George Square (Map 7, K6; May, June & Sept Mon–Sat 9am–6pm, Sun 10am–6pm; July & Aug Mon–Sat 9am–8pm, Sun 10am–6pm; Oct–April Mon–Sat 9am–6pm; ⓣ0141/204 4400, ⓦwww.seeglasgow.com).

For train timetable enquiries, telephone ⓣ0845/748 4950. For buses, call ⓣ0141/332 7133

Getting around

Despite the fact that it gets pretty hilly in the western part of the city centre and around the University, **walking** is the best way of exploring any one part of Glasgow, but as the main sights are scattered throughout the city – the West End, for example, is a good thirty-minute walk from the centre – you'll probably need to make use of the **Underground**, whose stations are marked with a large orange U. There's a flat fare of 90p, or you can buy a **day ticket** for £1.60 (Mon–Fri after 9.30am and all day weekends). The most useful stations are **Buchanan Street** (Map 7, J5), which is near George Square and connected to Queen Street railway station by a moving walkway; **St Enoch** (Map 7, J7), at the junction of Buchanan Street pedestrian precinct and Argyle Street; and **Hillhead** (Map 7, C2), bang in the heart of the West End. Black **taxis** are common and can be hailed from the street – to order one, call ⓣ0141/429 7070.

A selection of brief tours of Glasgow operate from the tourist information office on George Square, including hop-on hop-off bus tours, guided historical walking tours and solo audioguided walking tours.

The City Centre

Glasgow's large **city centre** is the densest in Scotland, with offices, shops and traffic bound in a rigorous grid-pattern of streets – possibly inspired by Edinburgh's New Town. Glasgow has one of the best collections of Victorian buildings in the world; the city's booming trade and industry at the end of the nineteenth century and beginning of the twentieth allowed merchants to commission the finest architects of the day. Nowhere is the confidence of the era more apparent than in **George Square** (Map 7, K6), a continental-style plaza dominated by the grandiose Italian Renaissance facade of the **City Chambers**, opened in 1888, at the square's eastern end.

CHARLES RENNIE MACKINTOSH'S GLASGOW

Glasgow is synonymous with the work of architect Charles Rennie Mackintosh (1868–1928), whose idiosyncratic fusing of Scots Baronial with Gothic and Art Nouveau makes him one of the most important designers of the twentieth century – outstanding examples of his work are found all over the city.

The finest display of his visionary style is surely the Glasgow School of Art at 167 Renfrew Street (Map 7, H4; ⓦwww.gsa.ac.uk), designed in 1896. Student-led guided tours (Mon–Fri 11am & 2pm, Sat 10.30 & 11.30am; July & August also Sat 1pm, Sun 10.30 & 11.30am; book ahead on ⓣ0141/353 4526; £5) offer a taste of his innate ability to blend function with superb artistry. Another early commission, The Lighthouse, on Mitchell Lane (Map 7, J6; Mon, Wed, Fri & Sat 10.30am–5.30pm, Tues 11am–5.30pm, Thurs 10.30am–7pm, Sun noon–5pm; free; ⓦwww.thelighthouse.co.uk), now houses Scotland's Centre for Architecture, Design and the City, and incorporates a Mackintosh Interpretation Centre (£2.50), an exhaustively informative exhibi-

GLASGOW

The grid of streets that lies immediately southeast of the City Chambers, known as the **Merchant City**, is where wealthy eighteenth-century tobacco merchants built warehouses and homes. In the last decade or so it has been sandblasted and swabbed clean, and yuppie apartments, expensive designer shops and bijou cafés give the area a pervasive air of sophistication and chic. A *Merchant City Trail* leaflet, guiding you around a dozen of the most interesting buildings in the area, can be picked up from **Hutcheson Hall**, at 158 Ingram St (Map 7, K6; Mon–Sat 10am–5pm).

Just to the south of George Square on Royal Exchange Square (off Queen Street) is Glasgow's lively and off-beat **Gallery of Modern Art** (Map 7, J6; Mon–Thurs & Sat 10am–5pm, Fri & Sun 11am–5pm; free), a good place to

tion where you can learn more about the man and his work.

Other Mackintosh highlights around the city are the House for an Art Lover (April–Sept daily except Fri 10am–4pm; Oct–March Sat & Sun 10am–4pm but closed occasionally for functions; ☏0141/353 4449; £3.50), in Bellahouston Park on the south side of the Clyde, which was designed by Mackintosh in 1901 for a German competition but not actually built until 1996; and the Scotland Street School Museum of Education (Map 7, G9; Mon–Thurs & Sat 10am–5pm, Fri & Sun 11am–5pm; free), located opposite the Shields Road Underground station. At the Hunterian Art Gallery (Map 7, D2) next to the university you can see the Mackintosh House (Mon–Sat 9.30am–5pm; free); a re-creation of the interior of the now-demolished Glasgow home of the artist and his wife, Margaret, it has over sixty pieces of Mackintosh furniture spread over three floors. A popular place for tea, the Willow Tea Rooms, 217 Sauchiehall St (Map 7, I5; daily 9.30am–5pm), are a faithful reconstruction on the site of Mackintosh's 1904 original.

GLASGOW

catch up on works such as the large-scale, socially committed pieces of the "**Glasgow Pups**" – Peter Howson, Adrian Wiszniewski, Ken Currie and Stephen Campbell – as well as the evocative black-and-white urban photographs of **Sebastião Salgado** and the inspired art-from-nature installations of **Andy Goldsworthy**.

Glasgow Cathedral and the East End

The oldest part of the city lies to the east of the Merchant City, centred on the stumpy-spired **Glasgow Cathedral** (Map 7, N5; April–Sept Mon–Sat 9.30am–6pm, Sun 2–5pm; Oct–March Mon–Sat 9.30am–4pm, Sun 2–4pm). Dedicated to the city's patron saint and reputed founder, St Mungo, it dates back to the late fifteenth century and is the only Scottish mainland cathedral to have escaped the hands of religious reformers in the sixteenth century. Inside, the impressively lofty nave of the **upper church** contrasts with the **lower church**, with its dark and musty **chapel**; one of the most glorious examples of medieval architecture in Scotland, the latter houses the tomb of St Mungo. Next to the Cathedral the atmospheric **Necropolis** (Map 7, N6), a hillside graveyard filled with gloomy catacombs and Neoclassical temples, reflects the vanity of the nineteenth-century industrialists buried here. It's worth climbing to the summit for the superb views over the Cathedral and city.

Heading down the High Street from the Cathedral, you'll come to **Glasgow Cross** (Map 7, L7), the city's principal intersection until the middle of the nineteenth century. East of Glasgow Cross lies the **East End**, once a densely packed industrial area which essentially created the city's wealth. Today, isolated pubs, tatty shops and cafés sit amidst this dereliction, in sharp contrast to the gloss of neighbouring Merchant City. You definitely get the sense that you're off the tourist trail in these parts, but unless you're here after dark it's not as threatening as it may feel, and there's no doubt that the area advertises a rich flavour of working-class Glasgow. The nearby open spaces of **Glasgow Green** (Map 7, M8–L8), reputedly the oldest public park in Britain, offer a welcome contrast, and the **People's Palace Museum** (Mon–Sat 10am–5pm, Sun 11am–5pm; free), at the northern end of the Green, is a wonderfully haphazard evocation of the city's history. It was purpose-built back in 1898 – almost a century before the rest of the country caught on to the fashion for social history collections.

The best way to return to George Square is to head along the banks of the **Clyde**, a river whose intimate connections with the city range from the fish which appears on Glasgow's coat of arms, to the ships which once packed the quaysides from the centre all the way downriver to the Firth of Clyde.

The West End

The urbane veneer and leafy parks of Glasgow's **West End** (Map 7, E3) seem a world away from the tightly packed centre. In the 1800s, the city's focus moved west as wealthy merchants established huge estates away from the soot and grime of city life, and in 1870 the ancient university was moved from its cramped home near the cathedral to a spacious new site overlooking the River Kelvin. The hub of life in this part of Glasgow is **Byres Road** (Map 7, C2), running down from Great Western Road past Hillhead Underground station, where shops, restaurants, cafés, some enticing pubs and hordes of roving young people, including thousands of students, give the area a real sense of style.

The principal attraction in the district is the huge, red-brick fantasy castle of **Kelvingrove Museum and Art Gallery** (Map 7, D4; Mon–Thurs & Sat 10am–5pm, Fri &

Sun 11am–5pm; free), a brash statement of Glasgow's nine-teenth-century self-confidence, built to house the 1888 International Exhibition. Located in Kelvingrove Park, not far from the university, it's most easily reached from the centre by Underground to Kelvin Hall station; however, renovations mean that it's likely to be closed for much of 2003. The highlight of the ground floor is the airy central hall, which offers a soaring introduction to the museum. Most of the impressive art collection is upstairs, and includes paintings by **Botticelli**, **Rembrandt**, **Degas** and **Monet**, alongside a good representation of Scottish work, ranging from portraits such as **Sir Henry Raeburn**'s magnificent *Mr and Mrs Robert N. Campbell of Kailzie*, to the distinctive work of **Glasgow Boys** Guthrie, Lavery and Crawhall. Within the precincts of the university – Sir George Gilbert Scott's dramatic black Gothic quadrangle and spire perched on the hill behind Kelvingrove – is the **Hunterian Art Gallery** (Map 7, D2; Mon–Sat 9.30am–5pm; free). To get here from Kelvingrove, follow the tree-lined Kelvin Way then climb up University Avenue. The Hunterian is best known for its wonderful works by **James Abbott McNeill Whistler**, but also displayed are the quasi-Impressionist Scottish landscapes of **William McTaggart**, a forerunner of two important Scottish groups, the Glasgow Boys and the Scottish Colourists, both represented here.

The Burrell Collection

Mon–Thurs & Sat 10am–5pm, Fri & Sun 11am–5pm; free.
Glasgow's most outstanding collection of art is to be found at the **Burrell Collection**, the accumulated treasures of shipping magnate Sir William Burrell (1861–1958). The Burrell is located in Pollok Country Park, three miles

south of the city (and just off our map); to get there, either take the **train** from Central Station to Pollokshaws West station (not to be confused with Pollokshields West), or **bus** #45, #47, #48 or #57 from the city centre to the park gates on Pollokshaws Road, or a **taxi** (£12–14 from the centre). From the park gates, a **free minibus** runs every half-hour between 10am and 4.30pm to the gallery building; alternatively, you can do the pleasant walk in about twenty minutes.

Unlike many other art collectors, Sir William's only real criterion for buying a piece was whether he liked it or not; his tastes were eclectic and broad, and he acquired many "unfashionable" works. The collection is housed in a superbly designed space, built in 1983, with large picture windows giving sweeping views over the park and serving as a tranquil backdrop to the objects inside. A catch-all title for Greek, Roman and earlier artefacts, the **Ancient Civilizations** section includes an exquisite Roman mosaic cockerel from the first century BC and a 4000-year-old Mesopotamian lion's head. The large **Oriental Art** collection ranges from Neolithic jades and Tang funerary horses to cloisonné; **near Eastern art** is also represented, with a dazzling array of turquoise- and cobalt-decorated jugs and a swath of intricate carpets. A **sculpture court**, centred on the huge Warwick Vase from Hadrian's Villa in Tivoli, includes Rodin's *The Age of Bronze*, *A Call to Arms* and the famous *Thinker*, while nearby a trio of dark and sombre panelled rooms have been re-erected in faithful detail from the Burrells' Hutton Castle home, their heavy tapestries, antique furniture and fireplaces displaying the same extraordinary taste as the rest of the museum. Among the highlights of Sir William's weighty **painting collection** are one of Rembrandt's evocative early self-portraits, along with work by Degas, Pissarro, Manet and Boudin.

GLASGOW

141

Nightlife and entertainment

While Glasgow has nothing to match the Edinburgh Festival for a concentrated celebration of theatre and the arts, it still manages to pump out an impressive range of art, theatre, film and music right round the year, a cultural integrity recognized, and to some extent sustained, by the city's reign as European City of Culture in 1990. Glasgow is the home of both Scottish Opera and the Royal Scottish National Orchestra, and has two major **music venues** – the Royal Concert Hall (Map 7, J5) and the Clyde Auditorium (or the "Armadillo" as it's popularly known; Map 7, D6). It also boasts two of Scotland's most consistently innovative and trendy **theatres**, the Citizens' (Map 7, J8) and the Tramway, off our map at 25 Albert Drive (just over a mile south of the river near Pollockshields West train station). You can find **events details** in the *Herald* or *Evening Times* newspapers, or the comprehensive fortnightly listings magazine, *The List* (£2.20), which also covers Edinburgh. To book **tickets** for theatre productions or big concerts, call at the Ticket Centre, City Hall, Candleriggs (Map 7, L6; Mon–Sat 10.30am–6.30pm, Sun noon–5pm), or call Ticket Link on ☏0141/287 5511.

The city's **music and clubbing scene** is highly rated; Glasgow consistently attracts some of the world's top DJs, while various small live music venues have almost become used to nurturing local talent such as Travis, Texas, Belle & Sebastian and Deacon Blue. Most of Glasgow's nightclubs are in the heart of the main shopping areas off Argyle and Buchanan streets, with a further concentration on Sauchiehall Street near Charing Cross on the western side of the city centre. Some of the best nights happen at venues such as *The Arches* at 30 Midland Street (Map 7, I7; ☏0141/221 4001; ⓦwww.thearches.co.uk) and *Alaska* at 142 Bath Lane (Map 7, I5; ☏0141/248 1777). In general,

GLASGOW

establishments are pretty mixed, and although there's still a stack of outdated mega-discos with rigorous dress codes, the last couple of years have seen the arrival of far more stylish haunts. Hours hover from around 11pm to 3am, though some places are open until 5am, and cover charges are variable – expect to pay around £3 during the week, and up to £10 at the weekend.

Eating and Drinking

Eating and drinking also benefit from Glaswegians' renowned sense of style and love of a good night out. For an original dining experience right in the centre of the city, head to *Rogano* at 11 Exchange Place (Map 7, J6), a cocktail bar and pricey seafood restaurant decked out as an Art Deco replica of the *Queen Mary*, a ship built on Clydeside. The most fashionable bars (often referred to as "style bars") are found in the **Merchant City** – compare, for instance, designer *Bar 10* at 10 Mitchell St (Map 7, J6) with the opulent and ornate interior of *Corinthian* at 191 Ingram St (Map 7, K6); in this area of the city you'll also find a number of excellent restaurants such as sushi bar *Oko* at 68 Ingram St (Map 7, L6; ℡0141/572 1500) or modern Scottish *Farfelu* at 89 Candleriggs (Map 7, L6; ℡0141/552 5345). The **West End** is also a great place to head, with its mix of students and yuppies guaranteeing a lively atmosphere at places like the *Attic*, 44–46 Ashton Lane (Map 7, C2), or *Firebird*, near the Kelvingrove Museum at 1321 Argyle Street (Map 7, D4). For something to eat in the West End try *No. Sixteen* at 16 Byres Road (Map 7, C3; ℡0141/339 2544), which serves good-value modern Scottish food in a tiny two-level restaurant, or the curries at *Mother India*, 28 Westminster Terrace, off Sauchiehall Street (Map 7, E4; ℡0141/221 1663.

GLASGOW

STIRLING

Map 8.

With its crag-top castle, steep cobbled streets and mixed community of locals and students, **STIRLING** looks a bit like a smaller version of Edinburgh, and though the town lacks the cosmopolitan edge of the capital, it's rich in history, having been the scene of two of the most significant battles in Scottish history. A day-trip here should take in Stirling's **castle** – a more explorable and interesting citadel than even Edinburgh's – and either the **Wallace Monument**, the hilltop monolith built in memory of the Scottish leader William Wallace, or **Bannockburn**, the field where the famous Scottish victory under Robert the Bruce in 1314 was won.

From Edinburgh, there are regular trains (45min) and buses (1hr) to Stirling: the **railway station** (Map 8, F6) is near the centre of town on Station Road, while the **bus station** (Map 8, G7) is nearby on Goosecroft Road. The **tourist office** is in the heart of town at 41 Dumbarton Rd (Map 8, E7; July & Aug Mon–Sat 9am–7.30pm, Sun 9.30am–6.30pm; June & Sept Mon–Sat 9am–6pm, Sun 10am–4pm; Oct–May Mon–Sat 10am–5pm; ☏01786/475019, ⓦwww.scottish.heartlands.org).

Stirling is very compact and the sights are easily seen on **foot**, though to avoid the steep hills you could take advantage of the hop-on hop-off **open-top bus tours** (April–Sept 10am–5pm; £6.50) run by Guide Friday, whose circular route takes in the castle, Wallace Monument, Stirling University and the bus and train stations.

The Castle

Map 8, B4. Daily: April–Sept 9.30am–6.30pm; Oct–March 9.30am–5pm; £6.50.

STIRLING

As one of the most important bridging points across the **River Forth**, with the Highlands in view to the north and Edinburgh visible to the southeast, Stirling is one of the most strategically significant places in Scotland, and the possession of **Stirling Castle** was vital for any army wanting to control the gateway to the Highlands. The daunting rock on which it sits was first fortified during the Iron Age, though what you see now dates largely from the fifteenth and sixteenth centuries.

From the railway station, it's a ten-minute walk up the hill to the castle; the **visitor centre** on one side of the esplanade car park shows an introductory film giving a potted history of the castle, but the best place to get an impression of its gradual expansion is the **Outer Close**, the first main courtyard beyond the imposing inner gatehouse to the castle. Here you can join the **guided tours** (free), which leave every half-hour.

Looming over the courtyard is the magnificent **Great Hall**, dating from 1501–3; its creamy-yellow limewash cladding ensures that it stands out not just in the courtyard but across the whole town. The Great Hall's interior has been restored to its original state as the finest medieval secular building in Scotland, complete with five gaping fireplaces and an impressive hammerbeam ceiling. Most interesting of the castle's other buildings are the largest: the **Palace**, which dates from 1540–42 and is richly decorated with grotesque carved figures, and the **Chapel Royal**, which also faces onto the Inner Close (the sloping upper courtyard). This was built in 1594 by James VI for the baptism of his son, and boasts a delightful interior with a seventeenth-century fresco of elaborate scrolls and patterns. Alongside the chapel, and at the highest point in the castle, the **King's Old Building** now houses the **museum** of the Argyll and Sutherland Highlanders regiment. Don't miss the narrow passageway between the King's Old Building

STIRLING

and the Chapel Royal, through which you'll find the **Douglas Gardens**, a lovely, quiet corner with mature trees and battlements that afford splendid views of the rising Highlands beyond.

The rest of the town

Heading downhill from the castle along St John Street, you'll encounter the whinstone boulders of the **town walls**, built in the mid-sixteenth century and intended to ward off the advances of Henry VIII, who had set his sights on the young Mary as a wife for his son, Edward. A few minutes' walk further along St John's Street, past the junction with Broad Street, takes you to the best of the various historic buildings and museums in Stirling's old centre – the most interesting is the **Old Town Jail** (Map 8, D6; April–Sept daily 10am–5pm; Oct–March Mon–Sat 10am–5pm, Sat & Sun 11.30am–3pm; £3.95), where the history of the building is brought to life by enthusiastic actors. A glass lift goes up to the prison roof, where you can admire spectacular views across Stirling and the Forth Valley.

Stirling doesn't have a great selection of places to eat out: in the old town the best are the ground floor brasserie at *Hermann's* (Map 8, D5) and the *Yill & Kail* across Broad Street, which has a relaxed bar and restaurant serving moderately priced Scottish food.

Back on the ground, **Broad Street** (Map 8, D5) was the site of the marketplace and centre of the medieval town; the further downhill you go, the more recent the buildings become. These days, the town's main **shopping** area lies at the bottom of the hill along Port Street and Murray Place

STIRLING

(Map 8, F6–F7), while the **Smith Art Gallery and Museum** (Map 8, C6; Tues–Sat 10am–5pm, Sun 2–5pm; free) is a short walk west up Dumbarton Road. Founded in 1874, it houses "The Stirling Story", a reasonably entertaining whirl through the history of the town, balancing out the stories of kings and queens with social and domestic history.

The fifteenth-century **Old Bridge** (Map 8, F2) over the Forth lies to the north on the edge of the town centre, a twenty-minute walk from Murray Place. An earlier, wooden **bridge** nearby was the focus of the Battle of Stirling Bridge in 1297, where William Wallace (the subject of Mel Gibson's Oscar-winning but wildly inaccurate film, *Braveheart*) defeated the English. The victory at Stirling Bridge is marked by the prominent **National Wallace Monument** (daily: July & Aug 9.30am–6.30pm; June 10am–6pm; March–May & Sept–Oct 10am–5pm; Nov–Feb 10.30am–4pm; £3.95), a mile and a half north of here (and off our map) on the top of Abbey Craig, the place from which the Scottish hero led his troops to victory. If you can manage the climb – 246 spiral steps up – there are superb views across to Fife and Ben Lomond from the top of the 220-foot tower. A shuttle bus runs every 15 minutes from the base of the hill to the tower.

The Scots' other great battlefield triumph is remembered a couple of miles south of Stirling (and off our map), just north of the village of Bannockburn. While there's not a great deal to see other than the **Bannockburn Heritage Centre** (daily: April–Oct 10am–5.30pm; March, Nov & Dec 11am–4pm; £2.50), which recalls Robert the Bruce's victory on June 24, 1314, the battle site is fondly remembered by Scots as the place where their independence was won. Bannockburn can be reached by buses #51 and #52, which leave Stirling bus station every half-hour.

STIRLING

147

THE HIGHLANDS

With its beguiling mix of bare hills, green glens and silvery lochs and rivers, the spectacular scenery of the **Highlands** is one of Scotland's major draws. The distances involved, however, as well as the relative infrequency of public transport, mean that only certain parts of the region are achievable in a day-trip from Edinburgh.

The most accessible area from the capital is the **Trossachs**, situated in the centre of the country to the northwest of Stirling. The two focal points here are the towns of **Callander** and **Aberfoyle**, both of which have tourist information centres where you can pick up details about good local walks and viewpoints. Though it's most easily accessed by car, you can get a **bus** direct to Callander from Edinburgh's St Andrew Square (Scottish Citylink #913, Fri–Sun & Mon only departing at 9.15am), though there are more regular services if you get the hourly First Edinburgh #38 from St Andrew Square to Stirling and connect with the hourly First Edinburgh #59 from Stirling to Callander. From Stirling there's also a two-hourly service (First Edinburgh #11) to Aberfoyle, while in the summer months (July to mid-Sept) the useful *Trossachs Trundler* loops round Callander, Loch Katrine and Aberfoyle four times a day (not Wed) – for further details contact Callander's tourist office (☎01877/330342).

In the central Highlands, a reasonable target is the town of **Pitlochry**, 25 miles north of Perth on the main A9 towards Inverness, and served by both trains and buses from Edinburgh. While its centre is rather overrun by tourist shops, Pitlochry lies close to some lovely elevated countryside, and there are some pleasant hill and forest walks from Killiecrankie Visitor Centre, on the northern side of Loch Faskally, north of Pitlochry.

If you're prepared to spend a lot of time on the road, a

good option for a packed day of Highland sightseeing is to join a **guided minibus day-tour** from Edinburgh. Various daily trips to places such as Glencoe, Loch Tay and Loch Lomond are offered by Rabbies Trail Burners (☎0131/226 3133) and Timberbush Tours (☎0131/555 4075) – both charge £20–30 per person. For a taste of hill walking in the Highlands, there are also companies that offer **guided day-walking trips** from around £40, with transport included: in Edinburgh contact Walkabout Scotland (☎0131/661 7168), while from Stirling try C-N-Do (☎01786/445703).

ST ANDREWS

Only thirty miles northeast of Edinburgh as the crow flies, though frustratingly tiresome to get to by road or rail, **ST ANDREWS** is Scotland's oldest university town and a pilgrimage centre for golfers from all over the world. Confident, poised and well-groomed, if a little snooty, the town is most often compared to Oxford or Cambridge for its intimate, collegiate feel (and for the fact that the student population has a significant proportion of English undergraduates, among them, famously, Prince William). It isn't a large place, with only three main streets and an open, airy feel encouraged by the long stretches of sand on either side of town and the acreage of golf links all around. The **tourist office** is at 70 Market Street (July & Aug Mon–Sat 9.30am–7pm, Sun 10am–5pm; May & June Mon–Sat 9.30am–5.30pm, Sun 11am–4pm; Sept Mon–Sat 9.30am–6pm, Sun 11am–4pm; April Mon–Sat 9.30am–5pm, Sun 11am–4pm; Oct–March Mon–Sat 9.30am–5pm; ☎01334/472021, ⊛www.standrews.com).

St Andrews is not on the rail network. The nearest **train station** is on the Edinburgh–Dundee line at Leuchars, five miles northwest across the River Eden, from where regular buses make the fifteen-minute trip into town. When you buy your rail ticket to Leuchars, ask for a St Andrews Rail-bus ticket, which includes the bus fare. Stagecoach services #X59 and #X60 provide a regular direct bus service from Edinburgh's St Andrew Square to St Andrews; both terminate at the bus station on City Road at the west end of Market Street.

St Andrews has no shortage of places to eat and drink: for ambitious modern Scottish fare, try *West Port* at 170–172 South St, while the *Inn on North Street* at 127 North St is a lively spot serving good pub grub.

The Town

According to legend, St Andrews was founded in the fourth century, when St Regulus, a custodian of the bones of the apostle Andrew, was instructed in a vision to carry the relics to the edge of the western world, but was shipwrecked on rocks close to the present harbour. He built a shrine to the saint on what subsequently became the site of the cathedral; St Andrew became Scotland's patron saint and the town its ecclesiastical capital. The centre of St Andrews still follows its medieval layout, with three main thoroughfares, North Street, South Street and Market Street, running west to east towards the ruined cathedral. Narrow alleys connect the cobbled streets, while attic windows and gable ends shape the rooftops, and here and there you'll see old wooden doors with heavy knockers and black iron hinges.

Chief among the town's early medieval sights are the ruined Gothic **St Andrews Cathedral** at the eastern end of the old town (April–Sept Mon–Sat 9.30am–6pm, Sun noon–6pm; Oct–March Mon–Sat 9.30am–4pm, Sun 2–4pm; £1.80, joint ticket with St Andrews Castle £3.50; cathedral grounds Sun only 9am–6.30pm; free), once the

GOLF IN ST ANDREWS

St Andrews' **Royal and Ancient Golf Club** (or "R&A") is the international governing body for golf, and dates back to a meeting of 22 of the local gentry in 1754, being "admirers of the ancient and healthful exercise of golf". The approach to St Andrews from the west runs adjacent to the famous **Old Course**, one of seven courses in the immediate vicinity of the town. The British Open Championship was first held here in 1873, and since then it has been held at St Andrews regularly, pulling in enormous crowds. Pictures of golfing greats from Tom Morris to Tiger Woods, along with clubs and a variety of memorabilia donated by famous players, are displayed in the admirable **British Golf Museum** on Bruce Embankment, along the waterfront below the clubhouse (see below) (April to mid-Oct daily 9.30am–5.30pm; rest of year Thurs–Mon 11am–3pm; £3.75).

If being in St Andrews inspires you to take to the fairways, it is possible to **play** any of the town's courses, ranging from the nine-hole Balgove course (£10 per round) to the venerated Old Course itself – though for the latter you'll need a valid handicap certificate and must enter a daily ballot for tee times; if you're successful the green fees are £85 in summer. All this and more is explained at the clubhouse of the **St Andrews Links Trust** (Ⓦwww.standrews.org.uk), located alongside the fairway of the first hole of the Old Course.

Arguably the best golfing experience in St Andrews, even if you can't tell a birdie from a bogey, is the **Himalayas**, a fantastically lumpy eighteen-hole putting course in an ideal setting right next to the Old Course and the sea. Officially the Ladies Putting Club, founded in 1867, with its own clubhouse, the grass is as perfectly manicured as the championship course, and you can have all the thrill of sinking a six-footer in the most famous location in golf, all for just 80p per round.

ST ANDREWS

largest cathedral in Scotland, and the nearby remains of **St Andrews Castle** (same hours; £2.50 to visit the castle alone), hemmed in by a drop to the sea on three sides and a moat on the fourth. The **university** is scattered around town, but you can take a **guided tour** of the more interesting buildings (June–Aug Mon–Fri 11.30am & 2pm; £4) from the International Office, Butts Wynd, near St Salvator's Chapel about halfway along North Street.

There are plenty of excellent **walks** around the town, in particular the clifftop path between the castle and the harbour, and along either of the town's superb sandy beaches: the East Sands stretch south from the harbour, while the West Sands run along the seaward edge of the Old Course.

WEST LOTHIAN

To many, **West Lothian** (Map 1, A3–B3), the county immediately to the west of Edinburgh, is a poor relative to the rolling, rich farmland of East and Midlothian, with a landscape dominated by motorways, industrial estates and giant hillocks of ochre-coloured mine waste called "bings". However, anywhere this close to the centres of power through Scottish history would find it hard not to have something to show for itself, and in the ruined royal palace at **Linlithgow** the area boasts one of Scotland's more magnificent ruins. Not far away is one of Scotland's most impressive engineering feats, the **Forth Rail Bridge**, best seen from the parallel Road Bridge which crosses the Forth from the village of **South Queensferry**. Also accessible from South Queensferry is the ruined abbey on the island of **Inchcolm**, and **Hopetoun House**, one of Scotland's grandest stately homes. Both Linlithgow and South Queensferry are well served by frequent trains from Edinburgh's Waverley and Haymarket stations.

Linlithgow Palace

Map 1, A2. April–Sept daily 9.30am–6.30pm; Oct–March Mon–Sat 9.30am–4.30pm, Sun 2–4.30pm; £2.80.

Fifteen miles west of Edinburgh in the ancient royal burgh of Linlithgow is **Linlithgow Palace**, a splendid fifteenth-century ruin romantically set on the edge of Linlithgow Loch, and associated with some of Scotland's best-known historical figures – including Mary, Queen of Scots, who was born here in on 8 December 1542 and became queen six days later. James I began construction of the present palace in the fifteenth century, a process that continued through two centuries and the reign of no fewer than eight monarchs. From the top of the northwest tower, Queen Margaret looked out in vain for the return of James IV from the field of Flodden in 1513 – indeed, the views from her bower, six giddy storeys up from the ground, are exceptional. Bonnie Prince Charlie visited during the 1745 rebellion, and a year later the palace was burnt, probably accidentally, whilst occupied by General Hawley's troops.

This is a great place to take children: the rooflessness of the castle creates unexpected vistas and the elegant, bare rooms echo with footsteps and the fluttering of birds flying out through the empty windows, while there's a labyrinthine feel to the place, with its spiral staircases and endless nooks and crannies. The galleried **Great Hall** is magnificent, as is the adjoining kitchen, which has a truly cavernous fireplace. Don't miss the dank downstairs **brewery**, which produced vast quantities of ale; 24 gallons was apparently a good nightly consumption in the sixteenth century.

Adjacent to the palace, **St Michael's Church** is one of Scotland's largest pre-Reformation churches, consecrated in the thirteenth century. The present building was completed three hundred years later, with the exception of the hugely

WEST LOTHIAN

incongruous aluminium spire, tacked on in 1946. Inside, decorative woodcarving around the pulpit depicts queens Margaret, Mary and Victoria.

For good pub food in Linlithgow try *The Four Marys*, opposite the Cross on High Street, while *Marynka* at 57 High Street is a brighter, more modern bistro-style place. Best of all is *Champany Inn* (☎01506/834532), just outside Linlithgow on the way to Blackness, which serves delicious steaks, chops and seafood.

South Queensferry and around

Eight miles east of Linlithgow and much the same distance northwest of central Edinburgh, **SOUTH QUEENSFERRY** (Map 1, C2) is a compact little town used by St Margaret as a crossing point for her frequent trips between her palaces in Edinburgh and Dunfermline. Squeezed into the narrow gap between the seashore and the hillside above, the **High Street** is lined by a picturesque array of old buildings, among them an unusual two-tiered row of shops, the roofs of the lower level serving as the walkway for the upper storey. The small **museum** at 53 High St (Mon & Thurs–Sat 10am–1pm & 2.15–5pm, Sun noon–5pm; free), contains relics of the town's history and information on the building of the two bridges which loom over the village. A dedicated museum to the bridge can be found over the water in North Queensferry (see opposite).

The rail and road bridges
Map 1, C2

Stretching from South Queensferry across the width of the Forth estuary to North Queensferry on the southern shore of Fife, the cantilevered **Forth Rail Bridge** ranks among the supreme achievements of Victorian engineering. Built between 1883 and 1890 by Sir John Fowler and Benjamin Baker, some 50,000 tons of steel were used in the construction of a design that manages to express grace as well as might. Derived from American models, the suspension format chosen for the **Forth Road Bridge** alongside makes an interesting modern complement to the older structure. Erected between 1958 and 1964, it finally killed off the 900-year-old ferry, and now attracts a heavy volume of traffic.

The *Hawes Inn* at South Queensferry was used by Robert Louis Stevenson in his adventure story, *Kidnapped*, and you can still visit the whitewashed pub on the shore almost underneath the rail bridge.

While the geometric girders of the rail bridge are one of the most spectacular sights in Scotland, particularly after dark now that they're **floodlit**, the road bridge which parallels it is grand but comparatively dull. The only way to cross the rail bridge is aboard a train heading to or from Edinburgh, though inevitably this doesn't allow much of a perspective of the spectacle itself. For the best **panorama** of the rail bridge, make use of the pedestrian and cycle lane on the east side of the parallel road bridge. The **Forth Bridges Exhibition** (daily 9am–9pm; free), occupying a couple of rooms tacked onto the modern *Queensferry Lodge Hotel* in North Queensferry, provides background to the construction of the bridges. As well as perusing a series of storyboards, photographs, models and displays, you can contemplate various mind-boggling statistics such as the fact that there are six and a half million rivets in the rail bridge, and that a shower of rain adds around 100 tons to its weight.

WEST LOTHIAN

THE FORTH RAIL BRIDGE

The late-Victorian railway boom saw the development of train lines to many parts of Scotland, as well as continual investment to upgrade and improve important existing routes. One of the most important of these was the East Coast line from Edinburgh to Aberdeen, which took a long diversion around the Firth of Forth via Stirling. The first plans for a suspension bridge to carry a railway line across the Firth of Forth were ripped up in 1879, when the collapse of the Tay Rail Bridge over the Tay Estuary at Dundee shocked the authorities into commissioning John Fowler and Benjamin Baker's dramatic cantilevered steel bridge, which was made twice as strong as experts deemed it needed to be. Its construction was eagerly followed by the inhabitants of Edinburgh and Fife, and after it was opened in 1890, people would take a train to North Queensferry simply to say they'd crossed the bridge. It was widely acknowledged as a triumphant symbol of Scottish engineering prowess, with the great French engineer Alexandre-Gustave Eiffel describing it as "the greatest wonder of the century". Not everyone took to it, however: the artist William Morris called it "the supremest specimen of all ugliness". The bridge is renowned for taking so long to paint that as soon as the job is finished, it's time to start again; however, there are plans to replace the old paint with a high-tech, long-lasting coating that will render the continuous painting process redundant.

Inchcolm

Map 1, D1.

From South Queensferry's Hawes Pier, just west of the rail bridge, pleasure boats (Easter, May & June Sat & Sun; July to mid-Sept daily; confirm sailing in advance on ☏0131/331 4857; £10) head out onto the Forth in the direction of the island of **Inchcolm**. The beautiful ruined

Abbey here was founded in 1123 by King Alexander I in gratitude for the hospitality he received from a hermit when his ship was forced ashore in a storm; the hermit's cell survives at the northwestern corner of the island. The best preserved medieval monastic complex in Scotland, the Abbey's surviving buildings date from the thirteenth to the fifteenth centuries, and include a splendid octagonal chapterhouse. Although the church is almost totally dilapidated, its tower can be ascended for a great aerial view of the island, which is populated by a variety of nesting birds and a colony of grey seals. Hawes Pier is a pick up point for Seafari (℡0131/331 5000) which also operates out of Newhaven harbour (see p.122), and offers high-speed wildlife-spotting trips out past Inchcolm and round various other islands in the estuary.

Hopetoun House

Map 1, C2. April–Sept daily 10am–5.30pm; £5.30 house and grounds, £2.90 grounds only.

Immediately beyond the western edge of South Queensferry, just over the West Lothian border, **Hopetoun House** is one of Scotland's grandest stately homes. The original house was built at the turn of the eighteenth century, for the first Earl of Hopetoun, by architect of Holyroodhouse Sir William Bruce. A couple of decades later, William Adam carried out an enormous extension, engulfing the house in a curvaceous main facade and two projecting wings – superb examples of Roman Baroque pomp and swagger. Particularly impressive are the Red and Yellow Drawing Rooms, with their splendid ceilings by the young Robert Adam. Among the house's furnishings are seventeenth-century tapestries, Meissen porcelain, and a distinguished collection of paintings, including portraits by Gainsborough, Ramsay and Raeburn.

The **grounds** of Hopetoun House are also open, with

WEST LOTHIAN

magnificent walks along the banks of the Forth and great opportunities for picnics.

MIDLOTHIAN

Map 1, E5.
Immediately south of Edinburgh lies the old county of **Midlothian**, once called Edinburghshire. It's one of the hilliest parts of the Central Lowlands, with the Pentland chain running down its western side, and the Moorfoots defining its boundary with the Borders to the south. Though predominantly rural, Midlothian contains a belt of former mining communities which are struggling to come to terms with the recent decline of the industry. Such charms as it has are mostly low-key, with the exception of the riotously ornate chapel at **Roslin**.

Dalkeith and around

Map 1, E4–F4.
Despite its Victorian demeanour, **DALKEITH**, eight miles southeast of central Edinburgh – to which it is linked by very regular buses (#3, #30, #82) – grew up in the Middle Ages as a baronial burgh under the successive control of the Douglases and Buccleuchs. It's a bustling shopping centre today, with an unusually broad High Street at its heart.

At the far end of the street is the entrance to **Dalkeith Country Park** (April–Oct daily 10am–6pm; £2), the estate of the Dukes of Buccleuch, whose seat, the early eighteenth-century **Dalkeith Palace**, can only be seen from the outside. You can, however, visit the estate's one-time chapel, now the Episcopalian parish church of **St Mary**, adorned inside with extremely rich furnishings, which is located near the entrance to the park at the northern end of the High Street. Further north, Robert Adam's

MIDLOTHIAN

Montagu Bridge straddles the River North Esk in a graceful arch; beyond are some derelict but once wonderfully grandiose garden follies. There's also a large woodland playground, suitable for all but the youngest children.

A mile or so south of Dalkeith is **NEWTONGRANGE**, whose Lady Victoria Colliery is now open to the public as the **Scottish Mining Museum** (Map 1, F4; daily: Feb–Oct 10am–5pm, Nov–Jan 11am–4pm; £4), with a 1625-foot shaft and a winding tower powered by Scotland's largest steam engine. A great place for kids, the visitor centre brings the mine and the local community to life with "magic helmets", which enable you to go on shift and experience a virtual-reality tour of life below ground.

Roslin

Map 1, E4.

The tranquil village of **ROSLIN** lies seven miles south of the centre of Edinburgh, from where it can be reached by bus #37A or First Edinburgh service #315 from St Andrew Square. An otherwise nondescript place, the village has two unusual claims to fame: it was near here, at the Roslin Institute, that the world's first **cloned sheep**, Dolly, was created in 1997; the village also boasts the mysterious, richly decorated late-Gothic **Rosslyn Chapel** (Mon–Sat 10am–5pm, Sun noon–4.45pm; £4). Only the choir, Lady Chapel and part of the transepts were built of what was intended to be a huge collegiate church dedicated to St Matthew: construction halted soon after the founder's death in 1484, and the vestry, built onto the facade nearly four hundred years later, is the sole subsequent addition. After a long period of neglect, a massive restoration project has recently been undertaken: a canopy has been placed over the chapel, which will remain in place for several years in order to dry out the saturated ceiling and walls, and other

MIDLOTHIAN

essential repairs are due to be carried out to the interior.

The outside of the chapel bristles with pinnacles, gargoyles, flying buttresses and canopies, while inside the foliage carving is particularly outstanding, with botanically accurate depictions of over a dozen different leaves and plants. Among them are cacti and Indian corn, providing fairly convincing evidence that the founder's grandfather, the daring sea adventurer Prince Henry of Orkney, did indeed, as legend has it, set foot in the New World a century before Columbus. The rich and subtle figurative sculptures have given Rosslyn the nickname of "a Bible in stone", though they're more allegorical than literal, with portrayals of the Dance of Death, the Seven Acts of Mercy and the Seven Deadly Sins.

The greatest and most original carving of all is the extraordinary knotted **Prentice Pillar** at the southeastern cor-

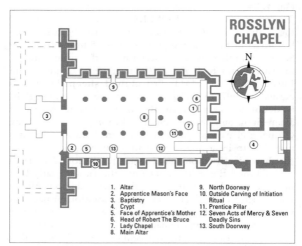

ROSSLYN CHAPEL

N

1. Altar
2. Apprentice Mason's Face
3. Baptistry
4. Crypt
5. Face of Apprentice's Mother
6. Head of Robert The Bruce
7. Lady Chapel
8. Main Altar
9. North Doorway
10. Outside Carving of Initiation Ritual
11. Prentice Pillar
12. Seven Acts of Mercy & Seven Deadly Sins
13. South Doorway

MIDLOTHIAN

ner of the Lady Chapel. According to local legend, the pillar was made by an apprentice during the absence of the master mason, who killed him in a fit of jealousy on seeing the finished work. A tiny head of a man with a slashed forehead, set at the apex of the ceiling at the far northwestern corner of the building, is popularly supposed to represent the apprentice, his murderer the corresponding head at the opposite side. The entwined dragons at the foot are symbols of Satan, and were probably inspired by Norse mythology.

The chapel's unconventional and sometimes disturbing carvings and designs have led to all kinds of theories about its function, symbolism and hidden secrets. A number of books have been published in recent years about the building, drawing on everything from Freemasons and the Turin Shroud to the True Gospels and the regular sightings of UFOs over Midlothian. Others speculate that it's the home of the Ark of the Covenant or the real Stone of Destiny. Conspiracy theories notwithstanding, Rosslyn is very definitely worth a visit.

EAST LOTHIAN

Map 1, I3.

East Lothian consists of the coastal strip and hinterland immediately east of Edinburgh, bounded by the Firth of Forth to the north and the Lammermuir Hills to the south. Often mocked as the "home counties" of Edinburgh, there's no denying its well-ordered feel, with prosperous farms and large estate houses dominating the scenery. The most immediately attractive part of the area is the coastline, extending from **Musselburgh**, all but joined onto Edinburgh, round to **Dunbar**, birthplace of naturalist John Muir. This stretch includes the wide sandy beaches by **Aberlady**, the famous golf courses of **Gullane**, the enjoyable Seabird Centre at **North Berwick**, which looks out to the volcanic plug of the Bass Rock, and the dramatic – and romantic – clifftop ruins at **Tantallon**. Meandering buses from Edinburgh connect with most settlements in East Lothian; you can also catch a train to North Berwick or Dunbar.

Musselburgh to Dirleton

Though strictly the largest town in East Lothian, with a long history connected to the development of mussel beds at the mouth of the River Esk, you're unlikely to linger long at **MUSSELBURGH** (Map 1, F3), if only for the feeling that you've hardly shaken off the dust of Edinburgh. There is, however, a **race course** here, one of the busiest in Scotland, with a regular programme of decent quality National Hunt and Flat meetings. For details of what's on, call ☎0131/665 2859.

Bypassing the chimneys of the Cockenzie power station, the East Lothian coastline takes a turn for the better by **ABERLADY** (Map 1, G2), an elongated conservation village of Gothic-style cottages and mansions just sixteen miles east of Edinburgh. Aberlady served as Haddington's port until its river silted up in the sixteenth century, and the salt marshes and sand dunes of the adjacent **Aberlady Bay Nature Reserve**, a bird-watchers' haven, mark the site of the old harbour.

From the nature reserve, it's a couple of miles to **GULLANE** (pronounced "Gillin"; Map 1, G1), the location of the famous shoreline links of **Muirfield Golf Course**, home course of the grandly named Honourable Company of Edinburgh Golfers and venue for the Open Championship in 2002. If golf isn't your thing (there are three other courses around Gullane, not to mention dozens more around East Lothian), you might prefer the fine sandy **beaches** of Gullane Bay, great for blustery walks and views out across the Firth of Forth, or one of the museums which lie inland. A half-mile detour off the Aberlady–Gullane road just after you pass the Nature Reserve takes you to the **Myreton Motor Museum** (Map 1, G2; daily: Easter–Oct 10am–6pm; Nov–Easter 10am–5pm; £3), a small stash of vintage cars, motorbikes, military vehicles and motoring memorabilia. A few miles east of this, by East Fortune, the **Museum of Flight** (Map 1, H2; daily 10.30am–5pm; £3), has over fifty vintage aircraft including a Vulcan bomber, a Comet airliner, a Spitfire and a Tigermoth packed into old World War II hangars.

Two miles east of Gullane lies the genteel hamlet of **DIRLETON** (Map 1, H1), where you'll find **Dirleton Castle** (daily: April–Sept 9.30am–6.30pm; Oct–March 9.30am–4.30pm; £2.80) a romantic thirteenth-century ruin, with beautifully laid-out gardens leading to a volcanic knoll crowned by the Cromwell-shattered remains. Scrambling round the castle is fun, and if the weather's good you can take the mile-long path from the village church to the sandy, rock-framed beach at **Yellowcraigs**, which overlooks **Fidra Island**, a large lump of basalt that's home to thousands of noisy seabirds. In the village, opposite the castle, the splendid *Open Arms Hotel* has every luxury, including a fantastic restaurant serving moderate to expensive food from a varied and imaginative menu.

North Berwick

Map 1, H1.
Two miles east of Dirleton, **NORTH BERWICK** has a great deal of charm and a somewhat faded, old-fashioned air, its guesthouses and hotels extending along the shore in all their Victorian and Edwardian sobriety. The town's small harbour is set on a headland which cleaves two crescents of sand, providing the town with an attractive coastal setting,

EAST LOTHIAN

though it's the two nearby volcanic heaps, the **Bass Rock** and **North Berwick Law**, which are the North Berwick's defining physical features. The Bass Rock's summer population of gannets can be closely observed from North Berwick's principal attraction, the Scottish Seabird Centre, located by the harbour. The small **museum** on School Road (April–Oct daily 11am–5pm; free), housed in the old school house, displays local curios including the old town stocks.

Scottish Seabird Centre and the Bass Rock

Daily: April–Oct 10am–6pm; Nov–March 10am–4pm; £4.50.

Located in an sensitively designed, bright new building by the harbour, the **Scottish Seabird Centre** offers an introduction to all the types of seabird found around the Scottish coast, particularly the 100,000-plus gannets and puffins which nest on the Bass Rock every summer. Such is the connection between the rock and its annual visitors that the gannet, once known as the solan goose, takes its Latin name, *Morus bassana*, from the Bass Rock. Thanks to a live link from the centre to cameras mounted on the volcanic island, you're able to view close-up pictures of the birds in their nesting grounds. Elsewhere in the centre, hands-on games and exhibits explain more about different seabirds, and a mock-up of a cliff face has various stuffed specimens nesting on it – all the birds, the centre insists, have been ethically gathered.

North Berwick is served by a regular half-hour train from Edinburgh Waverley, with special travel and entry deals available for those heading for the Seabird Centre (ask at Waverley ticket offices).

Resembling a giant molar, the **Bass Rock** itself rises 350ft above the sea some three miles east of North

Berwick. This massive chunk of basalt has had an interesting history, having held out as a Jacobite stronghold for six years longer than anywhere else in the country; it later served as a prison, a fortress and a monastic retreat. The last lighthouse keepers left in 1988, leaving it, quite literally, to the birds – Bass Rock is Scotland's second-largest gannet colony after St Kilda off the west coast of Scotland, and also hosts razorbills, terns, puffins, guillemots and fulmars. If you're not content with viewing the birds on the video link-up in the Seabird Centre, there are, weather permitting, **boat trips** round the island from North Berwick harbour (daily, from Easter to Sept; £5) – contact Fred Marr on *Sula* (℡01620/892838).

North Berwick Law
Map 1, H1.
The other volcanic monolith, 613ft-high **North Berwick Law**, which dominates the Lothian landscape for miles around, is about an hour's walk from the beach (take Law Road off High Street and follow the signs). On a clear day, the views out across the Firth of Forth, Fife and the Lammermuirs make the effort worthwhile, and at the top you can see the remains of a Napoleonic watchtower and an arch made from the jawbone of a whale.

With panoramic views over the beach, one of the best cafés in North Berwick is at the Seabird Centre; it's also open as an evening bistro (May–Sept Wed–Sat; for bookings and winter opening hours call ℡01620/893342). In town, the *Grange* at 35 High St (closed Mon) is a pleasant restaurant serving good quality, moderately priced meals, while both the *Tantallon Inn* on Marine Parade and the *Marine Hotel* on Cromwell Road do decent bar food.

EAST LOTHIAN

Tantallon Castle

Map 1, I1. April–Sept daily 9.30am–6.30pm; Oct–March Mon–Wed
& Sat 9.30am–4.30pm, Thurs 9.30am–noon, Fri & Sun 2–4.30pm;
£2.80

The melodramatic pinkish sandstone ruins of **Tantallon
Castle**, three miles east of North Berwick on the A198,
stand on the precipitous cliffs facing the Bass Rock. With a
sheer drop down to the sea on three sides and a sequence of
moats and ditches on the fourth, the castle's desolate invin-
cibility is daunting, especially when the wind howls over
the remaining battlements and the surf crashes on the rocks
far below. Built at the end of the fourteenth century, the
castle was a stronghold of the Douglases, the Earls of Angus,
one of the most powerful noble families in Scotland.
Besieged several times, it was finally destroyed by Cromwell
in 1651 after a twelve-day bombardment. The ruins enjoy a
wonderfully photogenic setting, with the Bass Rock and
the Firth of Forth in the background.

You can reach Tantallon Castle from North Berwick by
the Dunbar **bus** (Mon–Sat 6 daily, Sun 2 daily), which
takes fifteen minutes, or you can walk there from town
along the cliffs in around an hour.

Dunbar

Twelve miles further along the coast (and just off our map)
lies **DUNBAR**, which bears some resemblance to North
Berwick with a wide, recently spruced-up High Street
graced by several grand old stone buildings. One of the oldest is the **Town House** (April–Oct daily 12.30–4.30pm;
free), formerly a prison and now home to a small archeolo-
gy room and local history centre. Of greater significance is
the three-storey **John Muir House**, 128 High St (call
℡01368/860187 for opening hours; free), birthplace of the

explorer and naturalist who created the United States national park system. Recently refurbished, the house now acts as an interpretative and education centre inspired by the pioneer's life and legacy. A more appropriate tribute, in some respects, is the nearby **country park** in Muir's honour, where an easy three-mile walk west of the harbour takes you along a rugged stretch of coast to the sands of Belhaven Bay. Set beside the shattered remains of the castle, the delightfully intricate double **harbour**, with its narrow channels, cobbled quays and roughened rocks, merits a stroll. The town's one other claim to fame is as the home of **Belhaven beers**, which are still made on the original site of the monks' brewery, signposted off the Edinburgh road (guided tours can be arranged for groups; phone ☏01368/864488 for details).

EDINBURGH'S MALT WHISKY

Southeast of Edinburgh, about six miles west of East Lothian's county town of Haddington, the village of Pencaitland is the closest place to Edinburgh where malt whisky is made. Set in a peaceful dip in the rolling countryside about two miles outside Pencaitland, the Glenkinchie Distillery (Map 1, G4; March–May Mon–Fri 10am–5pm; June–Oct Mon–Sat 9.30am–5pm, Sun noon–5pm; Nov–Feb Mon–Fri 11am–4pm; £3.50) is one of only a handful found in the Lowlands of Scotland. It's a worthwhile place to visit, particularly if you're not going on to visit whisky distilleries elsewhere in Scotland, though here, of course, they emphasise the qualities which set Glenkinchie, a lighter, drier malt, apart from the peaty, smoky whiskies of the north. As part of the tour, you see an impressive scale model of a distillery, allowing you to place all the different processes in context, and get an explanation of the art of blending.

EAST LOTHIAN

THE BORDERS

South of Edinburgh, beyond the Pentland hills, nestles the valley of the **Tweed River**, the heart of the **Borders** region of Scotland, an area which boasts some of the most tranquil and beguiling scenery in the country. Broadly known as the Southern Uplands, the Border hills are characteristically bare and rounded – in contrast to the craggier peaks of the Highlands – and form the backdrop to a rich, turbulent history of border skirmishes and religious and internecine feuding.

From the capital, the most worthwhile targets of a day-trip are one or more of the famous ruined **abbeys** of **Melrose**, **Dryburgh** and **Jedburgh**, along with the impressive stately homes of **Abbotsford**, Sir Walter Scott's beloved country seat, and **Traquair**, with its appealingly quirky history and tiny brewery. The whole region is also great for **walking**, either up into the hills or along sections of riverside, particularly the Tweed, which has a well-marked walkway and cycle path.

The region isn't that well served by **public transport**. There are no trains, and while buses run south from Edinburgh to Galashiels on a fairly regular basis, picking up connections to places beyond this normally requires some careful planning. For full details contact Traveline (☎0800/232323).

Melrose Abbey

Map 1, G7. April–Sept daily 9.30am–6.30pm; Oct–March Mon–Sat 9.30am–4.30pm, Sun 2–4.30pm; £3.50

Tucked in between the Tweed and the gorse-backed Eildon Hills, minuscule **Melrose** is the most beguiling of towns, with its mix of pretty little cottages and tweedy shops alongside high-standing Georgian and Victorian facades. Its chief draw are the pink- and red-tinted stone ruins of **Melrose Abbey**, by far the best of the Border abbeys, which soar above their riverside surroundings. Founded in 1136 by King David I, Melrose was the first Cistercian settlement in Scotland and grew rich selling wool and hides to Flanders. Most of the present remains date from the fifteenth century, when extensive rebuilding abandoned the original Cistercian austerity for an elaborate, Gothic style inspired by the abbeys of northern England. The sculptural detailing at Melrose is of the highest quality, but it's easy to miss if you don't know where to look, so taking advantage of the free audioguide, or buying yourself a guidebook at the entrance (£2.50), is a good idea.

Dryburgh Abbey

Map 1, I7. April–Sept daily 9.30am–6.30pm; Oct–March Mon–Sat 9.30am–4.30pm, Sun 2–4.30pm; £2.80.

If you're driving the three miles from Melrose to Dryburgh, you'll pass **Scott's View**, a viewing point overlooking the Tweed Valley, where Sir Walter Scott often picnicked and where his horse stopped out of habit during the great writer's funeral procession. The tiny village of **DRYBURGH** is on the other side of the Tweed from St Boswells, and hidden away in a U-bend in the river, the remains of **Dryburgh Abbey** occupy an idyllic position against a hilly backdrop, with ancient cedars, redwoods, beech and lime trees and wide lawns flattering the pinkish-red hues of the stonework. The ruins of the **Abbey Church** are much less substantial than those of Melrose or Jedburgh, and virtually nothing survives of the nave, though the transepts have fared better, their chapels now serving as private burial grounds for, among others, Sir Walter Scott and Field Marshal Haig, the World War I commander whose ineptitude cost thousands of soldiers' lives.

THE BORDERS

Jedburgh Abbey

Map 1, I7. April–Sept daily 9.30am–6.30pm; Oct–March Mon–Sat
9.30am–4.30pm, Sun 2–4.30pm; £3.30.

Eight miles south of Dryburgh and just ten miles north of
the border with England, **JEDBURGH** nestles in the valley of the Jed Water near its confluence with the Teviot.
Despite its ruinous state, **Jedburgh Abbey** still dominates
the town; founded in the twelfth century as an Augustinian
priory by King David I, it's the best-preserved of all the
Border abbeys. Entry is through the **visitor centre** at the
bottom of the hill, which has a viewing room overlooking
the site. Jedburgh's chief glory is really its **Abbey Church**.
Built in red, yellow and grey sandstone, it can appear by
turns gloomy, calm or richly warm, depending on the
weather and the light. Splendidly preserved, it's a fine
example of the transition from Romanesque to Gothic
design, with pointed window arches surmounted by the
round-headed arches of the triforium, which, in turn, support the lancet windows of the clerestory.

Abbotsford House

Map 1, G7. June–Sept daily 9.30am–5pm; mid-March to May & Oct
Mon–Sat 9.30am–5pm, Sun 2–5pm; £4.

Memorably set on the banks of the Tweed between
Galashiels and Melrose, **Abbotsford House** was designed
to satisfy the Romantic inclinations of Sir Walter Scott,
who lived here from 1812 until his death twenty years later.
The building took twelve years to evolve, and is covered
with the fanciful turrets and castellations of the Scots
Baronial exterior; look out also for the entrance porch,
which imitates Linlithgow Palace and a screen wall in the
garden echoing Melrose Abbey's cloister. Despite all the

THE BORDERS

exterior pomp, the **interior** is surprisingly small and poky, with just six rooms open for viewing, including the heavy wood-panelled library, which boasts Scott's collection of more than nine thousand rare books and an extraordinary assortment of memorabilia, from a lock of Bonnie Prince Charlie's hair to a piece of oatcake found in the pocket of a dead Highlander at Culloden.

Traquair House

Map 1, D7. Daily: April, May, Sept & Oct 12.30–5.30pm; June–Aug 10.30am–5.30pm; £5.30; grounds only £2. ⓦwww.traquair.co.uk.

Peeping out from the trees a mile or so south of Innerleithen, a town twelve miles west of Galashiels and six miles east of Peebles, **Traquair** (pronounced "tra-kware") **House** is the oldest continuously inhabited home in Scotland, and has been in the hands of the same family – the Maxwell Stuarts – since 1491. The whitewashed facade is strikingly handsome, with narrow windows and trim turrets surrounding the tiniest of front doors – an organic, homogeneous edifice that's a welcome change from other grandiose stately homes. Inside, the house has kept many of its oldest features, including a carefully camouflaged priest's room where persecuted Catholic chaplains lived in hiding. In the surrounding **gardens** you'll find a hedge maze, several craft workshops and a **working brewery**, dating back to 1566 but reopened in its present form in 1965. You can taste the ales in the brewery shop. Look out too for the locked **Bear Gates**; Bonnie Prince Charlie, who stayed here for a night in 1745 while his army was in Edinburgh, left the house through the gates, and the then owner promised to keep them locked till a Stuart should ascend the throne.

THE BORDERS

LISTINGS

LISTINGS

Accommodation

A s befits its status as a busy tourist destination and important commercial centre, Edinburgh has a greater choice of **accommodation** than any other place in Britain outside London. **Hotels** (and large backpacker **hostels**) are essentially the only options you'll find right in the heart of the city, but within relatively easy reach of the centre the selection of **guesthouses**, **B&Bs**, **campus accommodation** and even **campsites** broadens considerably.

Many of Edinburgh's large central hotels are notable landmarks in themselves, and these are the most upmarket and expensive places to stay. You can remain in the heart of the city for less by checking into one of the string of bland modern hotel chains or one of the guesthouses or small

ACCOMMODATION PRICE CODES

Accommodation **prices** have been graded with the codes below, according to the cost of the least expensive double room in high season.

- ① under £40
- ② £40–50
- ③ £50–60
- ④ £60–70
- ⑤ £70–90
- ⑥ £90–110
- ⑦ £110–150
- ⑧ £150–200
- ⑨ £200 and over

FINDING ACCOMMODATION DURING THE EDINBURGH FESTIVAL

Whether you're in Edinburgh to take part, take in some shows or are simply passing through, there's no getting past the fact that accommodation isn't easy to find during the Edinburgh Festival. Before August, the tourist office telephone and online booking services (see opposite) can be helpful, but by the time the Festival has started these tend to get swamped. Other resources worth trying are the accommodation bulletin board on the Fringe website (ⓦ www.edfringe.com) or Festival Beds (ⓣ 0131/225 1101, ⓦ www.festivalbeds.co.uk), another clearing house for B&Bs. If you're up in Edinburgh for more than a couple of days, self-catering accommodation is worth considering: The Festival Partnership (ⓣ 0131/478 1294; ⓦ www.edinburghfestival.net) and Factotum (ⓣ 0131/220 1838; ⓦ www.factotum.co.uk) both specialize in longer-term Festival accommodation.

hotels found within a mile's radius of the centre. The highest concentration of these can be found immediately north of Haymarket Station, in the eastern and northern reaches of the New Town, and in the south around the suburbs of Bruntsfield and Newington. Other popular areas, slightly further out, are Ferry Road, to the north of town, and the seaside suburbs of Portobello and Joppa – around three miles from the centre. Edinburgh's decent bus service means that even if you're staying beyond walking distance from the centre, it's still fairly easy to get around.

ACCOMMODATION

There's a list of gay-oriented accommodation options on p.257.

You should be able to find accommodation reasonably easily for most of the year. However, **advance reservations** are recommended during summer months, especially during the **Festival** (see box opposite). The **tourist office** (℡ 0131/473 3800, ⊛ www.edinburgh.org) sends out accommodation lists for free, and can reserve any type of accommodation in advance for a non-refundable £5 fee: call in personally when you arrive or contact the office in advance, stating requirements. In Waverley Station, Capital Holidays runs an accommodation reservation service (daily 9am–5pm; ℡ 0131/556 0030) which makes no charge for bookings but requires the first night to be paid in full in advance by credit card.

HOTELS

In the centre of the city, Edinburgh's **hotels** tend to fall into two categories: grand and traditional at the upper end of the market, and budget chain hotels (see box below) in the middle-to-low price range. A number of the new breed of modern designer hotels have recently arrived just

---

BUDGET HOTEL CHAINS

All the following budget hotel chains have large properties in or around the centre of Edinburgh. While they are generally lacking in charm or character, they invariably offer useful central locations, inexpensive room rates (£45–65 per room per night is typical, depending on time of year) and efficient booking and check-in systems.

Novotel/Ibis ℡ 020/8283 4530, ⊛ www.accorhotels.com
Travelodge ℡ 0870/085 0950, ⊛ www.travelodge.co.uk
Travel Inn ℡ 0870/242 8000, ⊛ www.travelinn.co.uk
Holiday Inn Express ℡ 0800/897121, ⊛ www.hiexpress.com

HOTELS

outside the city centre in places such as Leith and the West End, while in the suburbs and beyond, the country-house hotel style dominates.

Note that smaller hotels have generally been included in the guesthouse section (see pp.183–189).

ROYAL MILE AND THE OLD TOWN

Apex International Hotel

Map 3, C5. 31–35 Grassmarket ⓣ0131/300 3456, ⓦ www.apexhotels.co.uk. Student residence turned 175-bed business-orientated hotel with decent rooms, some with views to the Castle. The best views of all are from the top-floor *Heights* restaurant, while the street-level *Metro* brasserie looks out through plate glass windows to the happening Grassmarket. ⓺

Point Hotel

Map 3, A5. 34–59 Bread St ⓣ0131/221 5555, ⓦ www.point-hotel.co.uk. Former department store that's now one of the city's truly hip hotels. Rooms are large, well equipped and memorably stylish, with minimalist lines, cool lighting and designer touches. In the same thoroughly modern vein are the popular bar and an excellent restaurant at street level. ⓺

The Scotsman Hotel

Map 3, G2. 20 North Bridge ⓣ0131/556 5565, ⓦ www.thescotsmanhotel.co.uk. The most talked-about new hotel in Edinburgh, a plush, smart but non-stuffy new occupant of the grand old offices of the *Scotsman* newspaper. The marble staircase and walnut panelled lobby have been retained, but elsewhere the rooms are full of contemporary style, and you can sleep in what was the editor's office. ⓼

Tailors Hall Hotel

Map 3, F4. 139 Cowgate ⓣ0131/622 6800, ⓦ www.festival-inns.co.uk.

Though located in the otherwise dingy Cowgate, this mid-range hotel in a recently converted 1621 trades hall and brewery has modern if quite small en-suite rooms. Larger rooms sleeping three and four are available in addition to doubles. In the same building is the lively mock-Gothic *Three Sisters Bar*, which spills onto a large courtyard in summer. **6**

NEW TOWN

Balmoral Hotel

Map 4, L6. 1 Princes St ⓣ 0131/556 2414, ⓦ www.rfhotels.com. Originally known as the *North British*, this elegant Edinburgh landmark is the finest grand hotel in the city. Nearly two hundred rooms with all the extras including computers and huge TVs, full business facilities, a swimming pool and gym, and two highly rated restaurants. **8**

Bonham Hotel

Map 2, G5. 35 Drumsheugh Gardens ⓣ 0131/226 6050, ⓦ www.thebonham.com. One of Edinburgh's most stylish modern hotels, cheekily hiding behind a grand West End Victorian facade. The rooms, all with cable TV, DVD and PCs, feature an interesting mix of period features and modern designer furniture, with strong, bold colours next to ornate cornices and work by up-and-coming Scottish artists on the walls. **8**

Caledonian Hilton

Map 4, B9. Corner of Princes St & Lothian Rd ⓣ 0131/459 9988, ⓦ www.hilton.com. Built by the railway for the well-to-do travelling between London and their Highland estates, this eight-storey red-sandstone building, with some 250 rooms, lords it over the west end of Princes Street. Despite its five-star status, it isn't as plush or stylish as its competitors, though it's still popular with visiting celebrities. The

HOTELS

recent take-over by the Hilton Group promises to sharpen things up. ⑨

Christopher North Hotel
Map 4, B2. 6 Gloucester Place
ⓣ 0131/225 2720,
ⓦ www.christophernorth.co.uk.
Small, elegant and comfortable townhouse hotel in a typical New Town Georgian terrace, with neat en-suite rooms. Decor is fairly up-to-date and dramatic, if a little overwhelming, with bold stripy wallpaper, lots of gold paint and velvet curtains. ⑥

Frederick House Hotel
Map 4, E5. 42 Frederick St
ⓣ 0131/226 1999,
ⓦ www.townhousehotels.co.uk.
A reasonably priced if slightly plain mid-range hotel with 45 rooms above an unassuming entrance-way just off George Street. All the rooms are en-suite, with satellite TV, fridges and modem socket, though the decor isn't all that elegant or harmonious. For breakfast, a voucher system is operated

with *Café Rouge* across the road. ④

Howard Hotel
Map 4, G1. 34 Great King St
ⓣ 0131/557 3500,
ⓦ www.thehoward.com.
Highly refined, top-of-the-range townhouse hotel, with fifteen exclusive rooms lavishly decorated in classically elegant style. Stuffed with antiques, oil paintings and chandeliers, the overwhelming atmosphere here is of a terribly well-looked-after Georgian home. Rooms have the usual top-notch technological touches, and though there's no restaurant, room service is available 24 hours. ⑨

Melvin House Hotel
Map 2, G5. 3 Rothesay Terrace ⓣ 0131/225 5084,
ⓦ www.melvinhouse.co.uk.
One of Edinburgh's grandest Victorian terrace houses, with exquisite internal wood panelling, a galleried library and decent en-suite rooms, some with outstanding views

over Dean Village and the city skyline. Guests get use of a pleasant lounge and fairly basic restaurant. ❼

Old Waverley Hotel
Map 4, I6. 43 Princes St
Ⓣ 0131/556 4648,
Ⓦ www.paramount-hotels.co.uk.
Rather old-fashioned and plainly furnished but ideally placed grand hotel with 66 rooms, right across from Waverley Station and with sweeping city views. The lounge bar and restaurant aren't up to much (other than for the views), and leisure facilities are located five minutes walk away at the linked *Calton Hotel*. ❽

Parliament House Hotel
Map 2, I4. 15 Calton Hill
Ⓣ 0131/478 4000,
Ⓦ www.scotland-hotels.co.uk.
The parliament is no longer planned for Calton Hill, but this neat hotel in a discreet but central location not far from Princes Street remains pleasant and well run, with 53 rooms (including three for disabled guests) and a

slightly garish modern bistro. ❽

LEITH

Malmaison
Map 6, H3. 1 Tower Place
Ⓣ 0131/468 5000,
Ⓦ www.malmaison.com.
Chic modern hotel, in a converted harbourside building, with bright, bold decor and furnishings in each room, as well as CD players and cable TV. Also has a gym, room service, a Parisian brasserie and a café-bar serving lighter meals. ❼

SOUTH OF THE CENTRE

Allison House Hotel
Map 2, J6. 15–17 Mayfield Gardens, Mayfield
Ⓣ 0131/667 8049,
Ⓦ www.allisonhousehotel.com.
Quite a grand affair for what is a family-run, suburban hotel, but the standards of hospitality are high and it's comfortable throughout.

HOTELS

181

The 23 rooms all have showers, there's an honesty bar and a restaurant serving "taste-of-Scotland" style meals and breakfasts. It's conveniently located on one of the main bus routes into town, too. ❹

Braid Hills Hotel
Map 2, G8. 134 Braid Rd, Braid Hills ⓣ 0131/447 8888, ⓔ bookings@braidhillshotel .co.uk.
Old-fashioned baronial-style hotel perched on the top of one of Edinburgh's seven hills – the views, and walks on the neighbouring public golf course, are good. All 68 rooms have en-suite facilities as well as satellite TVs, and there's plenty of free car parking. ❼

Bruntsfield Hotel
Map 2, G6. 69–74 Bruntsfield Place, Bruntsfield ⓣ 0131/229 1393, ⓦ www.thebruntsfield.co.uk. Large, comfortable and unexpectedly peaceful hotel overlooking Bruntsfield Links, a mile south of Princes Street. Rooms are plain but adequate in the best traditions of the Best Western group; there's a bar serving above-average grub and a modern Scottish restaurant with a large conservatory in the basement. Good standby rates. ❻

Prestonfield House Hotel
Map 2, J6. Priestfield Road, Bruntsfield ⓣ 0131/668 3346, ⓦ www.prestonfieldhouse.com. This seventeenth-century mansion set in its own park below Arthur's Seat, with upmarket rooms in the main house and a tasteful annex, is a unique Edinburgh hotel. Peacocks strut around on the lawns and Highland cattle low in the adjacent fields. ❼

Simpson's Hotel
Map 3, A6. 79 Lauriston Place ⓣ 0131/622 7979, ⓦ www.simpsons-hotel.com. Well-priced and smart yet unfussy medium-sized hotel, located in a former maternity hospital near Tollcross and the Meadows. Offers double,

HOTELS

triple, family and disabled rooms, all en-suite, and there's a café-bar for breakfast, snacks and evening meals. Named after Sir James Young Simpson, pioneer of modern anaesthetics. **5**

WEST OF THE CENTRE

The Original Raj Hotel
Map 2, F5. 6 West Coates ☎0131/346 1333.
Imaginatively conceived and lavishly executed, this townhouse hotel has seventeen rooms themed on India and the splendour of the Raj, featuring colourful Indian fabrics and embroidery, impressive rugs and lovely colonial furniture. Meals for residents are prepared by award-winning chef/proprietor, Tommy Miah. **6**

Ramada Jarvis Edinburgh
Map 2, D5. 4 Ellersly Rd, Corstorphine ☎0131/337 6888, Ⓦwww.jarvis.co.uk.
Ivy-covered Edwardian country mansion set in a walled garden in quiet suburban Corstorphine, between the city centre and the airport. Inside it has less character but proves perfectly adequate for its predominantly business clientele, with a restaurant, bar, 24-hour room service and plenty of parking. **7**

GUESTHOUSES

Edinburgh's vast range of **guesthouses**, **small hotels** and **bed & breakfast** establishments generally offer much better value for money and a far more homely experience than the larger city hotels. While a handful of notably upmarket options are found right in the heart of the city, there's a much wider choice of guesthouses, many in large, elegant Georgian or Victorian houses, located within easy reach of the centre. The best balance between accessibility and good value can be found in the New Town or inner city suburbs such as the Grange and Bruntsfield, but there are many others within easy reach of the centre by bus. The tourist office has fuller lists of approved B&Bs, and can help with bookings (see p.177).

ROYAL MILE AND THE OLD TOWN

Bank Hotel
Map 3, F8. 1 South Bridge
Ⓣ0131/556 9043,
Ⓦwww.festival-inns.co.uk.
Notable location in a 1920s former bank at the crossroads of the Royal Mile and South Bridge, with *Logie Baird's* bar downstairs and nine unusual but comfortable rooms upstairs on the theme of famous Scots. ❺

The Witchery Apartments
Map 3, C8. Castlehill, Royal Mile Ⓣ0131/225 5613,
Ⓦwww.thewitchery.com.
Two riotously indulgent apartments above the famously spooky Royal Mile restaurant, jammed full of antiques and tapestries, baroque designs and gilded bookcases. Among the features are a bed-head created out of an old church pulpit and a freestanding roll-top bath. Top of the range, unique and memorable. ❽

NEW TOWN

Ardenlee Guest House
Map 2, H4. 9 Eyre Place
Ⓣ0131/556 2838.
Welcoming, non-smoking guesthouse on the northern edge of the New Town, with exceptionally comfortable and spacious rooms. Breakfast includes some vegetarian options, and large family rooms are available. ❸

Brodies Guest House
Map 2, H4. 22 East Claremont St Ⓣ0131/556 4032,
Ⓔrose.olbert@saqnet.co.uk.

Friendly non-smoking B&B in a Victorian terraced house near the Broughton area (on the eastern edge of the New Town), with fairly standard single, double, triple and family rooms. Children are welcome. **❸**

Davenport House

Map 4, F1. 58 Great King St Ⓣ 0131/558 8495, Ⓔ davenporthouse@btinternet .com.

Grand, regally decorated guesthouse in an attractive New Town townhouse that makes a well-priced and intimate alternative to some of the nearby hotels. The en-suite rooms have typical Georgian features such as high ceilings and old fireplaces, as well as a decent range of facilities including TVs. **❹**

Galloway Guest House

Map 2, G4. 22 Dean Park Crescent Ⓣ 0131/332 3672. Friendly, family-run option in elegant Stockbridge, an area with some fine shops and restaurants but also within walking distance of the centre. **❷**

Gerald's Place

Map 4, I2. 21b Abercromby Place Ⓣ 0131/558 7017, Ⓦ www.scotland2000.com /geraldsplace.

A real taste of New Town life at an upmarket but wonderfully idiosyncratic, hospitable and comfy basement B&B full of bookcases, lived-in antiques and original art. The fact that there are only two double rooms adds to the homely feel. **❺**

Greenside Hotel

Map 2, I4. 9 Royal Terrace Ⓣ 0131/557 0022, Ⓦ www.townhousehotels.co.uk. One of a number of small hotels on Calton Hill with great views from the top floors – in this case across to Leith and beyond to the Firth of Forth. The rooms are all en-suite, and though the decor is rather traditional and uninspiring they offer good value for money considering the location. **❹**

GUESTHOUSES

Rick's Restaurant With Rooms
Map 4, E5. 55a Frederick St
Ⓣ 0131/622 7800,
Ⓦ www.ricksedinburgh.co.uk.
Four much sought-after
rooms at the back of the
popular New Town bar and
restaurant. Beautifully styled
and fitted with walnut
headboards and top quality
fabrics, they look out onto a
cobbled lane behind. ❻

Six Mary's Place
Map 2, G4. Raeburn Place
Ⓣ 0131/332 8965,
Ⓦ www.sixmarysplace.co.uk.
Collectively run
"alternative" guesthouse
with very tasteful, simply
designed rooms; there's a
no-smoking policy and
excellent home-cooked
vegetarian meals are on offer
–including breakfast, which
is served in the bright
conservatory. ❹

Stuart House
Map 2, H4. 12 East Claremont
St Ⓣ 0131/557 9030,
Ⓔ stuartho@globalnet.co.uk.
Homely and bright Georgian

house on an attractive
cobbled street in the
Broughton area. The rooms,
with their slightly over-
elaborate decor, are located
on the first or second floor.
No smoking. ❹

LEITH AND INVERLEITH

A-Haven Town House
Map 6, D4. 180 Ferry Rd, Leith
Ⓣ 0131/554 6559,
Ⓔ reservations@a-haven.co.uk.
Terrifically friendly and well-
run, this is among the best of
a number of guesthouses
along one of Edinburgh's
main east–west arteries. A
total of 14 bedrooms, some
of which are en suite;
evening meals are served by
arrangement. ❺

Ashlyn Guest House
Map 2, G2. 42 Inverleith Row,
Inverleith Ⓣ 0131/552 2954.
An elegant, intimate place
with eight rooms, some of
which have period Georgian
features and nice views out
over the greenery. Right by

the Botanic Garden, it's a half-hour walk or an easy bus trip from the centre. Non-smoking. ❸

Bar Java

Map 6, H4. 48–50 Constitution St, Leith ☎ 0131/467 7527, Ⓦ www.java-bedandbreakfast .com.

A step above a backpacker hostel, offering simple but brightly designed rooms above one of Leith's funkiest bars. Great breakfasts served, and food and drink available till late in the bar itself. ❷

SOUTH OF THE CENTRE

- -

Ashdene House

Map 2, I6. 23 Fountainhall Rd, Grange ☎ 0131/667 6026, Ⓔ Ashdene_House_Edinburgh @compuserve.com.

Well-run, non-smoking and environmentally conscious guesthouse in the quiet southern suburbs. Five en-suite rooms with pleasant, unfussy decor. ❸

Cluaran House

Map 2, G6. 47 Leamington Terrace, Viewforth ☎ 0131/221 0047, Ⓦ www.scotland2000 .com/cluaran.

A very pleasant guesthouse in a quiet side street near Brunstfield, with plenty of nice touches including stained glass, wooden shutters and stripped floors. The rooms have neat, clean decor and wholefood breakfasts are served. No smoking. ❸

The Greenhouse

Map 2, G6. 14 Hartington Gardens, Viewforth ☎ 0131/622 7634, Ⓔ greenhouse_edin @hotmail.com.

A fully vegetarian/vegan guesthouse, right down to the soaps and duvets, though a relaxed rather than right-on atmosphere prevails. The rooms are neat and tastefully furnished, with fresh fruit and flowers in each. ❸

Hopetoun Guest House

Map 2, I6. 15 Mayfield Rd, Mayfield ☎ 0131/667 7691, Ⓔ hopetoun@aol.com.

GUESTHOUSES

Bright, friendly non-smoking guesthouse with just three rooms. Great views of Arthur's Seat and Blackford Hill; various buses run past the front door into town. ➋

International Guest House

Map 2, J6. 37 Mayfield Gardens, Mayfield ⓣ 0131/667 2511, ⓔ intergh@easynet.co.uk. One of the best of the guesthouses on this busy arterial road leading into Edinburgh. The en-suite rooms are comfortable, with TVs and some interesting plasterwork. No evening meals. ➋

The Stuarts B&B

Map 2, H6. 17 Glengyle Terrace, Bruntsfield ⓣ 0131/229 9559, ⓔ reservations @the-stuarts.com. A five-star bed and breakfast in central Edinburgh, with three comfortable and well-equipped rooms in a basement beside Bruntsfield Links. ➎

Teviotdale House Hotel

Map 2, I6. 53 Grange Loan, Grange ⓣ 0131/667 4376, ⓔ teviotdale.house@btinternet .com. Peaceful, non-smoking small hotel, offering luxurious standards at reasonable prices. Particularly good (and huge) home-cooked Scottish breakfasts. ➌

EAST OF THE CENTRE

Joppa Turrets Guest House

Map 2, N5. 1 Lower Joppa, Joppa ⓣ 0131/669 5806, ⓦ www.joppaturrets.demon .co.uk. The place to come if you want an Edinburgh holiday by the sea: a quiet establishment right by the beach in Joppa, five miles east of the city centre. Though the rooms (all non-smoking) are quite small, all have sea views. ➋

Portobello House

Map 2, N4. 2 Pittville St, Portobello ⓣ 0131/669 6067.

Pleasant rooms, including some en suite and a family room, as well as good organic breakfasts at this family-run, non-smoking guesthouse. Located in a quiet cul-de-sac only two minutes from Portobello's promenade and beach. ❷

Stra'ven Guest House
Map 2, N5. 3 Brunstane Rd North, Joppa ☎0131/669 5580. Splendid lounge and friendly service in an elegant, well-kept guesthouse. Useful buses into town run from only one block away. No smoking. ❷

SELF-CATERING APARTMENTS

Self-catering apartments offer good value if you're in a group or looking for a level of independence and privacy you can't always get in guesthouses or hotels. Centrally located, custom-built self-catering apartments full of mod-cons are mostly popular with business travellers, but with no minimum let they make viable alternatives to guesthouses, particularly if you're in a group of four or more. They're also well worth considering for longer stays, for example during the Festival.

Canon Court Apartments
Map 2, H3. 20 Canonmills ☎0131/474 7000, ⓦwww.canoncourt.co.uk. Two modern blocks of smart, comfortable self-catering apartments with one or two bedrooms on the northern edge of the New Town, near the Water of Leith. All units have decent modern

furnishings, cable TV, CD hi-fi, modem point and full kitchen facilities. There's also free parking alongside. Prices start at £87 per night for a studio apartment sleeping two.

National Trust for Scotland
Map 3, D8. 5 Charlotte Square ☎0131/243 9331, ⓔholidays@nts.org.uk.

A two-room apartment in Gladstone's Land (the finest house on the Royal Mile). Fairly simply furnished with few frills – the important thing here is the historic setting and the great location. Minimum rental period is one week in summer and three nights in winter, but to secure it you'll have to book well in advance. Sleeps two and costs from £240 per week.

Royal Garden Apartments

Map 4, I3. York Buildings, Queen St ⓣ 0131/625 1234, ⓦ www.royal-garden.co.uk. Comfortable, stylish and modern one- and two-bedroom apartments with cable TV, CD players and all mod cons in the kitchen. In-house *Marshall's Cafe* at street level is open for breakfasts and light snacks through the day. Very centrally located opposite the National Portrait Gallery. Prices start at £150 per night for a studio apartment, though discounts are often available at weekends.

West End Apartments

Map 2, F4. c/o Brian Matheson, 2 Learmonth Terrace, Comely Bank ⓣ 0131/332 0717 or ⓣ 0131/226 6512, ⓔ brian@sias.co.uk. Five apartments in a West End townhouse; most have only one bedroom (with a sofabed in the lounge), though the flat on the top floor has one twin and one double room; minimum let two nights. The furnishings aren't as modern and slick as the city centre apartment blocks but there's a homelier feel and the units are all well equipped. Prices start at around £200 per week for a one-bedroom apartment.

CAMPUS ACCOMMODATION

With a large number of students studying in Scotland's capital, **campus accommodation** is available in the city during the Easter (early April) and summer holidays (mid

July to mid September), though generally it's not as cheap an option as might be expected, and the standard of accommodation is commonly plain and characterless. What's available is generally bed-and-breakfast accommodation in small single or twin rooms located along long, lonely corridors in student halls, or self-catering in fairly spartan flats with single rooms and kitchen-living rooms.

Napier University
Map 2, G6. 219 Colinton Rd, Merchiston Ⓣ 0131/455 4331, Ⓦ www.napier.ac.uk/business /holiday.htm.
No-frills B&B rooms in Bruntsfield student halls, or tiny three- to five-person self-catering flats in the Tollcross/ Bruntsfield area of the city. Minimum stay is one week, and rates start at £315 per week for a three-person unit.

University of Edinburgh Pollock Halls of Residence
Map 5, B7. 18 Holyrood Park Rd, Newington Ⓣ 0131/651 2007 or Ⓣ 0800/028 7118, Ⓦ www.edinburghfirst.com.
Unquestionably the best setting of any of the campuses, right beside the Royal Commonwealth Pool and Holyrood Park, but relatively expensive (Ⓢ; rates are for bed and breakfast). Also available are self-catering student flats in various modern blocks in Newington on the south side of the city.

HOSTELS

Edinburgh now has a wealth of **hostels**, including two grand SYHA(Scottish Youth Hostel Association)-run establishments and a cluster of independent outfits on or near the Royal Mile. All have dorms with bunkbeds, as well as large communal kitchens and living areas. Most hostels provide bedding, and many have **private four-bed or double rooms** available, though these tend to be priced at the same

HOSTELS

level as cheaper guesthouses. Expect to pay £10–12 a night for a dorm bed, though prices rise during the Festival by a couple of pounds, and some places now charge more in a bid to make the hostel slightly more upmarket. The hostels listed here are open all year round unless otherwise stated; we've also indicated those that have a curfew.

Argyle Backpackers Hotel

Map 2, H6. 14 Argyle Place, Marchmont ⒯ 0131/667 9991, ⓦ www.argyle-backpackers .co.uk.

A discerning choice offering a quieter, less intense version of the typical backpackers' hostel, with small dorms with single beds and a dozen double/twin rooms (❶), though across the board, prices are a pound or two higher than the city centre hostels. Neatly decorated, *Argyle* has a conservatory and small garden, and is pleasantly located near the Meadows in studenty Marchmont, with shops and pubs nearby.

Belford Hostel

Map 2, F5. 6–8 Douglas Gardens, West End ⒯ 0131/225 6209; booking hotline ⒯ 0800/096 6868,

ⓦ www.hoppo.com.

Housed in a converted Arts and Crafts church, just west of the centre close to St Mary's Cathedral and the Gallery of Modern Art, the four- to ten-bed dorms here are in box rooms with the vaulted church ceiling above. There are also six reasonable twin or double rooms (❶), as well as a lounge and bar with a pool table, and a bit of space outside for summer barbecues.

Brodies Backpackers Hostel

Map 3, G8. 12 High St, Old Town ⒯ 0131/556 6770, ⓦ www.brodieshostels.co.uk.

Tucked down a typical Old Town close, *Brodies* has four fairly straightforward dorms, limited communal areas and few facilities. However, being smaller than many others

HOSTELS

makes it feel a little bit more homely and genuinely friendly.

Bruntsfield Hostel

Map 2, H6. 7 Bruntsfield Crescent, Bruntsfield ⓣ0131/447 2994 or ⓣ0870/155 3255, ⓦwww.syha.org.uk.
Large, recently upgraded SYHA hostel a mile south of Princes Street overlooking Bruntsfield Links; take bus #10, #11 or #16. Accommodation is mostly in large dorms, and there are no dining facilities, but the small size and pleasant location make this a more discerning choice than its sister *Eglinton* hostel (see p.194).

Castle Rock Hostel

Map 3, D3. 15 Johnston Terrace, Old Town ⓣ0131/225 9666, ⓦwww.scotlands-top -hostels.com.
Busy, central 200-bed hostel

tucked below the Castle ramparts. Dorms are large and bright, and the communal areas include a games room with pool and ping-pong tables.

Cowgate Tourist Hostel

Map 3, F4. 94–116 Cowgate, Old Town ⓣ0131/226 2153, ⓦwww.cowgatetouristhostel .co.uk.
Basic but usefully central accommodation in rather small, dark and spartan three- four- and five-bedroom apartments with kitchens, in the heart of the Old Town. Beds are sold singly, like a normal dorm, though you can arrange to rent a whole apartment.

Edinburgh Backpackers Hostel

Map 3, F2. 65 Cockburn St, Old Town ⓣ0131/539 8695; booking hotline ⓣ0800/096 6868, ⓦwww.hoppo.com.

During July and August, SYHA take over two central student residences, one on The Pleasance and one on Cowgate; both have over 100 single bedrooms for around £16 per night. Call ⓣ0131/556 5566 for more info.

HOSTELS

Big hostel with a great central location in a side street off the Royal Mile. Accommodation is mostly in large but bright dorms, although a few doubles (❷) are available in a separate self-catering apartment nearby. There isn't much of a communal lounge, but the adjacent *Southern Cross Café* serves coffee and good food from breakfast till late.

Eglinton Hostel

Map 2, F5. 18 Eglinton Crescent, Haymarket ⓣ0131/337 1120 or ⓣ0870/155 3255, ⓦwww.syha.org.uk. Slightly more expensive but the more central of the two main SYHA hostels (the other is *Bruntsfield*; see p.193), in a characterful townhouse west of the centre, near Haymarket Station. Dining facilities are available, though they're often dominated by the large groups which are a common feature here.

High Street Hostel

Map 3, H3. 8 Blackfriars St, Old Town ⓣ0131/557 3984, ⓦwww.scotlands-top-hostels .com. Large but lively and well-known hostel in a sixteenth-century building just off the Royal Mile. There's a large and permanently busy ground-floor lounge and bar with windows looking out to the pavement, from where backpacker minibus tours seem to be constantly arriving or departing. Linked to *Castle Rock* and *Royal Mile Backpackers*.

Royal Mile Backpackers

Map 3, G8. 105 High St, Old Town ⓣ0131/557 6120, ⓦwww.scotlands-top-hostels .com. Small, friendly hostel popular with a large percentage of longer-term residents. It has limited communal areas, but residents mostly gravitate to the lounge and bar at its sister *High Street Hostel*, just over the road.

St Christopher's Inns

Map 3, F2. 9–13 Market St, Old Town ⓣ0131/226 1446, ⓦwww.st-christophers.co.uk. Edinburgh's first sighting of

HOSTELS

the mega-hostels now common in London; 110 beds (all bunks) with smaller twin rooms (**❶**) as well as dorms. There's a small communal area and a noisy bar for beer and food on ground level. A little corporate but clean and with good service; slightly more expensive than most other hostels.

CAMPSITES

There are three well-equipped caravan parks with **campsites** on the fringes of Edinburgh: one in the west, one in the east and two in the north of the city. Although each is a fair distance from the centre of town, all are well served by buses. You can expect to pay under £10 a night to pitch your tent.

Davidson's Mains Caravan Site

Map 2, D2. Marine Drive, Silverknowes ☎0131/312 6874. Edinburgh Caravan Club site in a pleasant location close to the shore in the north-western suburbs, a thirty-minute ride from the centre by bus #14. Only a basic shop on site. Open year-round.

Drummohr Caravan Park

Map 1, F3. Levenhall, Musselburgh ☎0131/665 6867. A large, pleasant site in this coastal satellite town to the east of Edinburgh, with excellent transport connections to the city, including buses #15, #15A, #26, #44, #66 (SMT) and #85. Open March–Oct.

Mortonhall Caravan Park

Map 1, F3. 38 Mortonhall Gate, Frogston Rd East ☎0131/664 1533. A good site, five miles south of the centre, near the Braid Hills; take bus #11 from Princes Street. Open March–Oct.

Eating

I t wasn't that long ago that eating out in Edinburgh meant either a stuffy, expensive restaurant or a tearoom serving little but sad-looking sandwiches and mugs of tea. However, the last decade has seen an upsurge in style, sophistication and good taste in Edinburgh's cafés and restaurants. Café culture has hit the centre of the city, with

MODERN SCOTTISH CUISINE

Traditionally, Scotland was a fully paid-up member of British cuisine's club for overcooked vegetables and stodgy puddings. As chefs everywhere began to adopt original ideas and wider influences during the 1990s, however, those in Scotland tied this freedom of expression to the country's native products, including Aberdeen Angus steaks, smoked fish, shellfish, molluscs, venison and grouse – high-quality products, most of which are farmed or live wild in remote parts of the country. So "Modern Scottish" cooking came about, creating dishes such as haggis in filo pastry with a plum sauce, salmon with a Thai salsa or venison in a dark chocolate sauce, and it has since been enthusiastically adopted not just by most of the best restaurants in Edinburgh, but also by many less expensive bistros and more adventurous cafés.

EDINBURGH'S BEST ALFRESCO DINING

Café Hub – for great views down the Royal Mile. See p.199.

Mamma's American Pizza Company – for all the hubbub of the Grassmarket. See p.200.

Oloroso – chic modern dining high above the New Town, with sweeping views of the Forth and Leith. See p.210.

The Tower – for a great rooftop outlook over the Old Town. See p.204.

Terrace Café – set in the Botanic Garden, and boasting the best views of Edinburgh's dramatic skyline. See p.213.

Pizza Express, Stockbridge – an unexpected riverside hideaway. See p.214.

Waterfront Wine Bar – as close as Leith gets to bijou, with a conservatory if it gets nippy. See p.221.

tables spilling onto the pavements in the summer, and this has been matched by the rise of a clutch of original, upmarket and stylish restaurants, many identifying their cuisine as contemporary or modern Scottish, and championing top-quality meat, game and fish. As with most large cities in Britain, the culinary map of Edinburgh is colourful and global, with long-established Chinese, Indian and Mexican places competing with Thai, Japanese, North African and Spanish cuisine.

Generally, small **diners** and **bistros** predominate, many adopting a casual French style and offering good-value set menus. Traditional **Scottish cooking** can still be found at some of the more formal restaurants, and inevitably some tourist-oriented places offer haggis and other classic clichés. Edinburgh excels in **vegetarian** restaurants (including a couple of classic Indian veggie places), and is equally notable for **seafood** – long a speciality of the **Leith** water-

EATING

front, and now served up by a number of great seafood bistros in the centre of town as well. It's worth bearing in mind that most **pubs** (which are covered in the following chapter) serve food, and that while the large city-centre **hotels** have restaurants, most of these are extremely expensive, and not always good value for money.

More cafés and restaurants are listed in the "Gay Edinburgh" and "Kids' Edinburgh" chapters; see p.254 & p.265.

In the listings below, we've used broad **price categorizations** to indicate how much you can expect to pay for a two-course meal, excluding the cost of drink: **inexpensive** means you can expect to pay under £10; **moderate** £10–20; **expensive** £20–30; and **very expensive** over £30. Some places will add on a ten percent service charge to the bill; if they haven't, it's usual to leave a **tip** of around the same amount.

Most of Edinburgh's cafés are open from 9am to 5pm, while restaurants serve from noon to 2.30pm and 6pm to

HANDY PLACES FOR LATE-NIGHT NIBBLES

Elephant House – coffee and cakes till 11pm. See opposite.

The Witchery by the Castle – great value post-theatre meals. See p.204.

Loon Fung – chopsticks clicking till midnight in Canonmills. See p.209.

Modern India – late-night curry in the east end of town. See p.212.

blue – smart snacks in theatreland. See p.215.

Lazio's – last orders for pizza and pasta on Lothian Road. See p.216.

Favorit – milkshakes and munchies till 3am. See p.218.

EATING

10pm; we've included a number of places which are open outside these times as well. During the **Festival**, the majority of restaurants keep longer hours, but they are also much busier; we've given phone numbers for places where you're likely to need to make a **reservation**.

THE ROYAL MILE AND THE OLD TOWN

Generally, the cafés and restaurants of the **Royal Mile** are less obviously tourist traps than the shops, and you can find plenty of places brimming with character and imagination. Many are tucked away down the lanes and closes of the Old Town, or have set up shop in unusual and interesting buildings. In summer, this is the busiest part of Edinburgh, so it's advisable to book a table for an evening meal at all of the restaurants listed below (the cafés and bistros are better bets for a walk-up, though they can still be busy).

BISTROS, CAFÉS AND DINERS

Café Hub
Map 3, C8. The Hub, Lawnmarket ☎ 0131/473 2067. Tues–Sat 9.30am–10pm, Sun & Mon 9.30am–6pm. Inexpensive. Colourful, well-run café-bistro in the Edinburgh Festival centre, with light modern meals such as mussel and saffron risotto or salmon, pak choi and Asian noodles served right through the day and evening. Teas, coffees, snacks and drinks are also available, there are sofas to sink into and original art on the walls, and the large terrace is usefully central on sunny days.

Elephant House
Map 3, E4. 21 George IV Bridge. Daily 8am–11pm. Inexpensive. Popular café near the Museum of Scotland which gets most things right, from its large selection of coffees

and teas to filling sandwiches, light meals such as home-made quiches or pasta bakes and big cakes. The cavernous back room is a great spot for reading newspapers or ear-wigging on philosophical discussions.

Khushi's Lothian Restaurant
Map 3, H4. 16 Drummond St. Mon–Sat noon–3pm, 5–9pm. Inexpensive.

One of the first Indian places to open in the capital, *Khushi's* is still essentially a basic cafeteria with melamine tables, long benches and few frills, but it's a characterful and friendly place. Reliable, cheap and delicious, the Punjabi-style meat curries are laid out in large dishes for you to help yourself. Bring your own drink.

Lower Aisle
Map 3, E8. High Kirk of St Giles, High Street. Mon–Fri 8.30am–4.30pm, Sun 9am–2pm. Inexpensive.

Popular with bewigged advocates from the High Court,

this café in the crypt, with its wooden tables and tiny stained glass windows, serves straightforward, good-value light lunches: soups, baked potatoes and a dish of the day – kedgeree or casseroles are common. Also does excellent home-baked cakes, scones and treats.

Mamma's American Pizza Company
Map 3, C4. 30 Grassmarket ☎ 0131/225 6464. Sun–Thurs noon–midnight, Fri & Sat noon–1am. Inexpensive–moderate.

The best pizzas in this part of town, *Mamma's* is disarmingly friendly and genuine – always buzzing with groups of students, tourists and families, but rarely loud or chaotic. Pizzas arrive onto a raised platter in the middle of your table – ideal for sharing – and come with an exhausting range of toppings from the sublime (smoked salmon) to the ridiculous (haggis). The house wine is reasonably priced and there are outside tables in the summer.

Ortegas

Map 3, G9. 38 St Mary's St
☎0131/557 5754.
Tues–Sat 5.30–10pm.
Moderate.

Pleasantly designed and friendly new bistro; although the name sounds Spanish, the food isn't easily pigeonholed, with some refreshingly original dishes such as venison stroganoff and avocado Thai green curry, while wild food such as dandelion leaves or hedgerow berries make unexpected appearances. Worth booking ahead.

Plaisir du Chocolat

Map 3, H8. 251–253
Canongate ☎0131/556 9524.
Mon–Wed & Sun 10am–6pm,
Thurs–Sun 10am–10pm.
Moderate–expensive.

Unexpectedly classy Parisian tearoom serving delicious, if expensive, lunches including filled brioches, omelettes and platters of Bayonne ham and salami. Equally appealing are the luxurious patisserie treats, an array of gourmet teas and properly made hot chocolate (though no coffee). Dinner menus depend on the chef's

shopping, but scallops in squid ink or fresh fish soup are the kind of thing he likes to cook.

Le Sept

Map 3, E8. 7 Old Fishmarket
Close ☎0131/225 5428.
Mon–Thurs noon–2pm &
6–10.30pm, Fri & Sat
noon–11pm, Sun noon–10pm.
Moderate.

Long-established French brasserie tucked down a cobbled close off the Royal Mile, with a pleasant bar alongside the plant-filled terrace and a cosy dining area in the arched cellars. Specializes in crepes, served both as main courses or dessert. Also on the menu are substantial mains of duck or game, as well as fresh fish such as sea bass or cod in simple French-style butter or white sauces.

Two Thin Laddies

Map 3, C4. 6 Grassmarket.
Daily: April–Oct 8am–7pm,
Nov–March 8am–4.30pm.

An antidote to chain coffee shops and plastic sandwich bars, this tiny Old Town café thrives on an irreverent attitude and a tasty range of sandwiches, snacks and daily specials such as roast pepper tortillas, locally made pork pies and home-baked muffins.

RESTAURANTS

Bann UK

Map 3, F8. 5 Hunter Square
℡0131/226 1112.
Mon–Sun 11am–11pm.
Moderate.
Thoroughly modern vegetarian restaurant, with interesting, non-conventional dishes, stylish design and a very contemporary feel. Sidesteps the boring veggie cliches with well-conceived and artfully presented dishes such as vegetable gateau with dauphinoise potato or woodland mushroom crepes. An all-day breakfast (till 5pm) includes vegetarian haggis and leek sausages.

Black Bo's

Map 3, G9. 57 Blackfriars St
℡0131/557 6136.

Sun–Thurs 6–10.30pm, Fri & Sat noon–2pm & 6–10.30pm. Moderate.
Inventive and friendly non-meat diner which, despite its earthy atmosphere (creaky wooden chairs and lots of candles at night) has plenty of intriguing and tasty dishes, such as pears grilled with blue cheese or smoked tofu and nori roulade.

Creelers

Map 3, F8. 3 Hunter Square
℡0131/220 4447.
Mon–Sat noon–9pm. Moderate.
The only specialist seafood place in the Old Town, with fresh produce brought in from a sister restaurant/fish shop on Arran. Best choices are its home-smoked fish (trout, salmon or herring), a great chowder and unfussed-over shellfish and fish dishes. A popular spot, but you can wait at the bar for tables to become available.

The Grain Store

Map 3, D3. 30 Victoria St
℡0131/225 7635.
Mon–Thurs noon–2pm &

6–10pm, Fri–Sun noon–3pm & 6–11pm. Expensive.

Often missed by passers-by, this unpretentious restaurant on eclectic Victoria Street is a relaxing haven above the tourist bustle of the Old Town, and serves fairly uncomplicated but good-quality modern Scottish food such as saddle of venison with shallots, and rosemary or pigeon with ginger, soy and sherry. Reasonable lunchtime and set-price options.

Igg's

Map 3, G8. 15 Jeffrey St ℡ 0131/557 8184. Mon–Sat noon–2.30pm & 6–10.30pm. Expensive.

The city's smartest Spanish restaurant, though in fact it's a bit of a hybrid, offering tapas snacks and Mediterranean dishes, such as aubergine and chick pea tagine, alongside locally influenced dishes such as duck with juniper berry jus. Exudes class with white linen, neat table settings and an impressive wine list, but not too intimidating.

Nicolson's

Map 3, H5. 6a Nicolson St ℡ 0131/557 4567. Mon–Sat noon–3pm & 5pm–late. Moderate.

Smartish Art Deco restaurant serving tasty if slightly over-ambitious modern Scottish food, such as mussels in coconut milk or duck in cep jus. *Nicolson's* is most famous these days as the site of the former tearoom where local author J.K. Rowling penned the first *Harry Potter* book between cappuccinos.

Suruchi

Map 3, H5. 14a Nicolson St ℡ 0131/556 6583. Closed Sun lunch. Moderate.

Refreshingly original curry house, in a plain upstairs room opposite the Festival Theatre, which serves genuine South Indian dishes – the menu is written in bizarre but entertaining broad Scots ("We bring ye the brawest Indian food"). Look out for cross-cultural specials such as tandoori trout or "Nirvana" – chicken with lemongrass, mustard seeds, curry leaves and creamy coconut.

The Tower

Map 3, E5. Museum of Scotland, Chambers Street ☎ 0131/225 3003.

Daily noon–11pm. Expensive.

Unique setting on Level 5 of the new Museum of Scotland; at night, you're escorted along the empty corridors to the classy restaurant, where spectacular views to the floodlit Castle are revealed. The excellent modern Scottish food does its best to match the setting, with top-quality steaks, oysters, scallops and venison, and one or two clever twists such as curried mussel broth or liquorice ice-cream.

Viva Mexico

Map 3, F2. 10 Anchor Close, off Cockburn Street ☎ 0131/226 5145.

Mon–Sat noon–2.30pm, 6.30–10.30pm, Sun 6.30–10.30pm. Moderate.

Long one of Edinburgh's best Mexican restaurants, with friendly, easygoing atmosphere that fortunately doesn't lay on the droopy moustache thing too thick. Serves up the staples such as fajitas and tortillas, though if you're after something more adventurous there's *mancha manteles*, a hearty chicken, pork and fruit stew. They can mix a mean margarita, too.

The Witchery by the Castle

Map 3, C8. 352 Castlehill, Royal Mile ☎ 0131/225 5613.

Daily noon–4pm & 5.30–11.30pm. Expensive.

A restaurant that only Edinburgh could create: all Gothic panelling, low ceilings, tapestries and heavy stonework, and only a broomstick-hop from the Castle. The superb fish and game dishes, including a spellbinding venison in chocolate sauce, are pricey, but you can steal a sense of it all with a pre- or post-theatre set menu (£10).

NEW TOWN AND WEST END

For eating places, as well as clubs and bars, the **New Town** and **West End** represent the most happening part of Edinburgh. Many nationwide chains have restaurants on George Street, and it's worth exploring some of the side streets and back lanes to find more authentic, homegrown places. Recently, Thistle Street Lane has established itself as a place to check out for its collection of bistros and restaurants – we've picked out the best below.

BISTROS, CAFÉS AND DINERS

Café Marlayne
Map 4, F5. 76 Thistle St
ⓣ 0131/226 2230.
Tues–Sat noon–2pm & 6–10pm. Moderate.
A very local feel to this intimate city-centre French bistro, where a short, daily changing menu concentrates on classic French farmhouse cooking such as snails in garlic butter, as well as plenty of hearty game and beef dishes.

Caffe DOC
Map 4, F5. 49a Thistle St
ⓣ 0131/220 6846.
Tues–Sat 10.30am–3pm & 7–10pm. Moderate–expensive.

Chic modern Italian dining space with a genuine dedication to good food, as evidenced by dishes such as *tagliata con la rucola* (Aberdeen Angus grilled on a bed of rocket and potatoes), but even the coffees and panini served at the sleek streetfront counter are an advert for Italian style and taste.

La Cuisine d'Odile
Map 2, G4. 13 Randolph Crescent, West End
ⓣ 0131/225 5685.
Tues–Sat noon–2pm. Closed for month of July. Inexpensive.
This plain little bistro in a West End basement under the French Institute is a tribute to simple but genuine French home cooking. Expect

savoury tarts and quiches, game casseroles, pan-fried pheasant or rabbit, and leave room for a helping of "choc Odile", as much a part of many locals' lunchtime as the One O'clock Gun. A real treat to discover, but you'll need to book.

Glass and Thompson
Map 4, G3. 2 Dundas St.
Mon–Sat 8.30am–5.30pm, Sun 11am–4.30pm. Inexpensive.
An unusually airy deli with huge bowls of olives and an extensive cheese counter; scattered tables and chairs mean you can linger over a made-to-order sandwich, or an irresistible cake and coffee.

Hadrian's
Map 4, L6. 2 North Bridge
⊤ 0131/557 5000.
Mon–Sat 7–10.30am, noon–2.30pm & 6.30–10.30pm, Sun 7.30–11am, 12.30–2pm & 6.30–10.30pm. Moderate.
Although it's strictly part of the upmarket *Balmoral Hotel*, this brasserie isn't too over-priced, and the elegance of the design and atmosphere, along with good quality modern British cooking, make it worth seeking out. Serves grand (though expensive) breakfasts.

Henderson's Salad Table
Map 4, G4. 94 Hanover St.
Mon–Sat 8am–10.30pm. Inexpensive/moderate.
Much-loved Edinburgh institution, with a self-service basement restaurant offering freshly prepared hot dishes such as vegetarian lasagne or sweet potato and cauliflower korma, plus a great choice of salads, soups, sweets and cheeses. The slightly anti-quated cafeteria feel can put people off, but the food is rarely short of outstanding, and there's live jazz every evening. Next door, *Henderson's Bistro* (⊤ 0131/225 2605; Sun, Tue & Wed noon–6pm, Thurs–Sat noon–10.30pm) offers similar, moderately priced food in a more formal setting, but has never been as popular.

L'Alba d'Oro
Map 2, H4. 5 Henderson Row, Canonmills.

Daily noon–midnight.
Inexpensive.

Italian voices fill the air in this classic takeaway, with fish and chips served on one side and pizzas, filled Italian rolls and ready-made pasta dishes on the other.

No. 28

Map 4, B7. 28 Charlotte Square ⓣ 0131/243 9339.
Mon–Sat 10am–5.30pm, Sun noon–5pm. Inexpensive–moderate.

Refined and very pleasant café within the Georgian National Trust for Scotland headquarters, serving classy light lunches featuring smoked salmon or locally made pâté. Tea and scones, or even porridge (served with double cream) are also on offer. By evening the two main rooms become *No. 27* (Tues–Sat 6–9.30pm), for evening dining featuring hearty Scottish numbers involving venison, pheasant or haddock.

Starbucks Coffee

Map 4, D8. Waterstone's, 128

Princes St.
Mon–Sat 7.30am–8pm, Sun 9.30am–6pm. Inexpensive.

One chain coffee shop worth mentioning, surrounded by books and with fantastic views across Princes Street Gardens to the Castle.

Niji

Map 4, G4. 25a Thistle St ⓣ 0131/220 5254.
Tues–Sat noon–2.30pm & 6–9pm. Inexpensive–moderate.

Tiny budget noodle bar offering filling meals from around £5. Engaging owner Katsuo Honjigawa will guide you through the more interesting dishes, including sushi and bento boxes.

RESTAURANTS

- - - - - - - - - - - - - - - - - - - -

Café Royal Oyster Bar

Map 4, K5. 17a West Register St ⓣ 0131/556 4124.
Daily noon–2pm & 7–10pm. Very expensive.

An Edinburgh classic, with its splendidly ornate Victorian interior (featured in *Chariots of Fire*), stained-

NEW TOWN AND WEST END

glass windows, marble floor and Doulton tiling. Classic seafood dishes, including freshly caught oysters, are served in a civilized, chatty atmosphere.

Café St Honoré
Map 4, F5. 34 Thistle St Lane ⓣ 0131/226 2211.
Mon–Fri noon–2.15pm & 5–10pm, Sat noon–2.15pm & 6–10pm. Expensive.
A classy little piece of Paris tucked away in a New Town back lane, this long-established brasserie with its black-and-white checked floor, old mirrors and wood panelling is full of atmosphere. On offer is fairly traditional French fare, with warm seafood salads, rump of lamb, pink Barbary duck, and calves' liver in red wine, but top quality. Cheaper *Après Cinq* menu operates between 5 and 7pm Mon–Fri.

Duck's at Le Marché Noir
Map 2, H4. 2–4 Eyre Place, Canonmills ⓣ 0131/558 1608.
Mon–Fri noon–2.30pm &

6–10.30pm, Sat 6–10.30pm, Sun 6–9.30pm. Expensive.
An upmarket Scottish/French restaurant with an endearingly unconventional attitude, with smartly dressed waiters, cartoons on the walls and ceramic ducks parked on the white linen tablecloths. Serves up high-quality dishes such as pork fillet with chilli and coriander mousse, or Thai seafood chowder. A great place too for discerning wine lovers.

Fishers in the City
Map 4, F5. 58 Thistle Lane ⓣ 0131/225 5109.
Daily noon–10.30pm. Expensive.
New Town incarnation of Leith's best-loved seafood bistro. This one has a sleek modern interior, great service and some stunning seafood – for a light meal try the superb fishcakes or chowder; going up a notch you can get Scottish langoustine, oysters on crushed ice, plates of grilled prawns and simply prepared line-caught fresh fish.

Howies at Waterloo
Map 2, I4. 29 Waterloo Place
☎ 0131/556 5766.
Mon–Sat 10am–2.30pm &
6–10.30pm, Sun noon–4pm &
5.30–10.30pm. Moderate.
Flagship restaurant of the
small local *Howies* chain, with
a contemporary dining area
in an old Georgian building
on the fringe of Calton Hill.
Howies specialize in comforting, reliably well-priced
modern Scottish food – the
likes of chicken supreme
stuffed with haggis with a
whisky and green peppercorn
sauce – which feels just a wee
bit special but finds favour
across the generations. Look
out for bargain house wine
and tasty desserts.

Kweilin
Map 4, F2. 19–21 Dundas St
☎ 0131/557 1875.
Tues–Thurs noon–11pm, Fri &
Sat noon–midnight, Sun
4–11pm. Moderate.
One of the most reliable
Chinese restaurants in town,
serving Cantonese and
Szechuan dishes in a traditional but bright dining room

just far enough away from the
city-centre hubbub. Though
slightly more expensive than
other Chinese places nearby,
the quality of the cooking is
high, and you can try things
like stewed duck feet.

Loon Fung
Map 2, H3. 2 Warriston Place,
Canonmills ☎ 0131/556 1781.
Mon–Fri noon–midnight, Sat
2pm–1am, Sun 2pm–midnight.
Moderate.
Near the eastern entrance to
the Botanic Garden, this has
been something of a trailblazer
for Cantonese cuisine in
Scotland, serving up memorably tasty dishes such as crispy
monkfish in honey sauce and
baked crab in ginger sauce.
Booking advised.

Mussel Inn
Map 4, F6. 61–65 Rose St
☎ 0131/225 5979.
Mon–Sat noon–10pm, Sun
1.30–10pm. Moderate.
After feasting on a kilo of
mussels and a basket of chips
for under £10, you'll realise
why there's a demand to get
in here. The fact that the

NEW TOWN AND WEST END

owners are west-coast shell-fish farmers ensures that the time from sea to stomach is minimal. Bright, relaxed and buzzy.

Oloroso

Map 4, D6. 33 Castle St ☏ 0131/226 7614.

Daily noon–10pm. Expensive.

An ambitious but much admired new restaurant featuring a stunning rooftop dining space floating over George Street, with plate glass walls and wide balconies, as well as stylish modern interiors. The food is by award winning Glaswegian chef Tony Singh, and shows no respect for categorization: Scottish lamb with a coriander pesto, chocolate samosas or a hearty dish of osso bucco. Lighter plates at the bar are particularly good value, and the wine is superb.

Songkran

Map 2, G5. 24a Stafford St, West End ☏ 0131/225 7889.

Mon–Sat noon–2.30pm &

5.30–11pm, Sun 5.30–11pm. Moderate.

A simple basement restaurant with authentic decor and great Thai food, including "banquet" options which give you the chance to try various dishes. Some bold, impressive cooking going on here – try the prawn tempura in a Thai beer batter served with sweet chilli sauce, or the extraordinary sounding (and tasting) *Pla Lard Prig*, a crispy deep fried whole trout topped with red curry paste and coconut milk.

Stac Polly

Map 4, I2. 29–33 Dublin St ☏ 0131/556 2231.

Mon–Fri noon–1.45pm & 6–10pm. Expensive.

Teetering on the edge of overbearing Scottishness, this atmospheric cellar with stone walls and clever lighting just avoids the kitsch. The hearty menu of game, fish and meat dishes is sparked into life by the long-term signature starter of haggis in filo pastry with a plum sauce.

BROUGHTON AND LEITH WALK

Occupying the eastern edge of the New Town, the area around **Broughton Street** is young, trendy and less upmarket than the very centre of the city. The city's gay community is an obvious influence here, and you'll find a strong Italian presence, including outstanding deli *Valvona and Crolla*. The restaurants at the top of **Leith Walk** may not be the most sophisticated in town, but many keep late hours, making this one of the livelier corners of town into the wee small hours, particularly on a Friday and Saturday night.

BISTROS, CAFÉS AND DINERS

Café Mediterraneo
Map 4, L1. 73 Broughton St
☎ 0131/557 6900.
April–Oct Mon–Sat 8am–10pm, Sun 9.30am–10pm; Nov–March Mon–Thurs 8am–6pm, Fri & Sat 8am–10pm, Sun 9.30–4.30pm. Moderate.
A great little Italian with a deli counter and a small dining space serving antipasto and a limited range of larger hot dishes such as seared tuna or warm salads in unpretentious style. Not a red-checked table cloth to be seen.

Lost Sock Diner
Map 2, H4. 11 East London St, Broughton ☎ 0131/557 6097.
Mon 9am–4pm, Tues–Fri 9am–10pm, Sat 10am–10pm, Sun 11am–5pm. Inexpensive.
While your dirty clothes take a spin in the adjacent laundrette, you can fill up on burgers, wraps and specials (mussels in white wine, or chicken skewers in a yoghurt and coriander marinade) chalked up on the blackboard, all at surprising low prices. Try the parsnip chips.

Valvona and Crolla
Map 2, I4. 19 Elm Row, Leith Walk ☎ 0131/556 6066.

Mon–Wed & Sat 8.30am–6pm, Thurs & Fri 8.30am–7pm. The best advert for this café at the back of Scotland's greatest Italian deli is the walk through the shop – which has food stacked from floor to ceiling, with display cabinets full of sublime olives, meats and cheeses. The café serves authentic and delicious breakfasts, lunches and snacks – the antipasto platters offer a taste of the deli counters while the gourmet pizzas are fresh from the V&C bakery.

RESTAURANTS

Marrakech
Map 2, H4. 30 London St, Broughton ⓣ 0131/556 4444. Mon–Sat 6–10pm. Moderate. Scotland's only Moroccan restaurant and very reasonably priced, dishing up superb, authentic couscous and tajines, plus a range of soups, fresh bread and pastries. Unlicensed, but you can take your own bottle and there's no corkage charge.

Modern India
Map 2, I4. 20 Union Place ⓣ 0131/556 4547. Mon–Thurs 11am–2pm & 5pm–midnight, Fri & Sat 5pm–1am, Sun 4pm–midnight. Moderate. Edinburgh's best example of the contemporary curry house, with bright modern decor and a menu daring to stray from the conventional, with things like Punjabi-style monkfish and chicken tikka salsa. A little bit of Bollywood right across from the Playhouse theatre.

The Tapas Tree
Map 4, L2. 1 Forth St, Broughton ⓣ 0131/556 7118. Daily 11am–11pm. Moderate. Authentic, lively and extremely friendly tapas bar, featuring Spanish guitar music on Wednesday evenings and flamenco on Thursday evenings, and kept fuelled by jugs of sangria and margarita.

STOCKBRIDGE AND AROUND

The New Town's northern fringe, **Stockbridge** is the home for many of the city's young professionals, who support a reliable if generally unadventurous clutch of restaurants, particularly along St Stephen Street. For many folk the area's most appealing aspect is that everything seems to operate at a much less frenetic pace than in the heart of the New Town.

BISTROS, CAFÉS AND DINERS.

Bell's Diner
Map 4, B1. 7 St Stephen St, Stockbridge ☎ 0131/225 8116.
Mon–Fri & Sun 6–10.30pm, Sat noon–10.30pm. Moderate.
This unpretentious little diner is a longstanding Stockbridge favourite, with none of the garishness which often comes with burger joints. Good, inexpensive burgers (including nut burgers for vegetarians), plus a wide choice of steaks with different sauces. If that doesn't fill you up, the pancakes and ice-cream surely will. Booking recommended.

The Gallery Café
Map 2, F5. Scottish National Gallery of Modern Art, Belford Road, Dean Village ☎ 0131/332 8600.
Mon–Sat 10am–4.30pm, Sun noon–4.30pm. Inexpensive.
Far more than a standard refreshment stop for gallery visitors, the cultured setting and strong menu of fresh soups, savoury tarts and casseroles attracts reassuring numbers of locals. As well as lunches you can stop for coffee and home-baked cakes, and there's some pleasant outdoor seating.

Terrace Café
Map 2, G3. Botanic Garden, Inverleith ☎ 0131/552 0616.
Daily 9.30am–6pm. Inexpensive.
Superior spot with outside tables offering stunning views

of the city skyline, but the food is not that exciting. The changing menu includes daily hot dishes such as pasta bakes or pies, as well as sandwiches and cakes.

RESTAURANTS

Blue Parrot Cantina

Map 4, C1. 49 St Stephen's St, Stockbridge ⓉⓇ 0131/225 2941. Mon–Thurs 5–11pm, Fri & Sat noon–11pm, Sun 5–10.30pm. Moderate.

Cosy Stockbridge basement restaurant, with a small, frequently changing menu

which deviates from the Mexican clichés with steaks in a spicy garlic sauce or *Pescado Baja* – haddock baked in a lime and coriander sauce.

Pizza Express

Map 4, A1. 1 Deanhaugh St, Stockbridge ⓉⓇ 0131/332 7229. Daily 11.30am–midnight. Inexpensive–moderate.

This member of the chain with the winning formula for smart interiors and decent pizza boasts a terrific location, in a clocktower building overlooking the Water of Leith.

LOTHIAN ROAD AND TOLLCROSS

Immediately to the west of the Castle and the Old Town, this is Edinburgh's theatre district, featuring sophisticated, lively places to eat and drink, and good-value pre- and post-theatre deals. **Lothian Road** is another of the city's popular late-night haunts, with a number of restaurants open past midnight, while **Tollcross**, a bit closer to the student areas of the Southside, is an up-and-coming area with a growing number of smart cafés and fresh new restaurants.

LOTHIAN ROAD AND TOLLCROSS

BISTROS, CAFÉS AND DINERS

----

blue

Map 2, G5. 10 Cambridge St
ⓣ 0131/221 1222.
Mon–Sat noon–3pm & 6–11pm.
Closed Sun. Moderate.
Longstanding café-bistro in
the same building as the
avant-garde Traverse Theatre.
Super-stylish minimalist
decor, and tasty modern dishes for under £10 per main
course – the likes of mussel
and prawn *laksa* noodles or
rabbit with leek and chorizo
risotto; posh bangers and
mash is a longstanding
favourite.

Ndebele

Map 2, G5. 57 Home St.
Daily 10am–10pm. Inexpensive.
Colourful African café offering sandwiches made with
home-baked bread and lots
of alternative fillings such as
pickled fish and baba
ganoush, along with imaginative salads and biltong for
homesick South Africans.
Each evening there are two
hot mains, from Durban
curries to Kenyan bean
stews.

RESTAURANTS

The Atrium

Map 2, G5. 10 Cambridge St
ⓣ 0131/228 8882.
Mon–Fri noon–2pm & 6–10pm,
Sat 6–10pm. Very expensive.
Resilient in its ranking
among the most impressive
restaurants in the city.
Quirky, arty design with
railway-sleeper tables, and
innovative nouvelle cuisine
with dishes such loin, cutlet
and navarin of lamb with
winter vegetables or ragout
of pigeon with mushroom
and foie gras sauce focusing
on high-quality Scottish produce. A special sommelier's
menu offers a set meal with a
different glass of wine for
each course.

Jasmine

Map 2, G5. 32 Grindlay St
ⓣ 0131/229 5757.
Mon–Fri noon–2pm &
5–11.30pm, Fri 5pm–midnight,

LOTHIAN ROAD AND TOLLCROSS

Sat 2pm–midnight, Sun 2–11pm. Moderate.

Modern looking, good-value Cantonese restaurant, with a strong line in fresh fish dishes such as crispy monkfish in a honey sauce and a clean-tasting shark-fin soup. Across the street from the Lyceum and the Usher Hall.

Lazio's

Map 2, G5. 95 Lothian Rd
ⓣ 0131/229 7788.

Mon–Thurs 5pm–1.30am, Fri–Sat noon–3am. Moderate.

Pick of the family-run trattorias on this block, handy for a late-night meal after a show in the nearby theatre district. What it lacks in sophistication it makes up for with slick service, reliable pastas and pizzas and great Italian ice-cream.

Marque Central

Map 2, G5. 30b Grindlay St
ⓣ 0131/229 9859.

Mon–Thurs noon–2.30pm & 5.45–10pm, Fri & Sat noon–2.30pm & 5.45–11pm. Moderate–expensive.

Sister restaurant to the original Southside venture, *Marque*

Central has proved a hit in the theatreland patch with its great value pre- and post-theatre deals. A place for imaginative modern Scottish food – the daily changing menu has treats such as baked salmon with aioli crumble or black pudding with parma ham galette.

Point Hotel

Map 2, H5. 34 Bread St
ⓣ 0131/221 5555.

Mon–Thurs noon–2pm & 6–10pm, Fri noon–2pm & 6–11pm, Sat 6–11pm. Moderate.

The in-house restaurant of Edinburgh's most stylish designer hotel. Oozing class with bold contemporary decor, white linen tablecloths and smartly dressed waiters, in addition to well-presented food based on fresh local fish and meat. One of the best-value deals in town: a three-course set menu is just £14.90.

The Rogue Restaurant

Map 2, G5. Scottish Widows Building, 69 Morrison St
ⓣ 0131/228 2700.

Mon–Sat noon–2pm & 6–10pm,

Sun 11am–3pm. Moderate.
A typically unconventional venture by Edinburgh's most adventurous restaurateur, David Ramsden. Inexpensive toasted panini is on the menu alongside sweetmeats or sumptuous lobster dishes, in a large avant-garde dining area with white linen and smooth service.

Shamiana
Map 2, G5. 14 Brougham Place,

Tollcross ☎ 0131/228 2265.
Mon–Sat 6–10pm, Sun 6–9pm. Moderate.
Long-established, first-class North Indian and Kashmiri restaurant located midway between the King's and Lyceum theatres. One of the more expensive places in this category, and an oddly stark interior, but well worth it for some assured cooking, often featuring milder spices and aromatic herbs.

SOUTHSIDE

As the student quarter of the city, the **Southside** boasts plenty of good-value places to eat, particularly among the vegetarian and Indian restaurants. However, it's also worth looking out for the ambitious, attractive modern-Scottish restaurants staked out here on the fringe of the more expensive city-centre area.

BISTROS, CAFÉS AND DINERS

The Apartment
Map 2, G6. 7–13 Barclay Place, Bruntsfield ☎ 0131/228 6456.
Mon–Fri 5.45–11pm, Sat & Sun

noon–3pm & 5.45–11pm. Moderate.
Hugely popular, highly fashionable modern diner, with IKEA furniture, sisal flooring and abstract modern art on the walls. Their "Chunky, Healthy Lines" menu features chargrilled kebabs of meat,

SOUTHSIDE

217

fish or vegetables, all served with pitta bread filled with apple and beetroot coleslaw. Otherwise there are lively salads, more substantial fish or steak dishes, and wonderfully gooey profiteroles.

Buffalo Grill

Map 2, I5. 14 Chapel St, Newington ☎ 0131/667 7427. Mon–Fri noon–2pm & 6–10.15pm, Sat 6–10.15pm, Sun 5–10pm. Moderate. Popular local steakhouse serving (they claim) "BSE – the best steaks in Edinburgh". It's indeed hard to look past the juicy steaks and filling burgers, though you can also get a salad of peeled prawns with lemon and lime mayonnaise, grilled chicken and veggie burgers named "Andybub" after the former employee who invented them.

Favorit

Map 2, G6. 30–32 Leven St, Bruntsfield. Daily 8.30am–3am. Inexpensive. Thoroughly modern café-diner dishing up coffees, fruit shakes, cakes and big sand-wiches, as well as alcohol, right through to the wee small hours, making it a hit with the post-club crowd.

Kaffe Politik

Map 2, H6. 146–148 Marchmont Rd, Marchmont. Daily 10am–10pm. Inexpensive. Café culture hits the student fiefdom of deepest Marchmont in a relaxed and stylish venue serving coffees and substantial snacks like pesto pasta and chicken Caesar salad. Weekend brunches offer porridge and cultured fry-ups.

Susie's Diner

Map 2, I5. 51 West Nicolson St, Newington ☎ 0131/667 8729. Mon–Sat 9am–9pm. Inexpensive. Popular café serving inventive soups, savouries and puddings, as well as a range of vegan food, to crowds of students. Head up to the counter and select from various large trays of sweet-and-sour tofu and vegetables or roti masala, with lots of different salad combos on the side.

SOUTHSIDE

RESTAURANTS

- - - - - - - - - - - - - - - - - - - -

Ann Purna

Map 2, I5. 45 St Patrick Square, Newington ☎ 0131/662 1807.
Mon–Fri noon–2pm & 5.30–11pm, Sat & Sun 5.30–11pm. Moderate.
A recent redesign has left this much-admired restaurant with a modern but slightly stark feel. Still, it's excellent value for authentic Gujarati and southern Indian cuisine (mainly vegetarian) – try the three-course set lunch for £4.95, or look to the house specials such as *Mili-juli-sabzi*, with aubergine, bhindi potato, peas and mushrooms.

Kalpna

Map 2, I5. 2 St Patrick Square, Newington ☎ 0131/667 9890.
Mon–Fri noon–2pm & 5.30–11pm, Sat 5.30pm–11pm. Moderate.
Outstanding vegetarian restaurant specializing in Gujarati dishes. In addition to the main menu there are four set meals, including a vegan option,
which are a great way to taste the range of the kitchen's output, with countless imaginative tricks using ingredients such as pistachios, home-made cheeses and coconut chutney.

King's Balti

Map 2, I5. 79 Buccleuch St, Newington ☎ 0131/662 9212.
Mon–Thurs noon–2pm & 5pm–midnight, Fri & Sat noon–midnight. Moderate.
Edinburgh's best balti establishment, *King's* is very popular with students and features an evening two-person banquet for £25.95, or you can try the *Sabzi Parsi* wedding dishes of chicken in a sweet and sour sauce with ginger, daal and lemon. You can bring your own alcohol, but 50p corkage per person is charged.

The Marque

Map 2, I6. 19–21 Causewayside, Newington ☎ 0131/466 6660.
Tues–Fri 11.45am–2pm & 5.45–10pm, Sat & Sun 12.30–2pm & 5.45–10.30pm. Moderate–expensive.

One of Edinburgh's best exponents of classy-but-casual dining: you're often given a tiny cup of frothy tomato cappuccino as a complimentary appetizer for the modern Scottish recipes, such as duck spring-rolls with wild mushrooms, or grilled turbot in a smoked haddock broth. If you're dining early or late they offer some top value pre- and post-theatre deals.

Phenecia
Map 2, I5. 55–57 West Nicolson St, Newington ☏ 0131/662 4493.
Mon–Sat noon–2pm & 6–11pm.
Moderate.
Basic, easygoing joint beside the main University campus, serving mostly Tunisian food, such as sweet tagine or couscous royale, but drawing on a variety of Mediterranean cuisines including Spanish and French; the three-course lunch for under £5 is very good value.

Sweet Melinda's
Map 2, H6. 11 Roseneath St, Marchmont ☏ 0131/229 7953.
Mon 7–10pm, Tues–Sat noon–2pm & 7–10pm.
Moderate.
Smart and confident seafood restaurant with a friendly neighbourhood feel, set in a single timber-panelled room. Dishes such as cod fillet with chorizo or canellini beans and tarragon are served with perfectly cooked vegetables, and desserts including lemon tart and cheese platters are equally assured.

LEITH AND AROUND

The area around the cobbled Shore of **Leith** (along the edge of the Water of Leith just as it reaches the sea) is the best known dining location in Edinburgh, and lives up to its billing with a string of good-quality, laid-back seafood bistros. It's worth coming down here at least once during your stay, especially on a summer evening when jazz drifts from some of the bars and seagulls swirl above.

LEITH AND AROUND

BISTROS, CAFÉS AND DINERS

- - - - - - - - - - - - - - - - - - - -

Daniel's
Map 6, G3. 88 Commercial St
Ⓣ0131/553 5933.
Daily 10am–10pm. Moderate.
Top-grade bistro in an attractive setting on the ground floor of a converted warehouse. Food is from the Alsace region of France; the *tarte flambée*, one of the specialist dishes, is a sort of pizza with a French name and German ingredients; it's perfect with a glass of beer and a bowl of rustic soup.

Ship on the Shore
Map 6, H3. 24–26 The Shore
Ⓣ0131/555 0409.
Daily noon–2.30pm &
6–9.30pm. Moderate.
The homeliest and least expensive of the waterfront brasseries, serving quality pub grub such as mussels or grilled salmon as well as more sophisticated combinations like sea bream with mango salsa. A handful of

meat dishes too, and there's a changing range of cask ales.

Skippers Bistro
Map 6, G3. 1a Dock Place
Ⓣ0131/554 1018.
Mon–Sat 12.30–2pm & 7–10pm,
Sun 12.30–2.30pm. Expensive.
More relaxed than it looks from the outside, with a vaguely nautical atmosphere and a superb fish-oriented menu that changes according to what's fresh – John Dory, turbot and lemon sole feature regularly. Worth booking ahead.

Waterfront Wine Bar
Map 6, G3. 1c Dock Place
Ⓣ0131/554 7427.
Daily noon–2.30pm &
6–9.30pm. Moderate.
Housed in a cute little red-brick cottage once used as ferry offices, you can eat in the wonderfully characterful wine bar (smoking) or non-smoking conservatory attached. Fish dishes such as devilled whitebait or halibut in basil butter dominate.

LEITH AND AROUND

RESTAURANTS

Britannia Spice
Map 6, F3. 150 Commercial St
℡0131/555 2255.
Daily noon–2.15pm &
5–11.45pm. Moderate.
The decor's nautical, the food
is prepared by specialist chefs
from the subcontinent and
the awards for this relatively
new but ambitious Indian
restaurant have been piling
up. The menu is huge and a
little bewildering – ranging
across Thai, Indian, Sri
Lankan and Nepalese dishes –
and for the most part reliable,
with filling and unusual dishes such as line-caught fish
marinated in Bangladeshi
spices or roast aubergine
masala.

Joanna's Cuisine
Map 2, J3. 42 Dalmeny St
℡0131/554 5833.
Mon, Wed & Sun 5–10.30pm,
Thurs–Sat 5–11.30pm.
Moderate.
Homely little Chinese place
on a side street leading east
off the middle of Leith Walk.

The menu includes wonder-
ful Pekinese specialities,
notably delicious duck
cooked with orange and
almonds or pickled with ginger and pineapple. A good
place to try Chinese tea, with
various blends specially
imported by the owner.

Restaurant Martin Wishart
Map 6, H4. 52 The Shore
℡0131/553 3557.
Tues–Fri noon–2pm & 7–10pm,
Sat 7–10pm. Expensive.
Edinburgh's only Michelin
star-holder wows the
gourmets with French-influ-
enced Scottish food served
right by the Water of Leith.
The cooking is incredible –
oysters are served with
smoked salmon and muscadet
jelly while pork cheek and
grilled langoustines come
with spiced aromatics and
honey-roast vegetables – but
the ambience is rather stark.
Booking is essential.

The Shore
Map 6, H3. 3 The Shore
℡0131/553 5080.

Daily noon–2.30pm &
6.30–10pm. Moderate.
An attractive, stylish restaurant with huge mirrors, wood panelling and aproned waiters who serve up adventurous fish dishes (salmon in a lime mascarpone with toasted almonds, for example) and decent wines. Live jazz, folk and general hubbub floats through from the adjoining bar, where snacks are also available.

Tinelli
Map 2, J3. 139 Easter Rd
ⓣ 0131/652 1932.
Tues–Sat noon–2.30pm &
6.30–11pm. Moderate.
Longstanding, very popular restaurant in an unlikely part of town near the Hibs football ground, *Tinelli* is reputed to be Edinburgh's best traditional Italian. The speciality is in northern Italian food – try the spinach and pumpkin-stuffed pasta.

Umberto's
Map 6, F6. 2 Bonnington Road Lane, Bonnington ⓣ 0131/554 1314.
Mon–Sat noon–2.30pm &
5–10pm, Sun noon–6pm.
Moderate.
The best place in Edinburgh for anyone with children. Indoor and outdoor play areas, sympathetic staff and good, if predictable, Italian food.

LEITH AND AROUND

Drinking

Drinking is one of Edinburgh's great traditions. Many of the city's pubs, especially in the Old Town, are hundreds of years old, while others, particularly in the New Town, are unaltered Victorian or Edwardian period pieces that rank among Edinburgh's most outstanding examples of interior design. Sometimes known as howffs (an old Scots word meaning "haunt" or "resort"), these older-style hostelries, with their hard-drinking edge, represent the quintessential Edinburgh pub, though there are now just as many trendy modern bars as likely to major in alcopops as in ales. The standard licensing hours are 11am–11pm Monday to Saturday, and 12.30–11pm on Sundays, but many pubs have extended licensing hours and you won't struggle to find places which stay open till at least 1am, particularly on a Friday and Saturday night, and every night during the Festival.

Edinburgh has a long history of brewing beer, though only two principal **breweries** remain: the giant Scottish and Newcastle (who produce McEwan's and Younger's) and the small independent Caledonian Brewery, which uses old techniques and equipment to produce some of the best beers in Britain. Look out too for the excellent beers made in nearby East Lothian at the independent Belhaven Brewery. All these breweries have their own version of the distinctive Scottish ale known as "**heavy**" (see box below); you'll find it in all the city's pubs. English **bitter**, a sharper drink than heavy, is much less commonly found, and you'll have to go to a decent real-ale pub to find a good selection of these. In addition, all pubs sell **stout** (normally Guinness) and **lager**, both on tap and in bottles. A pint of any beer costs anything from £1.50 to £2.50, depending on the brew and the locale of the pub. The selection of **whisky** is better in some pubs than others, and though a "nip" (or measure) of malt whisky will normally cost more than a standard blend, many pubs offer lower-priced "malt of the month" specials.

EDINBURGH'S BEERS

Traditional Scottish beer is a thick, dark ale, known as heavy. Quite different in taste from English bitter, heavy is a more robust, sweeter brew with less of an edge, and is served at room temperature from a distinctive tall font, in pints or half-pints with a full head. Scottish beers are graded by the shilling: a system used since the 1870s to indicate the level of potency – the higher the shilling mark (/-), the stronger, or "heavier", the beer. Both 60/-, often described as a "pale ale", and skull-splitting 90/- are rarely seen nowadays; 70/- and 80/- are by far the most commonly found. The main brands to look out for are those of Edinburgh-based McEwans, Tennants and the small independents from the Edinburgh area, Caledonian and Belhaven.

Your best chance of uncovering these beers is to head for pubs promising real or cask-conditioned ales. These are often pointed out in the listings below, though for a more comprehensive rundown covering the whole of the UK, get hold of a copy of the widely available *Good Beer Guide* (£12.99), published annually by the Campaign for Real Ale (CAMRA; ⓦ www.camra.org.uk).

DRINKING

A large number of bars and pubs serve **food**, most commonly "pub grub" fare such as pies or deep-fried haddock with chips and peas, though occasionally you'll find places serving more modern alternatives such as filled panini, pasta and fresh salads. Bar food is normally well priced with mains for under £5, and is served at lunchtimes (noon–2pm) and early evenings (6–8pm), though occasionally through the afternoon as well.

Gay-oriented bars are listed on p.255.

WHERE TO DRINK

Once upon a time, Edinburgh's main drinking strip was the near-legendary **Rose Street**, a pedestrianized lane tucked between Princes and George streets in the New Town – the ultimate Edinburgh pub crawl was to take a drink in each of its dozen or so establishments. Things are a bit more sophisticated these days, with **George Street** itself taking a lead: various former financial institutions here have been converted into bars, with a predictable invasion of suits by day and style by night. On the outer fringes of the New Town, **Stockbridge** has a number of less intense, more homely drinking establishments, while the **Broughton** area is one of the city's liveliest, as well as being the established meeting point for the local gay community. While many of the **Royal Mile**'s pubs aren't ashamed to make the most of historical connections to draw in the tourists, you don't have to travel far to find some lively places, notably the student-filled pubs in and around the **Grassmarket**, with a further batch on the studenty **Southside**. **Leith** has a wide range of bars, from rough spit-and-sawdust places to polished pseudo-Victoriana, and we've also listed a number of characterful places further away from the centre.

DRINKING

PUB AND BREWERY TOURS

A fun way to explore Edinburgh's pubs is to take the **McEwan's 80/- Edinburgh Literary Pub Tour**, a pub crawl – with culture – around Old and New Town watering holes. Led by professional actors, the trip takes you to various historic pubs in the city, with stops along the way where the guides act out scenes from the lives of major figures of Scottish literature, including Burns, Scott and MacDiarmid, and recite lines from their work. The two-hour tour starts from the *Beehive Inn*, 18–20 Grassmarket (March–May & Oct Thurs–Sun 7.30pm; June & Sept daily 6pm & 8.30pm; July & Aug daily 2pm, 6pm & 8.30pm; Nov–Feb Fri 7.30pm; £7 – not including drinks). You can just turn up, or book ahead by phoning ☎0131/226 6665, or by calling in at the tourist office on Princes Street.

The Caledonian Brewery, Slateford Road (Map 2, F6; ☎0131/623 8066) runs one-hour tours at 11am, 12.30pm and 2.30pm (Mon–Fri; £5) which offer a fairly conventional trot through the brewing process, though the Victorian brewing apparatus and giant copper vats are well worth seeing. It's best to phone ahead before you visit.

THE ROYAL MILE AND AROUND

Bannermans

Map 3, G3. 212 Cowgate. Once the best pub in the street, but the loud late-night music blaring out of the speakers has become a bit intrusive. *Bannermans* is still atmospheric, however – a former vintner's cellar, it has a labyrinthine interior deep under the Old Town and good beer on tap. Open daily till 1am.

Black Bo's

Map 3, H3. 55 Blackfriars St. No music, and no decent ales, but a good example of how to stay trendy without going minimalist. Next to, but separate from, the vegetarian restaurant of the same name.

Bow Bar

Map 3, D4. 80 West Bow. Wonderful old wood-panelled bar that won an award as the best drinkers' pub in Britain a few years back. Choose from among nearly 150 whiskies or a changing selection of first-rate Scottish and English cask beers. Closed Sunday afternoons.

City Café

Map 3, G3. 19 Blair St. Longstanding but determinedly trendy bar on the street linking the Royal Mile to the clubbers' hub along the Cowgate. The blue-baize pool tables are always popular, and you can buy candies behind the American-style bar.

Doric Tavern

Map 3, F2. 15 Market St. This long-established upstairs wine bar (open daily till 1am)

is a favoured watering hole of journalists and artists. The downstairs *McGuffie's Tavern* is a traditional Edinburgh *howff*, while the brasserie beside the wine bar serves reliable good quality Scottish food.

EH1

Map 3, F8. 197 High St. Wrought iron and cool aqua colours dominate in this contemporary Royal Mile bar, popular with a pre-club set. Serves up reasonably imaginative food throughout the day, plus pitchers of vividly coloured cocktails. Open daily till 1am.

Greyfriars Bobby

Map 3, E5. 34 Candlemaker Row.
Slightly nondescript but long-established favourite with both students and tourists, serving standard pub grub at lunchtime and in the early evening. Named after the statue outside, though happily there's not too much sentimental memorabilia associated with the famously faithful "wee dug" (see p.71). Open daily till 1am.

Hebrides Bar
Map 3, F2. 17 Market St.
Home from home for
Edinburgh's Highland
community; there's a ceilidh
atmosphere with lots of jigs,
strathspeys and reels and lots
of whisky), but no tartan
kitsch.

Jolly Judge
Map 3, D8. 7a James Court.
Atmospheric, low-ceilinged
bar in a close just down from
the Castle. Cosy in winter
and pleasant outside in
summer, with a typical Old

Town courtyard surrounded
by tall tenement buildings.

Last Drop
Map 3, D4. 74–78
Grassmarket.
The "Drop" refers to the
Edinburgh gallows, which
were located in front of the
building, and whose former
presence is symbolized in
the red exterior paintwork.
Cheapish pub food, and, like
its competitors in the same
block, patronized mainly by
students. Open daily till
1am.

NEW TOWN

Abbotsford
Map 4, I5. 3 Rose St.
Large-scale pub whose
original Victorian decor,
complete with wood
panelling and island bar, is
among the finest in the city.
Good range of ales, including
a house ale brewed by
Broughton, and the upstairs
restaurant serves hearty
Scottish food.

Café Royal Circle Bar
Map 4, K5. 17 West Register
St.
As notable as the *Oyster Bar*
restaurant next door (see
p.207), the *Café Royal* is
worth a visit just for its
Victorian decor, notably the
huge elliptical "island"
counter and the tiled portraits
of renowned inventors. Thurs
open until midnight, Fri &
Sat till 1am. Upstairs, the

NEW TOWN

Café Royal Bistro Bar is an unlovely rugby-themed affair.

Cumberland Bar

Map 2, H4. 1 Cumberland St. Mellow and highly regarded New Town bar with no jukebox, no TV and a wide variety of ales. There's a garden in the summer, and good, reasonably priced food is served from noon to 2pm Monday to Saturday.

The Dome

Map 4, I5. 14 George St. Opulent conversion of a massive New Town bank, thronging with well-dressed locals, though the ultra-chic atmosphere can be a bit intense. Probably the most impressive bar interior in Edinburgh, with Grecian columns and a huge glass dome, while the stylish side cocktail bar is reminiscent of a 1920s cruise ship. Open till 11.30pm Sun–Thurs, and till 1am Fri & Sat.

Indigo Yard

Map 4, A7. 7 Charlotte Lane, West End.

For many years one of Edinburgh's "it" bars, though now past its prime. Still busy and lively, though, with decent food as well as designer lager. Open daily till 1am.

Kay's Bar

Map 4, C3. 39 Jamaica St. Small, dark and civilized one-time wine shop, warmed by a roaring log fire in winter, and serving fine cask ales. Open till midnight Mon–Thurs, and till 1am Fri & Sat.

Milne's Bar

Map 4, H6. 35 Hanover St. Cellar bar once beloved of Edinburgh's literati, and known as "The Poets' Pub" courtesy of Hugh MacDiarmid et al. Recent redevelopment hasn't done it many favours, though, with chain-pub decor and special promotions doing their best to squeeze out what character remains. Serves a good range of cask beers.

Oxford Bar

Map 4, C6. 8 Young St.

Traditional city bar, unpretentious and something of a shrine for rugby fans, off-duty policemen and readers of the books of Ian Rankin. Open until 1am; sandwiches and hot pies are available till late.

Pivo Caffé
Map 2, I4. 2–6 Calton Rd.
The theme is essentially Czech, but the result is a laid-back and popular bar with good DJs. Eastern European food and beer is prominent. Open daily till 1am.

BROUGHTON

The Barony Bar
Map 4, L2. 81–85 Broughton St.
A fine old-fashioned bar, which manages to be big and lively while hanging onto its character and friendly atmosphere. Real ale and some good food, though it can be a wait to get served. Open daily till midnight.

The Basement
Map 4, L2. 10a Broughton St.
Packed out, especially at the

weekends, with a pre-club crowd, this trendy bar is run by young, enthusiastic staff and serves cheap Mexican food till 10pm every day. Open daily till 1am.

The Outhouse
Map 4, L2. 12a Broughton Street Lane.
Busy pre-club bar tucked away down a cobbled lane off Broughton Street, with a lively beer garden and funky music. Open daily till 1am.

STOCKBRIDGE

Baillie Bar
Map 4, B1. 2 St Stephen Street.
Traditional basement bar at

the corner of Edinburgh's most self-consciously Bohemian street. English and Scottish ales are available, as

BROUGHTON • STOCKBRIDGE

well as better-than-average pub grub. Open till midnight Mon–Thurs, till 1am Fri & Sat, and till 11pm Sun.

Bert's Bar

Map 2, G4. 2–4 Raeburn Place, Stockbridge.
Popular locals' pub, despite its relatively recent arrival. Serves excellent beer, tasty pies and strives to be an authentic, non-theme-oriented venue, though the telly rarely misses any sporting action.

Hector's

Map 4, A1. 47–49 Deanhaugh St.
A magnet for trendy Stockbridgers, full of tall stools, chocolate-coloured leather couches and rough-hewn walls. Good for weekend brunches; food is served all day in a dining area to the rear.

LOTHIAN ROAD AND TOLLCROSS

Bennets Bar

Map 2, G5. 8 Leven St, Tollcross.
Edwardian pub, with mahogany-framed mirrors and Art Nouveau stained glass, which gets packed in the evenings, particularly when there's a show at the King's Theatre next door. Opens till midnight from Monday to Saturday; lunch is also available on these days.

Blue Blazer

Map 3, A5. 2 Spittal St.
Traditional Edinburgh *howff* with an oak-clad bar and church pews; serves a good selection of ales including guest English bitters. Open till midnight Wed & Thurs, and till 1am Fri & Sat.

Cloisters

Map 2, H5. 26 Brougham Place, Tollcross.
Fine real-ale pub located in an old manse – the attitude to beer is appropriately reverential, with an open fire, comfy chairs, no loud music and a row of fonts serving interesting beer.

Monboddo

Map 3, A5. 36 Bread St.
Stylish modern bar on the
street level of the chic *Point
Hotel*. Serves fine food at
lunchtimes and beer in tall
glasses by evening. A drink
here and one in the *Blue
Blazer* across the road offers a
taste of both ends of the
Edinburgh drinking spectrum.

Traverse Bar Café

Map 2, G5. Traverse Theatre,
10 Cambridge St.
Much more than just a theatre
bar, attracting a lively,
sophisticated crowd – which
dispels any notion of a quiet
interval drink. Good food
available in the bar and at *blue*
(see p.215) upstairs. One of *the*
places to be during the Festival.

THE SOUTHSIDE

Drouthy Neebors

Map 2, I6. 1–2 West Preston
St, Newington.
What a Scottish theme bar
will look like when it's
exported around the world to
countries bored of Irish
theme bars, with oddly-
shaped whisky bottles and
deflated sets of bagpipes to
replace the shamrocks and
Gaelic footballs. Popular with
students, and often lively.
Open daily till 1am.

Human Be-In

Map 3, G6. 2–8 West
Crosscauseway, Newington.
Despite the odd name (it's a
Californian thing), this is one
of the trendiest student bars
in town, with huge plate glass
windows to admire the
beautiful people and tables
outside for summer posing.
Good food too. Open daily
till 1am.

Peartree House

Map 3, H7. 36 West Nicolson
St, Newington.
Fine bar in an eighteenth-
century house, with old
sofas and a large courtyard,
one of central Edinburgh's
very few beer gardens.
Budget bar lunches are on
offer. Open until midnight
Mon–Wed & Sun, and till
1am Thurs–Sat.

THE SOUTHSIDE

LEITH

Bar Java
Map 6, H4. 48–50 Constitution St.

Airy, modern and friendly bar in an area where you'd expect all the pubs to have sawdust on the floor. Serves decent food, has a small courtyard beer garden and even B&B rooms upstairs (see p.187). Open till midnight Sun–Wed, and till 1am Thurs–Sat.

Carriers' Quarters
Map 6, H4. 42 Bernard St.

Intimate pub that dates back to 1785 and retains many original features, including a tiny "snug" and blazing log fire. Open till 1am Fri & Sat.

Kings Wark
Map 6, H4. 36 The Shore.

Real ale in an atmospheric restored eighteenth-century pub right in the heart of Leith, with bar meals chalked up on the rafters. Open till midnight Fri & Sat.

Starbank Inn
Map 6, B2. 64 Laverockbank Rd, Newhaven.

Fine old stone-built pub overlooking the Forth, with a high reputation for cask ales and bar food. Open till midnight Thurs–Sat.

ELSEWHERE IN THE CITY

Athletic Arms
Map 2, F6. 1 Angle Park Terrace, Polwarth.

Out in the western suburbs, not far from Heart's football ground and Murrayfield rugby stadium, the *Athletic* is also known as *The Diggers*, a nickname which stems from its close proximity to a cemetery. For decades it has had the reputation of being Edinburgh's best pub for serious ale drinkers. Open till midnight Mon–Sat; and till 6pm Sun.

Caley Sample Room

Map 2, F6. 58 Angle Park Terrace, Polwarth.

The former sampling room and now showcase pub for the cask ales of the nearby Caledonian Brewery, full of old brewing artefacts and photographs. A good place to find a noisy crowd when there's a big rugby international on the telly, and also hosts ceilidhs occasionally. Open till midnight Mon–Thurs & Sun, and till 1am Fri & Sat.

Canny Man's (Volunteer Arms)

Map 2, G7. 237 Morningside Rd, Morningside.

Atmospheric and idiosyncratic pub/museum adorned with anything that can be hung on the walls or from the ceiling, ranging from old violins to assorted beer mugs. There's a pleasant beer garden for warm weather. Open till midnight Mon–Sat.

Crammond Inn

Map 2, A2. Crammond Village

An authentic old inn by the riverside at Crammond – the perfect place for a drink or a pub meal after a stroll along the coastal path.

Hawes Inn

Map 1, C2. Newhalls Road, South Queensferry.

Famous old whitewashed tavern virtually under the Forth Rail Bridge, immortalized by Stevenson in *Kidnapped*. The bar serves a wide range of food and drink, and the rambling complex also includes a hotel and restaurant.

Sheep Heid Inn

Map 5, G6. 43 The Causeway, Duddingston.

This eighteenth-century inn with a family atmosphere makes an ideal refreshment stop at the end of a tramp through Holyrood Park. Decent home-cooked meals are available at the bar, while the old-fashioned skittle alley is always popular with students.

Live music and clubs

Edinburgh's nightlife inevitably falls into two categories: the high-octane, non-stop action which takes place during the Festival, and the lineup during the other 49 weeks of the year – which can only ever pale by comparison. The Festival, though, is a misleading yardstick, as Edinburgh has a lot to offer year-round, especially in the realm of theatre and live music. You can hear live jazz, folk and rock most evenings in one or other of the city's hundreds of pubs, and while many of the big rock bands bypass Edinburgh altogether, making Glasgow their only Scottish date on a major international tour, some do perform at ad-hoc venues such as the Castle Esplanade or Murrayfield Stadium, and you'll find that plenty of smaller touring bands play the city's medium-sized clubs.

Edinburgh's gay clubs are listed on p.255.

Edinburgh's top **classical music** venue is the Usher Hall, where larger orchestras and choirs perform, while large-scale **opera and ballet** – performed both by the national companies Scottish Opera and Scottish Ballet, and by touring companies – are staged at the Festival Theatre. Smaller ensembles tend to perform at the Queens Hall, which also sees a fair bit of jazz and mellow rock, while choral and organ recitals are held at assorted venues, the best known being the High Kirk of St Giles. Tickets for the major shows and performances are around the £15–25 mark, dropping below £10 for the lesser venues.

It isn't always easy to get a grip on Edinburgh's **club scene**, partly because it offers an eclectic array of different styles and music, and partly because there aren't that many clubs or venues which have made such an impact that the crowds flock in, come rain or shine – as is the case in many other British cities. What you should find, however, is something covering most tastes, from reggae through hip-hop to rock; in the bigger venues, you may find different club nights taking place on each floor, and it's worth checking out where some of the city's best DJs, such as Eh-wun, Richie Rufftone or TPV, are playing. Look out, too, for the popular Seventies or Eighties nights with the emphasis firmly on fun, dressing up and drinking. Most of the city-centre clubs stay **open** till around 3am and charge around £5 to get in, though covers for the more popular and better-known nights can climb up towards £10.

The best way to find out **what's on** is to pick up a copy of *The List*, an excellent fortnightly listings magazine covering both Edinburgh and Glasgow (£2.20). Alternatively, get hold of the *Edinburgh Evening News*, which appears Monday to Saturday: its listings column gives details of all performances in the city that day. Information on nightclubs can also be found on posters and piles of leaflets distributed to most of the pre-club bars around town. Box offices of individual halls and theatres are likewise liberally supplied with promotional leaflets about forthcoming music and theatre, and some are able to sell tickets for more than one venue.

LIVE MUSIC VENUES

The Corn Exchange

Map 2, E7. New Market Road, Gorgie ☏ 0131/443 2437. Edinburgh's best mid-sized venue (capacity 2000), and visited by many well-known bands. Located 2.5 miles west of the city centre – buses #4 and #44 are your best bet.

Henry's Jazz Bar

Map 2, G5. 8 Morrison St, off Lothian Rd ☏ 0131/221 1288. Edinburgh's premier jazz and hip-hop venue, with live music every night and regular top performers.

The Liquid Room

Map 3, D4. 9c Victoria St ☏ 0131/225 2528. Good-size venue frequented by visiting indie and local R&B bands, while the occasional star act gets queues round the block.

On the Mound

Map 3, D3. 2–3 North Bank St ☏ 0131/226 6899. This "acoustic music café" is a good spot to stumble upon regular impromptu folk sessions; coffees and light meals are served.

The Queen's Hall

Map 2, I5. 37 Clerk St ☏ 0131/667 2019. Converted Southside church seating up to 800, with gigs from African, funk and rock bands on the way up or back down, as well as smaller jazz and folk concerts. Also hosts a lot of classical music performances (see opposite) and occasional comedy nights.

The Playhouse

Map 2, I4. 18–22 Greenside Place ☏ 0131/557 2692 (information), ☏ 0870/606 3424 (booking line). Large theatre mainly used for musicals but still popular with ageing re-formed rock acts and tribute bands.

Royal Oak

Map 3, G4. 1 Infirmary St ☏ 0131/557 2976.

A traditional pub hosting regular informal folk sessions and the "Wee Folk Club" on Sundays.

Sandy Bell's

Map 3, E5. 25 Forrest Rd
☎ 0131/225 2751.
A small, friendly bar, with folk music every night of the week. Tends to attract good local musicians.

The Venue

Map 2, I4. 15 Calton Rd
☎ 0131/557 3073.

Regular stop for up-and-coming indie bands, local and national, and the odd rock'n'roll legend. The dark and dingy setting is just right for raucous guitar-based music.

Whistlebinkies

Map 3, G3. 4–6 South Bridge
☎ 0131/557 5114.
One of the most reliable places to find live music every night of the week – often it's rock and pop covers, though there are some folk evenings. Daily till 3am.

CLASSICAL MUSIC VENUES

St Cecilia's Hall

Map 3, G3. Corner of Cowgate and Niddry St ☎ 0131/650 2805.
The oldest purpose-built concert hall in Scotland, now owned by Edinburgh University. The excellent collection of early keyboard instruments is used during the Festival and occasionally at other times. Acoustics are good, but traffic noise does sometimes intrude.

The Queen's Hall

Map 2, I5. 37 Clerk St
☎ 0131/667 2019.
Operates as the home-base of both the Scottish Chamber Orchestra and Scottish Ensemble, with regular seasons from both, as well as hosting touring performers and choirs.

Reid Concert Hall

Map 3, F6. Bristo Square
☎ 0131/650 2423.

Owned by Edinburgh University, this hall is used sparingly during the year for classical music concerts. Free lunchtime recitals of organ and piano music during university terms.

Usher Hall
Map 2, C7. Corner of Lothian Rd and Grindlay St ℡0131/228 1155.

Edinburgh's main civic concert hall, recently refurbished and seating over 2500. Excellent for choral and symphony concerts, but less suitable for solo vocalists. The upper circle seats are cheapest and have the best acoustics; avoid the back of the grand tier and the stalls, where the sound is muffled by the overhanging balconies.

NIGHTCLUBS

La Belle Angèle
Map 3, G4. 11 Hasties Close ℡0131/225 2774.

Long-established, well-run venue regarded as the city's premier underground club. Look out for the drum'n'bass night *Manga* (monthly on Fridays) and hip-hop *Scratch* (monthly on Saturdays), two of Edinburgh's most impressive club nights. Occasionally hosts well-known touring bands.

The Bongo Club
Map 3, I1. 14 New St ℡0131/556 5204.

Great venue (now under threat of closure) above a car park near Waverley Station, attracting some of the most interesting DJs around. Look out for reggae and dub from the mighty Messenger Sound System (monthly on Saturdays), and Club Latino (monthly on Fridays).

The Cavendish
Map 2, G5. 3 West Tollcross ℡0131/228 3252.

Slightly dingy but still a packed venue for the roots, ragga and reggae night on Fridays; the *Mambo Club* on Saturdays is Edinburgh's best venue for Latin and African rhythms.

The Citrus Club

Map 2, G5. 40–42 Grindlay St
Ⓣ 0131/662 7086,
Ⓦ www.citrusclub.co.uk.
Popular with students and
indie fans, this place in
Edinburgh's theatreland has a
large non-smoking bar area.
Best nights are the indie
Teasage on Saturdays or lo-fi
Genetic on Thursdays.

Club Java

Map 6, F3. 40 Commercial St,
Leith Ⓣ 0131/467 3810,
Ⓦ www.clubjava.co.uk.
Large converted church in
Leith with a big dance floor,
pleasant lounge area and
weekend restaurant. Out-of-
town apathy means it doesn't
always draw the crowds.

Club Mercado

Map 3, F2. 36–39 Market St
Ⓣ 0131/226 4224.
Cheesy music night starts at
5pm on Fridays for the after-
work crowd; other regular
nights *Eye Candy* (fortnightly
on Saturdays) and *Tackno*
(monthly on Sundays) are all
glam and kitsch.

Ego

Map 2, I4. 14 Picardy Place
Ⓣ 0131/478 7434.
A former casino, this
capacious venue hosts *Joy*,
one of the city's longest
running nights, which plays
house and trance to a gay and
mixed crowd monthly on
Saturdays. The smaller
Cocteau Lounge downstairs is
another popular venue for
smaller, less mainstream club
nights.

Honeycomb

Map 3, G3. 15–17 Niddry St
Ⓣ 0131/220 4381.
Attractively designed, almost
plush club, attracting a
sophisticated set to nights
such as *Sublime* on Fridays,
playing trance and techno,
and *Luvely* on Saturdays,
playing house to a gay and
mixed crowd.

The Liquid Room

Map 3, D3. 9c Victoria St
Ⓣ 0131/225 2564.
Large, longstanding venue,
aiming for the student crowd,
with indie, chart and dance
music nights. Big dance floor

NIGHTCLUBS

and a huge, powerful sound system. Also attracts a decent number of live gigs.

The Venue
Map 3, H1. 15 Calton Rd
ⓣ 0131/557 3073,
ⓦ www.edinburghvenue.co.uk.
A fairly seedy rock'n'roll pit which has its moments as a stomping nightclub, with room for 1000 over three floors. Best bet is the retro house night *Blitz* on Fridays.

Theatre, comedy and cinema

O utside the Festival, Edinburgh has a relatively small but thriving theatre and cinema scene. One of the most consistently exciting small theatres in Britain, the Traverse leads the way in original, cutting-edge drama; while the Royal Lyceum regularly stages top-quality mainstream plays, often with a Scottish theme; and the huge Festival Theatre presents the biggest and most prestigious touring shows, including opera and ballet. Big successes from London's West End tend to do runs at the Playhouse, while smaller, more innovative work can be found at venues such as the Theatre Workshop and Edinburgh University's Bedlam Theatre. Ticket prices for live theatre vary enormously, ranging from £5 to £25 depending on the venue and the production.

Edinburgh has several multiscreen venues and two excellent repertory **cinemas**, the Cameo and Filmhouse, both of which present a daily choice of art-house and mainstream films. You can expect to pay around £6 for an evening show, less during the day. Check with the venue or read *The List* (see p.237) or *The Scotsman* for details of performances, and special offers for previews or reduced tickets for those with student ID.

THEATRE AND COMEDY

Bedlam Theatre
Map 3, E5. 2a Forrest Rd ℡ 0131/225 9893.
Converted church which operates as the main venue for low-budget but enthusiastic and occasionally notable productions staged by Edinburgh University students.

W.J. Christie & Son
Map 3, B5. 27–31 West Port ℡ 0131/228 3765.
Small, intense cellar bar with raw comedy spots (Thurs–Sun only) and appearances from some of the better local comedians.

Church Hill Theatre
Map 2, G6. 33a Morningside Rd ℡ 0131/220 4349.
This Victorian church has been transformed into a rather utilitarian theatre, used mainly by local amateur dramatics groups and visiting Festival groups.

Dance Base
Map 3, C4. 14–16 Grassmarket ℡ 0131/225 5525.
Sleek new venue, with various studios, that opened in 2001 as a dance school and workshop, and is used occasionally as a performance space for modern dance, ballet and touring companies.

Festival Theatre
Map 3, G5. 13–29 Nicolson St ℡ 0131/529 6000.
Revamped music-hall theatre, now with a grandiose glass front following renovation in the 1990s, the Festival now has the largest stage in Britain. It's principally used for Scottish Opera's appearances in the capital and other major orchestral performances, but also for everything from the children's show *Singing Kettle* to concerts from the likes of Engelbert Humperdinck.

Guilded Saloon

Map 3, G4. 233 Cowgate ⓣ 0131/226 6550.
Attached to the better known *Guilded Balloon*, one of the essential Festival spots for comedy, the Saloon is open year round and hosts occasional comedy nights, poetry readings and guest DJs.

The Hub

Map 3, C8. Castlehill ⓣ 0131/473 2000.
Edinburgh's year-round Festival Centre, with a large performance space in the funkily renovated church hall upstairs, used for recitals, plays and shows. There's a shop, ticket office and decent café at ground level.

King's Theatre

Map 2, G6. 2 Leven St ⓣ 0131/529 6000.
Stately Edwardian civic theatre that offers the most eclectic programme in the city – includes major touring theatre companies, Shakespeare, slapstick Christmas pantomime and mainstream comedy and music-hall acts.

Netherbow Arts Centre

Map 3, G8. 43 High St ⓣ 0131/556 9579.
Compact Royal Mile venue offering a regular supply of adventurous drama, with storytelling, puppetry, children's theatre and Scots themes prevailing.

Playhouse Theatre

Map 2, I4. 18–22 Greenside Place ⓣ 0131/557 2692 (information), ⓣ 0870/606 3424 (booking line).
Restored following a serious fire in 1993, the Playhouse is a huge theatre, seating around 3000, and is used most of the year for popular West End musicals such as *Phantom of the Opera* and *Cats*.

Royal Lyceum Theatre

Map 2, G5. 30 Grindlay St ⓣ 0131/248 4848.
A fine Victorian civic theatre with a compact auditorium, this is the city's leading year-round venue for mainstream drama.

St Bride's Centre

Map 2, F6. 10 Orwell Terrace ⓣ 0131/346 1405.

THEATRE AND COMEDY

Another converted church that doubles as a busy community centre; it's used by school groups and local dramatic societies during the year, and for a variety of shows at Festival time.

The Stand Comedy Club
Map 4, J3. 5 York Place ℡ 0131/558 7272.

The city's top comedy spot, with a different act on every night and some of the UK's top comics headlining at the weekends. The bar here is a great place to eat and drink, even if the stage is quiet.

Theatre Workshop
Map 2, G4. 34 Hamilton Place ℡ 0131/226 5425.

Small but versatile venue staging enticing programmes of innovative international theatre and performance art all year round.

Traverse Theatre
Map 2, G5. 10 Cambridge St ℡ 0131/228 1404.

A byword in experimental theatrical circles, and unquestionably one of Britain's premier venues for new plays, The Traverse is going from strength to strength in its new custom-built home beside the Usher Hall, with a great bar downstairs and the inventive *blue* café-bar upstairs.

CINEMAS

Cameo
Map 2, G5. 38 Home St; info line ℡ 0131/228 2800, bookings ℡ 0131/228 4141.

A treasure of an art-house cinema: nothing great to look at, but the three-screen venue has a cultured vibe backed up by an inspiring, cultured programme. Shows new releases of art-house, independent and more challenging mainstream films, as well as a regular selection of cult movies and weekend late-night shows for devotees of the likes of *Betty Blue* and *Reservoir Dogs*, and interesting Sunday matinees. Tarantino's been here and thinks it's great.

CINEMAS

Dominion

Map 2, G7. 18 Newbattle Terrace, Morningside
☎ 0131/447 4771.
Still family owned, this is a genuinely old-fashioned cinema, which battles on showing popular new releases.

Filmhouse

Map 2, G5. 88 Lothian Rd
☎ 0131/228 2688.
Three screens showing an eclectic programme of independent, art-house and classic films. This is the main centre for the Edinburgh International Film Festival, and the café is a hangout for the city's dedicated film buffs.

Odeon

Map 2, I5. 7 Clerk St
☎ 0131/667 0971; info and credit card bookings
☎ 0870/505 0007.

Five-screen cinema showing the latest releases. The huge main auditorium makes it an electric place to watch a newly released blockbuster.

UCI

Map 2, L6. Kinnaird Park, Newcraighall Rd, Niddrie
☎ 0870/010 2030.
Soulless multiplex, showing all the big blockbusters, 4.5 miles southeast of the city; use buses #14, #32 and #C3 from Princes Street.

UGC

Map 2, F6. Fountainpark, Dundee St, Fountainbridge
☎ 0870/902 0417.
Big, reasonably central multiplex in a large modern entertainment complex. Buses #1, #28 and #34 (from Princes Street), and #35 (from the Royal Mile) go straight there.

CINEMAS

Art galleries

I
n addition to Edinburgh's four major houses of art – the National Gallery (see p.89), the Portrait Gallery (see p.100), the Gallery of Modern Art (see p.112) and the Dean Gallery (see p.114) – there are a number of impressive smaller art galleries around the city, where you can see both traditional Scottish painting, typified by landscapes of beautiful Highlands scenery, and more contemporary works by a new generation of successful young artists.

For updates and forthcoming exhibitions at Edinburgh's four main national galleries, visit Ⓦ www.natgalscot.ac.uk.

You're most likely to see important local or touring exhibitions at places such as the **City Art Centre**, an impressive six-storey venue right beside Waverley Station, or the **Fruitmarket Gallery**, opposite, with its attractive glass-fronted design and art bookshop. Other important shows are exhibited at the Talbot Rice Gallery (see p.81) in Edinburgh University's Old College, and the Royal Scottish Academy (see p.89) beside the National Gallery at the foot of the Mound, notable for its annual show by members and the occasional large Festival retrospective. Complementing these are a raft of commercial galleries, from ritzy upmarket venues such as the **Scottish Gallery** and the **Ingelby**

Gallery in the New Town, to more modern and trendier spaces like the **Collective Gallery** in the Old Town. Also in the Old Town are two dynamic photographic galleries, **Portfolio** and **Stills**. You can also stumble on interesting exhibitions at many of the city's arts venues, too, such as the Filmhouse (see p.247), Queen's Hall (see p.238) and, particularly, **Inverleith House** in the Royal Botanic Garden. Check *The List* or *The Scotsman* for details of current shows.

GALLERIES

City Art Centre
Map 3, F2. 2 Market St
Ⓣ 0131/529 3993.
Mon–Sat 10am–5pm, Sun noon–5pm. Entry charge for major exhibitions.
Big civic venue, with six exhibition halls, that is often used for blockbuster shows: notable successes have included *Star Trek* and *Scotland's Art*, mounted in the summer of Parliament's opening. On show are choice items from the council's own substantial collection of art, including fascinating paintings of Edinburgh in former times. Works by notable locals such as Fergusson, McTaggart and Bellany are also occasionally put on display.

Collective Gallery
Map 3, F2. 22–28 Cockburn St
Ⓣ 0131/220 1260.
Wed–Sat 10.30am–5pm, Sun 3–5pm. Free.
An avant-garde gallery, established in the mid-80s by a large group of artists, which shows conventional and mixed-media contemporary art. Changing exhibitions can be a bit hit-or-miss, but they're ready to tackle taboo subjects such as drugs and gay sex. The Project Room, a small space off the main room, is used for smaller exhibitions.

doggerfisher
Map 2, I4. 11 Gayfield Square
Ⓣ 0131/558 7110.

GALLERIES

Thurs–Sat 11am–6pm, Sun 2–5pm. Free.

Cutting edge contemporary gallery located in an old tyre garage on the edge of the New Town. Relatively little-known, single-artist exhibitions are the mainstay, and the ethos is to introduce serious, interesting and original contemporary British art to the buying public.

Edinburgh College of Art

Map 3, B6. Lauriston Place
℗ 0131/221 6032.
Mon–Fri 10am–4pm, Sat 9am–1pm. Free.

It's always worth checking out the degree show held here in the early summer, and there are regular exhibitions throughout the year, the most interesting often at the time of the Festival. Fabulous views of the castle from the upper floors.

Edinburgh Printmakers' Workshop

Map 2, I4. 23 Union St
℗ 0131/557 2479.
Tues–Sat 10am–6pm. Free.

Bustling working studio used predominantly by local artists, but there are always a couple of rooms displaying some excellent printmaking, and a special show is put on during the Festival. Good place to go to buy reasonably priced screen prints and lithographs, and the viewing gallery allows visitors to watch artists at work. Workshops and courses are on offer.

Fruitmarket Gallery

Map 3, F2. 45 Market St
℗ 0131/225 2383.
Mon–Sat 11am–6pm, Sun noon–5pm. Entry charge for some exhibitions.

Award-winning space, behind a giant glass frontage immediately opposite the City Arts Centre, presenting the best in adventurous contemporary and cutting-edge art from Scotland and abroad in a variety of media, with regular exhibitions from high-profile international names. On-site are an excellent art/architecture bookshop and a popular café (Mon–Fri 11am–3pm, Sat 11am–5pm, Sun noon–5pm).

Ingelby Gallery

Map 2, I4. 6 Carlton Terrace

Ⓣ 0131/556 4441.
Wed–Sat 10am–5pm and by appointment. Free.
Located on the far side of Calton Hill, in the ground floor of a family house on one of Edinburgh's grandest terraces, this impressive gallery stages temporary shows by contemporary stars such as Andy Goldsworthy, Callum Innes and Ian Hamilton Finlay.

Inverleith House
Map 2, G3. Royal Botanic Garden, Inverleith Row Ⓣ 0131/552 7171.
Tues–Sun 10.30am–3.30pm. Free.
This attractive old house in the heart of the Botanic Gardens is used for serious, thought-provoking exhibitions, often with a nature/botanical theme; it has also hosted important shows such as photographs by Stanley Kubrick.

Open Eye Gallery
Map 4, E1. 75–79 Cumberland St Ⓣ 0131/557 1020.
Mon–Fri 10am–6pm, Sat 10am–4pm. Free.

Charming commercial gallery at the lower end of the New Town, showing many leading Scottish artists and a good range of jewellery, ceramics and crafts. Sister gallery I2, immediately opposite at number 66, has more of the same.

Portfolio Gallery
Map 3, E4. 43 Candlemaker Row Ⓣ 0131/220 1911.
Tues–Sat noon–5.30pm. Free.
Small photographic gallery near the Grassmarket which holds consistently interesting and well-presented photographic exhibitions, often on local themes. Produces the lavish *Portfolio* magazine, in which the photos are accompanied by thoughtful essays and criticism.

Scottish Gallery
Map 4, F2. 16 Dundas St Ⓣ 0131/558 1200.
Mon–Fri 10am–6pm, Sat 10am–4pm. Free.
Edinburgh's longest-established fine-art dealers, in the heart of the commercial gallery district of the New Town. Shows both traditional

GALLERIES

and contemporary art, with cabinets of jewellery, ceramics or wooden crafts; a good place to find leading twentieth-century Scottish artists.

Stills Gallery
Map 3, F2. 23 Cockburn St
Ⓣ 0131/662 6200.

Tues–Sat 10am–5pm. Free.
A small but attractive space predominantly showing photography, but an array of exciting contemporary artists also exhibit here. Good café on the mezzanine level, and a small bookshop.

Gay Edinburgh

With an estimated homosexual population of 15,000–20,000, Edinburgh has a dynamic **gay** culture, which for years has centred round the top of Leith Walk and Broughton Street, an area known as the "Pink Triangle", where the city's first gay and lesbian centre appeared in the 1970s. The power of the pink pound has led to a proliferation of gay enterprises – some transitory, others

USEFUL CONTACTS

Important local contacts are: Lothian Gay and Lesbian Switchboard (daily 7.30–10pm; ☎ 0131/556 4049, ⓦ www.lgls.org); Edinburgh Lesbian Line (Mon & Thurs 7.30–10pm; ☎ 0131/557 0751); and Solas (Mon–Fri 9am–5pm; ☎ 0131/661 0982), an HIV and AIDS counselling service. Otherwise, the best place to get up-to-date information is the Lesbian, Gay and Bisexual Centre, which houses *Nexus Café* (see p.254), or *Blue Moon Café* (see p.254), just up the road. Useful websites include ⓦ www.scotsgay.co.uk, which has archives of the magazine, as well as lots of links; and ⓦ www.gayscotland.com, a gay guide to all the Scottish cities, with information on accommodation, bars, clubs and other contacts in Edinburgh.

more durable – ranging from gay-owned guesthouses and cafés to dedicated gay bars and club nights.

The most important single event for Scotland's gay community is the annual **Pride Scotland** march, which takes place in June and alternates between Edinburgh and Glasgow; visit ⓦ www.pridescotland.org or call ⓣ 0141/556 4340 for more details. For further **information** on gay life in Edinburgh, check out *The List* or *Scotsgay*, a bi-monthly magazine available in most pubs and clubs.

CAFÉS

Blue Moon Café
Map 4, K1. 1 Barony St (off Broughton St) ⓣ 0131/557 0911.
Mon–Fri 11am–10pm, Sat & Sun 9.30am–10pm.
Now a well-established Broughton Street landmark, with a relaxed, friendly vibe that's popular with many sections of the local arty establishment, not just the gay crowd – a good place to read up about the gay scene and watch the world go by over a coffee. Serves snacks and drinks through the day, and main meals at night, including a couple of decent vegetarian dishes.

Nexus Café Bar
Map 2, H4. 60 Broughton St ⓣ 0131/478 7069.
Daily 11am–11pm.
Pleasant and bright licensed café at the back of Edinburgh's long-running Lesbian, Gay and Bisexual Centre, with a striking ceiling mural titled *We are one*! There's useful information on all aspects of gay life in Scotland's capital, and a PC with internet access. All-day breakfasts and light meals of soups and bacon rolls are served, along with snacks and coffees; larger meals are available in the evenings.

Solas Café

Map 2, J4. 2–4 Abbeymount ℡ 0131/661 0982. Tues & Thurs 11am–8pm, Wed & Fri 11am–4pm. Support and information centre with a café open four days (and two evenings) a week for vegetarian home cooking; HIV groups also meet here.

CLUBS AND BARS

C.C. Bloom's

Map 2, I4. 23 Greenside Place, Leith Walk ℡ 0131/556 9331. Mon–Sat 6pm–3am, Sun 4pm–3am. Free.
Consistently Edinburgh's liveliest gay/lesbian bar, with a friendly, welcoming crowd and a disco every night, playing non-stop, sweaty dance music from 10.30pm to 3am. Karaoke nights on Thursdays and Sundays, male dancers on Sunday afternoons.

Claremont Bar & Restaurant

Map 2, H3. 133–135 East Claremont St ℡ 0131/556 5662. Daily 11am–1am.
A gay-owned and operated bar, though strictly gay nights happen only occasionally. The unusual sci-fi theme draws a mixed crowd and gives the place a pleasantly bizarre edge.

Habana

Map 2, I4. Greenside Place, Leith Walk ℡ 0131/558 1270. Mon–Sat noon–1am, Sun 12.30pm–1am.
Bright, friendly pre-club café-bar near *C.C. Bloom's*, particularly popular in summer when the tables and chairs spill out onto the pavement.

Joy

Map 2, I4. *Ego*, Picardy Place ℡ 0131/478 7434, ⓦ www.clubjoy.co.uk. Fortnightly on Saturdays.
A big, popular club night, advertised by a big pink bunny rabbit logo, which

draws a mixed crowd and plays a mix of music ranging from chart and pop to garage and house.

The Laughing Duck

Map 4, E3. 24 Howe St
Ⓣ0131/220 2376.
Mon–Thurs 11am–11pm, Fri & Sat 11am–1am, Sun 11.30am–11pm.
Edinburgh's most famous gay bar, recently reopened with a stylish new look. Attracts an eclectic range of folk, with a series of different events through the week including a quiz night and an acoustic jam session. Food is served day and night.

Luvely

Map 3, G3. *The Honeycomb*, 15–17 Niddry St Ⓣ0131/220 4381.
Monthly on Saturdays.
A big dressing-up night for gay, glammed-up, ultra-trendy clubbers. Music policy is funky-to-hard house.

Newtown Bar

Map 4, I2. 26a Dublin St
Ⓣ0131/538 7775.
Daily noon–1am.
Still very near to the Broughton Triangle, but more of a New Town feel to this smart, men-only bar, which attracts a high number of professionals. Downstairs, the aptly named Intense music night takes place from Wednesday to Sunday.

Planet Out

Map 2, I4. 6 Baxter's Place, Leith Walk Ⓣ0131/556 5991.
Mon–Fri 4pm–1am, Sat & Sun 2pm–1am.
Another venue beside the Playhouse, this is an easygoing, friendly bar, with tacky decor. Tends to attract a younger gay crowd, though it's also popular at weekends as a warm-up for *C.C. Bloom's* up the road.

Tackno

Map 3, F2. *Club Mercado*,

For up to date information on gay and lesbian club nights, check the Gay section of *The List* (see p.237), or posters in gay venues for forthcoming dates.

36–39 Market St ☏ 0131/226 4224.

Monthly on Sundays.

One of Edinburgh's best-known clubs, a lively, noisy, mixed crowd worshipping at the decks of DJ Trendy Wendy's inimitable lineup of kitsch classics.

Taste

Map 3, G3. *The Honeycomb*, 15–17 Niddry St ☏ 0131/220 4381, Ⓦ www.taste-clubs.com.

Weekly on Sundays.

Long-established gay club with a hedonistic reputation for its hard house music policy and full-on dancefloor antics.

SHOPS

Out of the Blue

Map 4, K1. 1 Barony St (off Broughton St) ☏ 0131/478 7048.

Daily noon–7pm.

Scotland's largest gay and les-bian shop, and the capital's prime gay sex shop, situated at the heart of the Pink Triangle in the basement below *Blue Moon Café*.

ACCOMMODATION

Alva House

Map 2, J4. 45 Alva Place, ☏ 0131/558 1382, Ⓦ www.gayscotland.com /alvahouse.

Stylishly designed with modern decor and original features, this gay male only guesthouse is about ten minutes away from Broughton Street. Non-smoking. ❶

Elm View

Map 2, I4. 42 Elm Row, ☏ 0131/556 1215, Ⓦ www.elmview.net.

A gay-owned, vegetarian B&B with one double guest bedroom. Located on Leith Walk, very close to the heart of the gay scene, and stylishly presented, with stripped floors and a rich burgundy colour scheme. ❷

SHOPS • ACCOMMODATION

Garlands Guest House

Map 2, I3. 48 Pilrig St
ⓉⒾ0131/554 4205, Ⓦwww
.garlands.demon.co.uk.
Named after Judy, this is a
neat gay and straight-friendly
guest house in a fairly grand
Georgian house, with six en-
suite rooms, located half way
down Leith Walk. Non-
smoking. ❸

Mansfield House

Map 4, I2. 57 Dublin St Ⓣ0131/
556 7980, Ⓦwww.mansfield
guesthouse.com.
Large, popular gay-only New
Town guesthouse opposite
the *New Town Bar*, so handy
for the Broughton Street
scene. Nine smallish rooms,
some with gorgeous furni-
ture; some have en-suite
bathrooms. ❷

Kids' Edinburgh

T he dramatic visual impact of Edinburgh and its plethora of fascinating historic buildings make it a place that **kids** are likely to enjoy and remember. Older children especially will appreciate many of the attractions covered in other parts of this book, particularly **Edinburgh Castle**, with its battlements, winding staircases and dungeons. Other places which kids are likely to connect with are the **Outlook Tower** (see p.34) on the Royal Mile; **Greyfriars Bobby** (see p.71) on George IV Bridge; and the **Scott Monument** (see p.88) on Princes Street, with its tight spiral staircase winding for ever up into the Edinburgh stratosphere. Also covered elsewhere in the guide, and popular with children, are the **Brass Rubbing Centre** in Trinity Apse (see p.48), the **Museum of Childhood** (see p.48) and **Our Dynamic Earth** (see p.60). Edinburgh also has plenty of handy green spaces where kids can let off steam: right in the centre of the city are **Princes Street Gardens**, with a play park at the western end and bridges with good views over the railway lines leading into Waverley station. There's also lots of open space around **Holyrood Park** at the bottom of the Royal Mile, as well as the strange buildings and open views on **Calton Hill**, a few hundred yards east of Princes Street.

The attractions we've listed in this chapter are either

directly targeted at younger children or have dedicated child-friendly sections. **Edinburgh Zoo** and **Gorgie City Farm** offer contrasting choices of wild and tame animals, while the extremely popular **Deep Sea World** is an imaginatively mounted display of all kinds of weird and colourful sea creatures. For animal-life on a smaller scale, try **Edinburgh Butterfly and Insect World** to the south of the city, or the **Scottish Seabird Centre** in North Berwick in East Lothian. There are a number of places which successfully make the historical aspect of Edinburgh more relevant to children, including the **National Museum of Scotland** and **Scotland's Black Diamonds**, a mining museum eight miles southeast of the centre in the village of Newtongrange. Meanwhile, there's plenty of good clean fun to be had at the city's two best swimming centres, **Leith Waterworld** and the **Royal Commonwealth Pool**.

If you're planning to visit more than a couple of these places during your stay in Edinburgh, it's worth getting hold of the tourist board's *Essential Guide to Edinburgh and Lothians* (£1), available at the Tourist Office, which has a centre pull-out with various **discounts** and offers, many relating to family attractions. For listings with details of children's shows, activities and events, look for the "Kids" pages in the fortnightly *List* magazine.

Look out also for child-friendly events in the **Edinburgh International Science Festival** (see p.299) in April, while the **Puppet and Animation Festival** in March (see p.299) and the **Children's Festival** (see p.300) give kids (and parents) a taste of the wall-to-wall entertainment of the grown-up Festival. During the grown-up Festival itself, in August, a separate programme entitled *Festival for Kids* (available from the Fringe office and principal venues), gives details of children's shows, though you'll also find children's listings in the regular Fringe programme and the daily

What's On guide. Also in August, a particularly strong roster of events for children is put on as part of the **Book Festival** (see p.294) in Charlotte Square, with various famous children's authors, such as J.K. Rowling, making appearances, along with other entertainers and participation events. Finally, both during the Festival and at other times of year, the **Netherbow Theatre** and the **Theatre Workshop** frequently put on children's shows (see the "Theatre, comedy and cinema" chapter for details).

ATTRACTIONS

Deep Sea World

Map 1, C2. North Queensferry, Fife; ☎ 01383/411880.
July & Aug daily 10am–6.30pm; April–June & Sept–Oct daily 10am–6pm; Nov–March Mon–Fri 11am–5pm, Sat & Sun 10am–6pm; £6.50, children £4.25, family tickets from £18.

One of the most popular children's attractions in Scotland, this is a well-thought-out, well-run high-tech aquarium showcasing all kinds of sea creatures. The highlight, suitable for all but the youngest children, is a moving walkway through a transparent acrylic tunnel underneath the huge main fish tank, which is filled with all sorts of creatures including conger eels and sharks. Knowledgeable staff are on hand to allow the inquisitive to touch some of the gentler fish in a rockpool; also among the exhibits are a piranha tank and various brightly coloured and poisonous reptiles. The nearest railway station is North Queensferry. By car, cross the Forth Road Bridge, leave the M90 at Junction 1 and follow signs.

Edinburgh Butterfly and Insect World

Map 1, E4. Melville Nursery, Lasswade, Midlothian ☎ 0131/663 4932.
Daily: April–Oct

9.30am–5.30pm; Nov–March 10am–5pm; £4.25, children £3.25, family tickets from £13. Hundreds of brightly coloured butterflies and moths inside a large glasshouse; streams and a bubbling mud pool add to the excitement. At the back, there's a "Nocturnal World", with bee hives, scorpions, snakes and ants. Buses #3 and #29 from Princes Street take you right here; by car, it's just beyond the city bypass (A720) on the Gilmerton Road (A772).

Edinburgh Zoo

Map 2, C5. Costorphine Rd ⓣ 0131/334 9171.
Daily: April–Sept 9am–6pm; Oct & March 9am–5pm; Nov–Feb 9am–4.30pm; £7, family tickets from £20.

Two miles west of the city centre on the main Glasgow road, Edinburgh's zoo is built on an eighty-acre site stretching up the side of Costorphine Hill. The zoo has over a thousand animals, including a number of endangered species such as white rhinos, red pandas, pygmy hippos and poisonous arrow frogs. The highlight for children, however, is the famous penguin parade (daily at 2.15pm from April to Sept, and on sunny March and Oct days), which attracts large crowds; other delights for young children include polar bears, sea lions and plenty of cheeky monkeys. The new African Plains Experience and a Lion Enclosure have viewing platforms over the animals, while other popular new additions include the Magic Forest, showcasing smaller primates, and a water-filled Evolution Maze – it's great fun, though fastidious parents should be warned that few children emerge with their clothes dry. The zoo is well served by a number of buses (#2, #26, #31, #36, #69, #85, #86).

Gorgie City Farm

Map 2, F6. 51 Gorgie Rd, Tynecastle Lane ⓣ 0131/337 4202.
Daily: March–Oct 9.30am–4.30pm, Nov–Feb 9.30am–4pm; free.

Lots of cute animals, including sheep, hens, ducks and rabbits, on a 2.5-acre site in the west of the city. There's an old tractor for clambering and a good picnic and play area. The adjacent *Farm Café* is well prepared for children. Some organic produce for sale. The farm is just west of the city centre near Hearts' Football Ground: any bus along Gorgie Road will take you there, including #3, #4, #21 and #25 from Princes Street.

National Museum of Scotland

Map 3, F5. Chambers St ℡ 0131/247 4422.
Mon–Sat 10am–5pm, Tues 10am–8pm, Sun noon–5pm; free.

A great place for children of most ages, with plenty of objects on display to capture the imagination and tell some of Scotland's story. When setting up the museum, selecting the objects to be displayed and writing the captions displayed beside them, the curators paid close attention to the comments of the NMS Junior Board, made up of schoolchildren of different ages from across Scotland. In addition to the displays, occasional interactive screens, the see-through lift and even the museum's unusual layout with tiny balconies and spiral staircases, are all big hits with children. There are also audio guides in plain English, special "Themed Pathways" around the museum with objects to hunt out and puzzles to complete, and various books about the museum aimed at children available in the shop. A particular highlight is the Discovery Centre on the third floor, which is specially aimed at 5–14-year-olds, with an assortment of puzzles, games, storyboards, computer challenges and dressing-up clothes related to both the themes and actual objects found in the museum. See p.74 for an account of the rest of the museum.

Newhaven Heritage Museum

Map 6, B1. 24 Pier Place, Newhaven ℡ 0131/551 4165.
Daily noon–5pm; free.

Fairly simple fishing museum

in the old fish market, with reconstructions of the lives of local fishermen and their families, and offering the chance to dress up in old costumes and check out the boats in the harbour alongside. An important part of the visit for many is *Harry Ramsden's* fish and chip café next door (see p.266). The most direct bus to Newhaven is the #11 from Princes Street or the top of Leith Walk; services #7, #10 and #16, also from Princes Street, go via Leith.

Scotland's Black Diamonds

Map 1, F4. Lady Victoria Colliery, Newtongrange, Midlothian ☎ 0131/663 7519. Feb–Oct daily 10am–5pm; Nov–Jan 11am–4pm; £4, children £2.20, family tickets from £10.

One of Scotland's best industrial heritage experiences for kids, this mining museum is on the site of one of the country's most important old collieries. A brand new visitors' centre helps bring the mine and the local community to life, helped by some entertaining innovations, including "magic helmets", with which you can experience a virtual reality tour of life below ground. Take the #3 bus from Princes Street; by car, the colliery is clearly marked from the main A7 route south just as you leave the village of Newtongrange.

ACTIVITIES

Leith Waterworld

Map 6, H7. 377 Easter Rd, Leith ☎ 0131/555 6000. During school term Wed & Thurs 10am–1pm, Fri–Sun 10am–5pm; during school holidays daily 10am–5pm; adults £2.40, children 5–17 £1.80.

Big new swimming complex in Leith with a main pool, flumes, a "learner lagoon" and a sloping "beach", suitable for babies. Also has a crèche and café. Catch any bus going down Leith Walk apart from #11.

ACTIVITIES

Royal Commonwealth Pool

Map 2, J6. 21 Dalkeith Rd, Newington ⊤ 0131/667 7211. Mon, Tues, Thurs & Fri 9am–9pm; Wed 10am–9pm, Sat & Sun (summer) 8am–7pm (winter) 10am–4pm; £2.90, children £1.50.

A complex built for the 1970 Commonwealth Games, now slightly tatty round the edges, but still a good venue with a large 50m pool, a separate diving pool, a baby pool, a play area for under eights and a fitness centre. Buses #14, #21 and #33 from Northbridge all stop right outside the door.

FOOD

The problems of taking young children out for a **meal** in Edinburgh are the same as anywhere in Britain, with many establishments unsuitable for or reluctant to accept kids under the age of ten. The restaurants below have been chosen for their child-friendliness and the acceptable quality of the food for both adults and children. Apart from this selection, the **Royal Museum** (see p.79) on Chambers Street, adjoining the National Museum, the **City Art Centre** (see p.249) and the **National Gallery of Modern Art** (see p.112) all have child-friendly cafés.

Est Est Est

Map 4, C6. 135a George St, New Town ⊤ 0131/225 2555. Mon–Sat noon–11pm, Sun noon–10.30pm. Moderate.

Large, bright, stylish chain serving slick pasta and interesting pizzas. Children are allowed to use crayons on the (paper) table cloths, and are invited over to the prep area to help design their own pizza. Non-smoking section.

Giuliano's on the Shore

Map 6, G4. 1 Commercial St, Leith ⊤ 0131/554 5272. Daily noon–10.30pm. Moderate.

Popular family-oriented Italian where children can assemble their own pizzas and check out the electronic board

FOOD

displaying birthday messages. The menu is mainly pizza and pasta, but there's normally a good range of seafood specials. Non-smoking section.

Harry Ramsden's

Map 6, B1. 5 Newhaven Place, Newhaven ☎ 0131/551 5566. Mon–Fri & Sun noon–9pm, Sat noon–10pm. Inexpensive.

Big, slick, well-run fish'n'chips emporium next door to the Newhaven Heritage Museum. A perennial winner with kids, grandparents and big groups, you'll find everything you need for children, from special menus to high chairs, and an in-house entertainer at weekends. There's also a big play ship outside and a play area inside for rainy days. Completely non-smoking.

Henderson's Salad Table

Map 4, G4. 94 Hanover St, New Town ☎ 0131/225 2131. Mon–Sat 8am–10.30pm. Inexpensive.

Great vegetarian institution in the city centre, with relaxed, canteen-style service and lots of scattered tables and chairs.

Children-friendly attitude includes a kids' menu offering lots of healthy options (no chips). Non-smoking section.

Luca's

Map 2, G6. 16 Morningside Rd, Morningside ☎ 0131/446 0233. Daily 9am–10pm. Inexpensive.

Edinburgh's best-loved ice-cream makers: grab a take-away cone downstairs or sit in upstairs, where an uncomplicated menu of pizzas, pasta and burgers, along with more extravagant sundaes, is on offer. Non-smoking section.

Mamma's American Pizza Company

Map 3, C4. 30 Grassmarket, Old Town ☎ 0131/225 6464. Sun–Thurs noon–midnight, Fri & Sat noon–1am. Inexpensive–moderate.

American-style pizzas with a bewildering choice of toppings, from smoked salmon to marshmallow, and a family-friendly atmosphere. Two other branches at 2 Broughton Place (Map 2, H4) and 1 Howard Street, Canonmills (Map 2, H3). Completely non-smoking.

FOOD

The Potting Shed

Map 2, G6. *Bruntsfield Hotel*,
69 Bruntsfield Place
☏ 0131/229 1393.

Daily 5.30–9.30pm, plus Sat &
Sun noon–2pm. Moderate.

Attached to a largish hotel
but still refreshingly individual, this pleasant, taste-of-
Scotland-style restaurant is a
lot more relaxed than many
smarter places in its attitude
to kids, with colouring
sheets, crayons and room to
run around outside.
Completely non-smoking.

Terrace Café

Map 2, G3. Botanic Garden
☏ 0131/552 0616.

Daily 9.30am–6pm.
Inexpensive.

Offering scones, cakes and
juices, soup, baked spuds and
coffee, the food's not stunning here but the setting is. If
you're lucky, the weather will
be mild enough to sit outside
and enjoy the fantastic view
across to the Old Town,
while the children gambol in
the gardens. Completely
non-smoking.

Traverse Bar Cafe

Map 2, G5. Traverse Theatre,
10 Cambridge St ☏ 0131/228
5383.

Mon–Wed & Sun 10.30am–midnight, Thurs–Sat 10.30am–1am.
Inexpensive.

Spacious but very hip, well-
designed bar that's long been
a hangout of the arty set. It
has a children's license till
8pm, and also serves coffees,
decent tapas-style dishes and
freshly prepared daily specials.

Umberto's

Map 6, F6. 2 Bonnington Rd
Lane ☏ 0131/554 1314.

Mon–Sat noon–2.30pm &
5–10pm, Sun noon–6pm.
Moderate.

Tucked away off Bonnington
Road on the way to Leith
and not that easy to find, but
among Edinburgh's non-
chain restaurants, this is the
most family-oriented, with
play areas both outside in the
enclosed garden and in the
upstairs dining area. Pasta
dishes start from about £6,
and there are decent, realistic
portions from around £2 for
the young ones. Non-smok-
ing section.

FOOD

Shopping

Despite the relentless advance of the big chains, central Edinburgh remains an enticing place for shopping, with many of its streets having their own individual character. Princes Street retains one or two distinctive emporia, including Jenners, the "Harrods of the North". Parallel to Princes Street, pedestrianized Rose Street and grand George Street both contain a number of more glamorous and upmarket boutiques, including designer clothes shops and large bookshops. At the eastern end of Princes Street is the underground Princes Mall, a glossy centre of specialist shops, while Cockburn Street, leading up from Waverley Bridge, is a hub for trendy clothes and record shops. There are several distinctly offbeat places among the tacky souvenir sellers on the Royal Mile, and down Victoria Street and in and around Grassmarket you'll find an eclectic range of antique and arts and crafts shops, plus some antiquarian booksellers. The main concentration of general, academic and remainder bookshops is in the area stretching from South Bridge to George IV Bridge, while the best areas for antique shops are St Stephen Street in Stockbridge and Causewayside in Southside. Thursday night is late-night shopping, with many of the larger shops open till around 8pm.

BOOKS AND MAPS

Edinburgh's city-centre **book** scene is dominated by the national group Waterstones, with only Ottakar's providing much alternative, but this does mean that the city centre has a number of well-stocked, efficiently run branches, open late most nights. Check the individual shops and the local press for details of regular promotional readings. Edinburgh also has numerous **secondhand bookshops**, many of which are to be found in the Grassmarket area; some of the best are listed below.

Carson Clark

Map 3, J2. 181–183 Canongate
☎ 0131/556 4710.
Mon–Fri 10am–5pm, Sat 10.30am–5.30pm.
Small but fascinating Royal Mile shop selling antique maps, charts and globes.

The Cooks' Bookshop

Map 3, D4. 118 West Bow
☎ 0131/226 4445.
Mon–Fri 10am–5.30pm, Sat 10.30am–5.30pm.
Owned by Clarissa Dickson Wright, of TV's *Two Fat Ladies* fame, this bright shop has an attractive, uncluttered display of new and second-hand books on every imaginable branch of cooking and type of food.

Ottakar's

Map 4, G5. 57 George St
☎ 0131/225 4495.
Mon–Fri 9am–10pm, Sat 9am–5.30pm, Sun 11am–5pm.
A recent arrival, taking over the central branch of long-established local booksellers James Thin in 2002 (Thin's other main branch in Edinburgh, on South Bridge, was sold to Blackwell's and caters mostly for university courses). As well as a wide selection of current and general titles, Ottakar's has a well-stocked Scottish interest section, holding a decent range of both fiction and non-fiction titles.

McNaughtan's Bookshop

Map 2, I4. 3a–4a Haddington Place, Leith Walk ☎ 0131/556 5897.

Tues–Sat 9.30am–5.30pm.

Capacious shop covering all the main areas of the art and literary worlds. Sections include history, travel, classics and an excellent choice of Scottish titles and antiquarian books, and searches are undertaken for that elusive long-lost work. A great place to browse, but not cheap.

Peter Bell

Map 3, C5. 68 West Port ☎ 0131/229 0562.

Mon–Sat 10am–5pm.

A wide selection of quality secondhand books, concentrating on the academic end of the market. Philosophy, science, literature and history are all well represented, with a healthy display of recent first editions.

Second Edition

Map 2, H3. 9 Howard Place ☎ 0131/556 9403.

Mon–Fri noon–5.30pm, Sat 9.30am–5.30pm.

A great location for an Edinburgh bookshop, opposite the house where Robert Louis Stevenson was born (8 Howard Place). There's a large collection of all sorts of secondhand books, said to number up to 20,000, and the owner's choice of jazz makes this a pleasant place to while away an afternoon.

Waterstones

128 Princes St ☎ 0131/226 2666 (**Map 4, D7**); 13–14 Princes St ☎ 0131/556 3034 (**Map 4, K6**); and 83 George St ☎ 0131/225 3436 (**Map 4, E6**).

Daily: varying hours.

The customarily tasteful Waterstones recipe of browser-friendly shops. Huge ranges in most subjects, and particularly good for Scottish books, both fiction and non-fiction. *Starbucks Coffee* have a café around the first-floor bay window of the branch at 128 Princes St, with great views over Princes Street Gardens to the Castle.

Word Power

Map 2, I5. 43 West Nicolson St ☎ 0131/662 9112.

Mon–Fri 10am–6pm, Sat 10.30am–6pm.

Small, well-laid-out radical bookshop close to the University, with titles on feminism, gay and lesbian studies, ecology, politics and black studies. Good general literature section, with a healthy input from small independent publishers.

CLOTHES

The usual rack of high street **clothes stores** can be found on Princes Street and in large shopping malls, but for something a bit different, it's worth checking out some of the **secondhand shops**, where you should be able to find anything from ball gowns to kitsch-wear for that Seventies disco.

Wm Armstrong

313 Cowgate ☎ 0131/556 6521 (**Map 3, H3**); 81–83 Grassmarket ☎ 0131/220 5557 (**Map 3, D4**); 64 Clerk St ☎ 0131/667 3056 (**Map 2, I5**). Mon–Fri 10am–5.30pm, Sat 10am–6pm, Sun noon–6pm.

The biggest of Edinburgh's secondhand clothes shops, selling a vast range of garb, of both refined and dubious taste. Take your pick from velvet or leather coats and jackets, denim shirts, jackets and trousers, and just about any other style and cut of the last fifty years.

Jenners

Map 4, I6. 48 Princes St ☎ 0131/225 2442. Mon, Wed, Fri & Sat 9am–5.30pm, Tues 9.30am–5.30pm, Thurs 9am–7.30pm.

Edinburgh's most prestigious department store is stocked with luxury items of every shape and size. There are racks of men's and women's designer-label fashions, as well as a fantastic food hall and a sumptuous selection of toys and gifts.

CLOTHES

271

Paddy Barrass
Map 3, C4. 15 Grassmarket
☎ 0131/226 3087.
Mon–Fri noon–6pm, Sat
10.30am–5.30pm.
Small establishment selling
vintage items such as clothing
from the Victorian and later
eras, including nightshirts,
kilts and dinner jackets. Also
on offer are small linen and
lace items, many of which are
displayed on the walls for
inspection.

Tiso
115–123 Rose St ☎ 0131/225
9486 (**Map 4, E6**); 41
Commercial St, Leith
☎ 0131/554 0804 (**Map 6, F3**).
Mon, Wed, Fri & Sat
9.30am–5.30pm, Tues
10am–7.30pm, Thurs
9.30am–7.30pm, Sun
noon–5pm.
Biggest city-centre selection
of good-quality outdoor gear,
including waterproof jackets,
boots, and more gadgets than
a team of sherpas could carry.
Also stocks maps, outdoor
books and ski-wear. The spacious Leith branch has a
walking track for trying out
boots.

SCOTTISH CRAFTS AND CLOTHING

Standard Scottish **tartans** and **woollens** can be found in
many outlets on the Royal Mile and Princes Street, but it's
worth looking out for the more interesting and better-qual-
ity shops found nearby. Specialist crafts and jewellery shops
aren't that common, which is disappointing given the
amount of tat sold off every day on the Royal Mile.

The Cashmere Store
2 St Giles Street ☎ 0131/225
5178 (**Map 3, E8**); 67 George St
☎ 0131/226 4861 (**Map 4, F5**).
Mon–Sat 10am–5.30pm.
Elegant if expensive cashmere

garments by top Scots designers, as paraded on catwalks in
Europe's most fashionable
cities and sold in chic outlets
around the world.

Clanranald Trading Post
Map 3, I8. 189 Canongate
℡ 0131/558 9191.
Daily 10am–5.30pm.
Where to stock up on *Braveheart*-style memorabilia from broadswords to bag-pipes, and they'll even teach you how to use them.

Clarksons
Map 3, D4. 87 West Bow
℡ 0131/225 8141.
Mon–Sat 10am–5pm.
Respected jeweller (there's a workshop immediately above the shop) selling modern Celtic designs and a nice mix of classic and contemporary styles.

Dickson & MacNaughton
Map 4, F6. 21 Frederick St
℡ 0131/225 4218.
Mon–Sat 9am–5.30pm.
Outfitter of tweeds and green wellies to the huntin', fishin' and shootin' set.

Geoffrey (Tailor)
Map 3, G2. 57–59 High St
℡ 0131/557 0256.
Mon–Sat 9am–5.30pm, Sun 10am–5pm.

One of the best of the Royal Mile Highland outfitters, and the place to go if you need to hire or buy a kilt. Tweed and tartan wear for men and women is made on the premises, and various Scottish gifts also on offer.

Kinloch Anderson
Map 6, F3. Corner of Commercial and Dock streets, Leith ℡ 0131/555 1390.
Mon–Sat 9am–5.30pm.
Set in a large warehouse in Leith, this is one of the best suppliers for made-to-mea-sure Highland wear, includ-ing kilts and full dress outfits. Also hires out Highland dress for formal wear.

National Museum of Scotland Shop
Map 3, E5. Chambers St
℡ 0131/247 4422.
Mon–Sat 10am–5pm, Sun noon–5pm.
As well as souvenirs and post-cards, the shop inside the National Museum for Scotland (free entry) stocks an impressive range of high-quality and unusual hand-

made modern crafts from around Scotland, including jewellery and basketwork.

Ness Clothing
Map 3, E8. 367 High St ⊤ 0131/226 5227.
Daily: Oct–April 10.30am–5.30pm; May–Sept 10am–7pm.
Alongside all the woollen-mill outlets offering dull, chunky jumpers, Ness sells a refreshingly upbeat, contem-porary collection of modern Scottish designer knitwear.

Number Two
Map 2, G4. 2 St Stephen Place, Stockbridge ⊤ 0131/225 6257.
Mon–Sat 10am–5.30pm.
Innovative and original Scottish knitwear design: jer-seys, dresses, hats and scarves in bright, unusual patterns, as well as traditional Fair Isle jumpers.

MUSIC

A wide range of mainstream music is available at branches of the **Virgin Megastore** at 131 Princes St and **HMV** in the St James Centre. For something more unusual, try one of the shops listed below.

Avalanche
17 West Nicolson St ⊤ 0131/668 2374 (**Map 2, H8**); 63 Cockburn St ⊤ 0131/225 3939 (**Map 3, F2**); 28 Lady Lawson St ⊤ 0131/228 1939 (**Map 3, A5**).
Mon–Sat 10am–6pm, Sun (West Nicolson St only) noon–6pm.
Three busy shops traditionally specializing in indie stuff, but nowadays also moving into the massive dance market. New and secondhand, with lots of bargains, especially in the West Nicolson Street branch, for anyone prepared to spend some time digging around.

Blackfriars Music Shop
Map 3, H3. 49 Blackfriars St ⊤ 0131/557 3090.
Mon–Sat 9.30am–5.30pm.

Welcoming and entertaining folk music shop, down a side-street off the Royal Mile. CDs, cassettes, sheet music, instruments and concert tickets, as well as lessons on instruments from the fiddle to the bodhran.

Coda

Map 3, E3. 12 Bank St
℡ 0131/622 7246.
Mon–Sat 9.30am–5.30pm, Sun noon–4pm.
Good selection of contemporary Scottish folk and roots music, with helpful staff.

Fopp

Map 3, F2. 55 Cockburn St
℡ 0131/220 0133.
Mon–Sat 9.30am–7pm, Sun 11am–6pm.
Good, broad range of cutting-edge and mainstream sounds, in rather more hip surroundings than the vast high street stores.

McAlister Matheson Music

Map 3, A5. 1 Grindlay St
℡ 0131/228 3827.
Mon–Wed 9.30am–7pm, Thurs & Fri 9.30am–7.30pm, Sat

9am–5.30pm, Sun 1–5pm.
The most pleasant and informed place to buy classical CDs in Edinburgh, with a notable selection of jazz and Scottish folk as well.

Underground Solu'shun

Map 3, F2. 9 Cockburn St
℡ 0131/226 2242.
Mon–Sat 10am–6pm, Sun 1–5pm.
On the city's best street for offbeat record shops, this is a great place for house, garage, techno and drum'n'bass vinyl, as well as info about the hottest clubbing venues in town.

Vinyl Villains

Map 2, I4. 5 Elm Row
℡ 0131/558 1170.
Mon–Fri 10.15am–6pm, Sat 10.15am–5.30pm, Sun noon–4pm.
Sizeable store still stubbornly clinging on to its core stock of secondhand records, but now moving with the times and selling CDs and all sorts of odd memorabilia. The stock is dominated by rock music, with a good range of old punk singles.

MUSIC

FOOD AND DRINK

On hot summer days, there are plenty of places to pick up tasty sandwiches and snacks for an impromptu **picnic** in one of the city's many open spaces. Some of the high-quality local delis, as well as specialists in everything from vegan foods to haggis, are listed below. For those in search of top local organic produce, **farmers' markets** take place on Johnston Terrace (Map 3, A4), usually on the first and third Saturdays of every month.

Charles MacSween & Co

Map 1, E4. Dryden Rd, Bilston Glen, Loanhead ⊤ 0131/440 2555.

Mon–Fri 9am–5pm.

Makers of the finest local haggis, Scotland's national dish. It's something of an acquired taste, though undoubtedly worth sampling, and there's even a passable vegetarian version with kidney beans and lentils instead of meat. You can buy it from the factory in the southeastern suburbs of Edinburgh, or look for the brand name in various outlets around town, such as the Food Hall in Jenners (see p.271), or Peckhams, 155–159 Bruntsfield Place (Map 2, G6).

Crombie's

Map 2, H4. 97–101 Broughton St ⊤ 0131/557 0111.

Mon–Thurs 8am–6pm, Fri 8am–7pm, Sat 8am–5pm.

Butchers selling local organic meat, though their specialities are sausages with imaginative ingredients such as wild boar or pork, mango and apple, as well as tasty meat and game pies.

Iain Mellis

30 Victoria St ⊤ 0131/226 6215 (**Map 3, D3**); 6 Bakers Place, Stockbridge ⊤ 0131/225 6566 (**Map 2, G4**); and 205 Bruntsfield Place ⊤ 0131/447 7414 (**Map 1, D5**).

Mon–Sat 9.30am–6pm.

Wooden shelves and fridges piled high with rounds and

wedges of delicious farm-house cheeses from all over Britain and Ireland, plus a few specially imported from the continent. The smells alone are wonderful, and the taste will make you swear off plastic supermarket cheese for ever. Also stocks various choice deli items such as salamis, freshly roasted coffee and vats of olive oil.

Lupe Pintos

Map 2, G6. 24 Leven St ⓣ 0131/228 6241.
Mon–Sat 10am–6pm.
Fabulous shop offering Spanish and Mexican delica-cies and mouth-stinging chilli with everything. Buy a sand-wich filled with Spanish cheese or guacamole and some Mexican beer and chill out on Bruntsfield Links just round the corner. If you're really thirsty, you could choose from the big selection of tequila, with prices rang-ing from £13 to £35.

Nature's Gate

Map 2, I5. 83 Clerk St ⓣ 0131/668 2067.
Mon–Sat 10am–7pm, Sun

noon–4pm.
Vegetarian and vegan delights next to the Queen's Hall and close to the Meadows. Organic wines and beers, a big range of Japanese macro-biotic food and all sorts of goodies for anyone on a spe-cial diet, whether sugar-, salt- or gluten-free. Plenty of choice also for lunches and snacks. *Isabel's Café* in the basement serves similarly tasty food.

Real Foods

37 Broughton St ⓣ 0131/557 1911 (**Map 4, L1**); and 8 Brougham St ⓣ 0131/228 1201 (**Map 2, H5**).
Mon–Fri 9am–6pm, Sat 9am–5.30pm, Sun 11am–5pm.
The place to stock up on dried fruits, cereals, spices and a good selection of organic fruit and veg. For more immediate pleasures, sandwiches, snacks and all kinds of refreshing drinks are available, including organic beers and wines. Also sells numerous health products. Don't miss the notice board for an insight into alternative Edinburgh.

FOOD AND DRINK

Royal Mile Whiskies
Map 3, E8. 379–381 High St
ⓣ 0131/225 3383.
Mon–Sat 10am–6pm.
Solve all your gift problems in
this specialist shop opposite St
Giles, with everything the
whisky enthusiast could ever
need. Recent and vintage
malt or blended whisky in
bottles and miniatures.
Smoked salmon and haggis
are also on offer.

William Cadenhead
Map 3, I8. 172 Canongate
ⓣ 0131/556 5864.
Mon–Sat 10am–5pm.
Dedicated and longstanding
whisky retailer selling single
malts from all over Scotland
as well as special and much-
sought-after bottlings under
its own shop label.

Valvona and Crolla
Map 2, I4. 19 Elm Row, Leith
Walk ⓣ 0131/556 6066.
Mon–Wed & Sat 8.30am–6pm,
Thurs & Fri 8.30am–7pm.
The finest Scottish Italian deli
anywhere, now ninety years
old, this is full of wallet-emp-
tying Italian wonders: fresh
bread, oozing cheeses, pasta
sauces and a huge selection of
wine. The wonderful choice
has been further enhanced by
the arrival of quality vegetables, fresh from the Italian
markets. Regular wine tast-
ings and cookery demonstra-
tions, as well as a café at the
back.

FOOD AND DRINK

The Edinburgh Festival

For the best part of August, Scotland's capital is completely transformed by the Edinburgh Festival. Every available performance space – from the city's grandest concert halls to pub courtyards – plays host to a packed programme of cultural entertainment, ranging from high drama to base comedy. The streets fill with buskers, hustlers, circus acts and craft stalls, and the capital's population swells to twice its normal size as tourists, celebrities, performers, media types and festival-goers throng the streets. Pubs and restaurants stay open later, posters plaster every vertical space, and the atmosphere in the centre of town takes on a slightly surreal, vital buzz.

The Edinburgh Festival is actually an umbrella term which encompasses different festivals taking place at around the same time in the city, principally the **Edinburgh International Festival** and the much larger **Edinburgh Festival Fringe**, but also **Film**, **Book**, **Jazz and Blues** and **Television** festivals, the **Military Tattoo** on the Castle Esplanade, and the **Edinburgh Mela**, a Southeast Asian festival normally held over the first weekend in September.

FINDING OUT WHAT'S ON

In addition to each festival's own programme (as detailed in this chapter), various publications give information about what's on day-by-day during the Festival. Produced daily by the Fringe Office, The Guide gives a chronological listing of virtually every Fringe show scheduled for that day. It's available free from the Office and hundreds of other spots around Edinburgh. Of the local newspapers, the best coverage is in The Scotsman, which issues an excellent daily Festival supplement; their reviews and star-rating system carry a lot of weight. The Herald, published in Glasgow, also has good if slightly detached coverage. Most London-based newspapers print Festival news and reviews, notably The Guardian, which publishes a daily Festival supplement, available only in Edinburgh. For a local view, the Edinburgh Evening News provides a no-nonsense round-up of news and Festival issues. The List, a locally produced arts and entertainment guide, comes out weekly during the Festival and manages to combine comprehensive coverage with a reliably on-the-pulse sense of what's hot and what's not. It's sold in newsagents throughout the city, and costs £2.20.

There's also Festival coverage on radio, TV and the internet. Radio Scotland (94.3FM and 810MW) and BBC2 TV cover the shiny end of the Festival spectrum with informed specialized arts shows. Radio Forth (97.3FM), Edinburgh's independent local radio station, is much less highbrow and likes to broadcast the latest Festival news and gossip. The Fringe's useful website (ⓦ www.edfringe.com) provides updates and listings as well as hosting a message board and a useful list of links to other online Festival stuff. From the World Art stage in Princes Street Gardens, live and recorded highlights are transmitted over the web (ⓦ www.worldart.com), on cable TV and sometimes via satellite link-up with locations outside Edinburgh, including a big screen in London's Covent Garden.

The Festival came into being in 1947, when, driven by a desire for postwar reconciliation and escape from austerity, the Viennese-born former manager of the Glyndebourne Opera, Rudolf Bing, invited a host of distinguished musicians from the war-ravaged countries of central Europe to perform in Edinburgh. At the same time, eight theatre groups turned up in the city, uninvited, performing in an unlikely variety of local venues; the next year a critic dubbed their enterprise "the fringe of the official festival drama", and the name and the spirit of the Fringe was born. Nowadays, the Festival is by some margin the largest arts event in the world, and remains one of Edinburgh's biggest draws.

For the visitor, the sheer volume of the Festival's output can be mind-boggling: virtually every branch of arts and entertainment is represented somewhere, and world-famous stars mix with pub singers in the daily lineup. It can be a struggle to find accommodation, get hold of the tickets you want, book a table in a restaurant or simply get from one side of town to another; you can end up seeing something truly dire, or something mind-blowing; you'll inevitably try to do too much, or stay out too late, or spend too much money – but then again, most Festival veterans will tell you that if you don't experience most of these things then you haven't really done the Festival.

The useful website ⓦ www.edinburghfestivals.co.uk acts as a gateway to the home pages of most of Edinburgh's main festivals, including those that take place outside August.

Note that dates, venues, names, star acts, happening bars and burning issues in the Festival change from one year to the next. This **unpredictable nature** is one of Edinburgh Festival's greatest charms, however, so while the information given in this chapter will help you get to grips with

THE EDINBURGH FESTIVAL

many aspects of the event, always be prepared for — indeed, enjoy — the unexpected.

Dates for the various Festivals vary from year to year: the International Festival runs during the final three weeks in August, while the three weeks of the Fringe culminates on the last weekend in August, traditionally an English (but, confusingly, not a Scottish) Bank Holiday weekend. The Fringe now tends to get going earlier in August with "Week 0", and in recent years the Jazz and Blues Festival has got the season underway in late July.

EDINBURGH INTERNATIONAL FESTIVAL

The legacy of Rudolf Bing's Glyndebourne connections ensured that, for many years, the **Edinburgh International Festival** (sometimes called the "Official Festival") was dominated by opera. Although a broader cultural mix of international theatre, ballet, dance and classical music was introduced in the 1980s, it's still very much a **highbrow** event, and forays into populist territory remain rare. However, organizers respond to the inevitable charges of cultural elitism by pointing to healthy box-office returns.

The International Festival attracts truly international stars, such as actress Vanessa Redgrave and conductor Simon Rattle, along with some of the world's finest orchestras and opera, theatre and ballet companies. Performances commonly take place at the city's larger **venues**, such as the Usher Hall (Map 2, G5) and the Festival Theatre (Map 3, G5), and while **ticket prices** at the top end balloon over £40, it is possible to see shows for £10 or less. The most popular events, however, are frequently sold out only a few days after tickets go on sale.

FESTIVAL FIREWORKS

The most popular single event in the Festival is the dramatic **Fireworks Concert**, held late at night on the final Saturday of the International Festival: the Scottish Chamber Orchestra belts out pop classics from the Ross Bandstand in Princes Street Gardens, accompanied by a spectacular fireworks display high up above the ramparts of the Castle. Unless you want a seat right by the orchestra, you don't need a **ticket** for this event: hundreds of thousands of people view the display from various vantage points throughout the city, the prime spots being Princes Street, Northbridge, Calton Hill or Inverleith Park and the Botanic Gardens by Stockbridge.

The International Festival's headquarters are at **The Hub** (Map 3, C8; see p.36) on the Royal Mile. Open year-round, the building houses an information centre and ticket office for the International Festival and various other events throughout the year. For further **information**, including the annual Festival programme – released in the spring – contact The Hub, Edinburgh's Festival Centre, Castlehill, Royal Mile, Edinburgh EH1 2NE (℡0131/473 2000, ⓦwww.eif.co.uk/thehub).

EDINBURGH FESTIVAL FRINGE

Even standing alone from its sister festivals, the **Edinburgh Festival Fringe** is easily the world's largest arts gathering, and while the headlining names at the International Festival reinforce the Festival's cultural credibility, it is the Fringe which dominates Edinburgh every August, giving the city its unique buzz. Each year sees over 15,000 performances from over 700 companies, with more than 12,000 participants from all over the world. There are something in the region of 1500 shows every day, round the clock, in 200 venues around the city.

For the first three decades of its existence, the Fringe was a fairly intimate affair, dominated by drama and peopled largely by graduating Oxbridge students and talent-spotting producers (often Oxbridge graduates themselves). The Fringe ballooned in the late 1970s as other forms of entertainment established themselves, notably new comedy, which over the next quarter of a century became almost synonymous with the event. Nowadays, the Fringe is *the* place where artists of every conceivable description come to get discovered or re-launched, and audiences can expect to see glimpses of the household names of today and tomorrow.

The first **Fringe Programme** appeared in 1951, the bright idea of a local printer. A single sheet of paper then, it's now a fat magazine crammed with information on most, though not all, participating shows. In 1959, the **Fringe Society** was founded by participants to provide basic marketing and co-ordination between events. Crucially, no artistic control was imposed on those who wanted to produce a show, a defining element of the Fringe which continues to this day – anyone who can afford the registration fee can take part. This means that the shows range from the inspired to the diabolical, and ensures a highly competitive atmosphere, in which one bad review in a prominent publication means box-office disaster. Many unknowns rely on self-publicity, taking to the streets to perform highlights from their show, or pressing leaflets into the hands of every passer-by. Performances go on round the clock: if so inclined, you could sit through twenty shows in a day.

PRACTICALITIES

The full Fringe **programme** is usually available in June from the Festival Fringe Office, Box YQ, 180 High St, EH1 1QS; you can also order a copy from the Fringe Programme Hotline (℡0907/159 2002) – calls from the UK cost approximately £2 to cover postage and packaging. Full listings are also posted on the Fringe's extensive website, ⓦwww.edfringe.com. Postal and telephone **bookings** for shows can be made immediately after the programme is released, while during the Festival itself, tickets are sold at the Fringe Box Office, 180 High Street (Map 3, E8; daily 10am–7pm; ℡0131/226 0000), the venue itself, or at various locations around the city – in recent years, James Thin Booksellers at 53–59 South Bridge (Map 3, G4), Waterstones at 83 George St (Map 4, E6) and HMV, 93 Princes St (Map 4, C8).

Ticket prices for most Fringe shows start at £6, and average from £9 to £12 at the main venues, with the better-known acts going for even more. Although some theatre and music acts can be longer, most performances are scheduled to run for an hour, which means that you can easily spend upwards of £50 on admission alone in the course of a hard day's festivalling.

THEATRE

Comedy grabs more headlines, but **theatre** still makes up the bulk of the Fringe. Right from the start, innovative, controversial, wonderful and sometimes downright terrible productions have characterized the drama content. In the late 1970s, director Ken Campbell's 22-hour epic *The Warp* was the toast of the town, while the play *Rooting* at the Traverse Theatre featured several pigs in its cast, and a six-

A FEW FESTIVAL SURVIVAL TIPS

1. Everyone else is completely bewildered too. Trust your judgement and ride your luck.

2. Accept that you're not going to see everything that sounds, or looks, or other people say is, good; go and see something rather than spending two hours frozen by indecision. It's part of the Festival experience to sit through a complete turkey of a show while the one you nearly went to gets rave reviews, is sold out for three weeks, goes on national tour and spawns a hilarious, groundbreaking TV series.

3. Don't try and see too much. Sometimes the best show is watching the world go by, and Edinburgh has plenty of non-Festival attractions, some of them free, such as climbing up Arthur's Seat and looking down on the madness below.

4. August weather in Edinburgh is notoriously fickle. Be prepared for both rain and sunshine.

5. Set a budget in advance and try to stick to it. Allow for outrageous temptations, because there will be plenty, and some of them will be worth it.

6. Don't give yourself a stiff neck starspotting – if they're that famous you'll see them on TV, and there are plenty more interesting people and places to look at.

7. Don't bother going to see anything with "searing" in the blurb. It will be ghastly.

8. Don't take front row seats in comedy shows unless you don't mind being material for the act.

9. Try to sleep at some point, even if it's during the day. The Festival works on LA time: if you try and stay on British Summertime you'll miss half the fun.

10. All sorts of people will offer you advice, recommendations, ten survival tips, that sort of thing. Ignore them all and remember tip no. 1.

hour Cambridge-student production called *The Burning Of Carthage* was hailed as the worst play in the Fringe's history. More recently, a trilogy of plays called *Glad*, *Mad* and *Bad*, involving local homeless men, won awards; and in 1998, *Soldiers*, featuring real-life fighters, was cancelled after one of the cast was recalled to active service in Bosnia. Content ranges from Molière to Berkoff, from Shakespeare to Beckett (someone, somewhere, always puts on *Krapp's Last Tape*). There are numerous student productions, as well as the appearance of Scottish favourites such as playwright Liz Lochhead or actor Russell Hunter. Unusual **venues** add spice to some productions: Inchcolm Island in the Firth of Forth has been used to stage *Macbeth*, while *2001: A Space Odyssey* was performed to an audience sitting in a Hillman Avenger. Current favourite venues include the back-room café at Valvona and Crolla's Italian delicatessen on Elm Row, and the Royal Botanic Garden in Inverleith.

One way of saving money on tickets is to look out for **two-for-one ticket offers**, usually advertised at venue box offices or in newspapers. In recent years, most shows performing in Week 0 of the Fringe in early August have also offered tickets on a two-for-one basis.

COMEDY

Comedy is the Fringe's success story. Until the 1970s the Festival was a rite of passage from the Cambridge Footlights or Oxford Revue to the BBC or the London stage, with teams such as Beyond the Fringe and Monty Python appearing in Edinburgh before making their big break on TV. Although this still happens, the arena opened out in the 1980s with an explosion of talent and opportunities for

MAKING IT BIG AT THE FESTIVAL

There's hardly a serious entertainer worth their salt who hasn't played the Edinburgh Festival. Best known are the satirists of *Beyond the Fringe*, the 1960 Edinburgh revue which launched the careers of Peter Cook, Jonathan Miller, Alan Bennett and Dudley Moore. Miller and Cook had come fresh from the Cambridge Footlights; other Footlighters have included the entire casts of Monty Python and The Goodies, as well as David Frost, Germaine Greer, Richard Harris, Douglas Adams, Clive James, Griff Rhys-Jones, Stephen Fry and Emma Thompson. From Oxford came Rowan Atkinson and Mel Smith, while Manchester University graduates Ben Elton, Rik Mayall and Adrian Edmondson were first seen in Edinburgh in a revue called *Twentieth Century Coyote*. They teamed up with a duo called The Outer Limits (Nigel Planer and Peter Richardson) to form The Young Ones.

Comedian Arthur Smith first attracted attention in the student revue *Hamalongayorick*, while Robbie Coltrane was seen in the Traverse's original *Slab Boys Trilogy* long before fame struck. Other celebs who got their break at the Fringe include Paul Merton, Jo Brand, Steve Coogan, Frank Skinner and drag queen Lily Savage, while various soap stars have arrived in Edinburgh to reinvent themselves, including Tom Watt (*Eastenders*), Dannii Minogue (*Home and Away*) and the most successful of the lot, Mark Little (*Neighbours*).

EDINBURGH FESTIVAL FRINGE

selling it, and the Fringe became a hothouse for a generation of new comics once known as "**alternative**" and now
mostly working for the BBC or Channel 4: performers
such as Stephen Fry, Jeremy Hardy, Steve Coogan and
Eddie Izzard all arrived with shows, and saw their careers
take off shortly afterwards. At the same time, the success of
the **Perrier Award** for new comedy heralded a symbiosis

between commercial sponsors and performers which had previously only been seen in sport.

Aside from a few variety artists, the entire UK comedy scene – plus many international acts – can be found in Edinburgh at some point during the Fringe season. Artists range from household names to wannabes who stand in line for their chance to tell a few shaggy dog stories at smaller stages and open-mic slots around town. The bigger names are booked by the Assembly Rooms, Pleasance or Gilded Balloon, while Edinburgh's own comedy club, *The Stand* (Map 4, J3), has become an increasingly viable alternative. Look out for "Best of the Fest" shows, held at the main venues, featuring a selection of the year's big names, or live recordings of BBC radio shows such as *Loose Ends* at the Pleasance.

MUSIC

While **classical music** fans will no doubt find something to drool over in the International Festival programme, the Fringe also offers a wealth of reasonably priced **recitals** and other **concerts** to choose from. Near-professional standards are reached by the **Rehearsal Orchestra**, which performs a two-week season of classical music concerts – possibly the oldest Fringe music event, running since 1956. Established for top amateur musicians and aspirant top-grade orchestral performers, the orchestra often plays the same pieces that are being performed in the International Festival – hence the name "Rehearsal" Orchestra. The annual **Festival of Youth Orchestras** at Tollcross, featuring orchestras from around the world, also sets high standards, and music lovers with a sense of humour should check to see if there's an appearance by the **Really Terrible Orchestra**, a recent Fringe sensation which brings together music-loving amateur players – often lawyers and doctors – who are given the chance to live out their dream. Despite their best efforts (and they do rehearse), the result is, well, really terrible.

Folk, **roots** and **world** music are always well represented. In past years, larger venues such as *Café Graffiti*, the *Famous Grouse House* and the *Acoustic Music Centre* provided a concentrated focus for this type of attraction, contributing greatly to music's overall rise in prominence within the Fringe over the past decade or so. In some years, one venue – such as one of those mentioned above – takes on the mantle of the Fringe's main roots venue, although the tendency has been for these genres to become more integrated into mixed programming at the major venues. At the more intimate end of the market, the usual places for folk musicians to congregate are the *Royal Oak* (1 Infirmary Street; Map 3, G4), *Whistlebinkies* (4–6 South Bridge; Map 3, G3), *On The Mound* (2–3 North Bank St; Map 3, D3) and the *Waverley Bar* (1 St Mary's St; Map 3, H2). A travelling venue with a strong musical lineup, The Famous Spiegeltent (a wooden Victorian circus tent) has parked in recent years above Princes Mall, near Waverley Station at the East End of Princes Street, where it plays host to a wide variety of performances from big bands to small duos, with a slight bias towards Australian acts.

Standing out in the lists of **rock** and **pop** events is the relative newcomer **Festival Flux**, a festival within a Festival which has brought serious credibility to the Fringe music scene, via performances from the likes of Pulp, Nick Cave, Ivor Cutler, Howard Marks, The Fall, Orbital and Ken Kesey. The Fringe has also witnessed the rise of the independent non-folk-singing **songwriter** as a performing force, with the success of shows by established artists such as Tom Robinson, Ray Davies, John Otway and Paul Kelly.

Though the greatest concentration of **jazz and blues** now takes place in early August (see p.296), late greats like Rory Gallagher and British blues' founding father Alexis

Korner stormed the Fringe in their day, while the hardiest perennial of all is gruff-voiced Scots bluesman and Hollywood character actor Tam White, whose stomping shows with the Celtic Groove Connection remain the most sought-after tickets in town.

DANCE AND PHYSICAL THEATRE

As with classical music, mainstream ballet tends to be the preserve of the International Festival. However, the Fringe attracts a small but entertaining programme of contemporary **dance** ranging from easy-watching box-office smashes like *Tap Dogs*, *Gumboots* and Harlem blues-tapper Will Gaines, through cutting-edge companies such as The Kosh to full-on participation shows by the likes of The Jiving Lindyhoppers. Companies like Trestle Theatre or Jim Rose's Circus blur the line between physical theatre, drama, circus and comedy, while events such as the Bangladesh Festival of Food and Culture at Leith's *Raj* restaurant, which took place during the 1999 Fringe, honoured the role of dance alongside food in traditional celebration ceremonies. The big-name dance shows are inevitably put on in the **venues** with larger stages, including the Playhouse Theatre (Map 2, I4) and George Square Theatre (Map 2, H5); among the smaller venues most focus will inevitably be on Dance Base, the new dance studio and venue in the Grassmarket (see p.244), which has already attracted some of the world's most important dance groups.

ART

When the entire capital is swarming with performing artists, it's sometimes hard for **visual artists** to get themselves noticed. Fortunately, Fringe art has an honourable tradition of providing some quiet space and respite from the

THE FRINGE – A BRIEF GUIDE TO WHERE IT HAPPENS

The four **main Fringe venues** are The Assembly Rooms, The Pleasance, The Gilded Balloon and the relative newcomer known as "C". Venue complexes rather than single spaces, the latter three colonize a growing collection of nearby spaces for the duration of the Festival. If you're new to the Fringe, these are all safe bets for decent shows and a bit of starspotting.

The atmosphere at the **Pleasance** (Map 3, I4) is usually less frenetic than at the other venues, with classy drama and whimsical appearances by media stars such as Radio 4's *Just A Minute* team and Channel 4 icon Richard Whiteley sitting easily alongside the wackier acts. The **Assembly Rooms** (Map 4, G6) provides a grand setting for top-of-the-range drama by companies such as the RSC and big-name music and comedy acts, while the Fringe's premier comedy venue, **The Gilded Balloon** (Map 3, G4) hosts the *Late and Live* show, crammed with TV performers and wannabes competing to be noticed.

"C" venues, which take their name from their former Fringe

frenetic festival atmosphere. Special festival exhibitions are mounted at many of the city's leading galleries, while visitors such as the Glasgow Printmakers Workshop literally set up shop in whatever vacant premises they can find in central Edinburgh. New technology has inspired some exciting interactive shows, and multimedia multi-arts are alive and well – most successfully in recent years at the *Bongo Club* (Map 3, I1) in New Street.

CHILDREN'S SHOWS

Children's shows at the Fringe range from those performed by people who want to (and sometimes do) work in children's television, to those which make their young

programme number, 100, are widely scattered across the centre of the city (and numbered C1, C2, etc), with their headquarters located at Adam House in Chambers Street (Map 3, G4).

Other venues worth a visit include Komedia Southside at 117 Nicolson Street (Map 2, I5), the temporary home of the Brighton-based cabaret venue. Nearby, the Queen's Hall (Map 2, I5) mounts high-quality jazz, blues and classical concerts, and the George Square Theatre (Map 2, H5) always has a good mainstream programme. Long a champion of new drama, the Traverse Theatre (Map 2, G5) combines avant-garde and slick presentation both in the theatre itself and in its bar. Less glam, but with an excellent lineup of thought-provoking drama, is the Theatre Workshop (Map 2, G4). Small-scale productions from Diverse Attractions at Riddles Court in the Lawnmarket, (Map 3, D8) give a real flavour of the spirit of Fringes past, while among the best of the late-nighters is Underbelly (Map 3, E3), in the vaults below the library on George IV Bridge.

audience members want to run away and join the theatre. The best of the latter are the memorable, award-winning musicals put on by the National Youth Music Theatre. Children's shows also take in puppetry, clowns, pantomime, magic and straightforward drama, and are staged mostly in the mornings.

EDINBURGH INTERNATIONAL FILM FESTIVAL

The **Edinburgh International Film Festival** is the longest continually running film festival in the world, having first been staged, like the International Festival and the Fringe, in 1947. It can also claim a distinguished history at the cutting edge of cinema, premiering American block-

EDINBURGH INTERNATIONAL FILM FESTIVAL

busters from directors like Stephen Spielberg and Woody Allen, discovering low-budget smashes such as *My Beautiful Laundrette* and *Strictly Ballroom*, and introducing serious contenders such as the *Blair Witch Project*, *The Full Monty* and *Billy Elliot*.

Held over the last two weeks of August, and normally finishing at around the same time as the Fringe, the Film Festival offers the opportunity to see some of the year's big cinema hits before they go on general release, along with a varied and exciting bill of reissued or reworked movies. For those in the industry, it's also a vital talking-shop, with debates, seminars and workshops, and is spiced up by the attendance of Hollywood stars at the succession of glittering parties which accompany the launches. Most of the action takes place at the Filmhouse (the main venue; Map 2, G5), as well as the UGC complex at Fountain Park, Fountainbridge (Map 2, G6), the *Sheraton Hotel* on Lothian Road (Map 2, G5) and the Cameo in Home Street (Map 2, G6). A charming antidote to the large-scale business of the Film Festival is the presence of La Cinerama – one of the smallest cinemas in the world, based in the back of a truck, which parks itself as close to the action as possible.

Tickets and information are available from the Filmhouse, 88 Lothian Rd, EH3 9BZ (℡0131/228 2688, Ⓦwww.edfilmfest.org.uk). The programme usually comes out in late June.

EDINBURGH INTERNATIONAL BOOK FESTIVAL

Established in 1983, the **Edinburgh International Book Festival**, which takes place in the last two weeks of August, is one of the largest of its type in the world. A model plugfest, it's held in a tented village in the douce setting of Charlotte Square, and offers talks, readings and signings by a star-studded lineup of visiting authors as well as panel discussions and workshops on as many subjects as there are books. Well-known local writers such as Iain Banks, Ian Rankin and A.E. Kennedy are good for an appearance most years, while visitors from further afield have included Doris Lessing, Louis de Bernières, Ben Okri, John Updike and Vikram Seth. In addition, there are cook-ups by celebrity chefs promoting their latest tomes, late-night musical events with a literary flavour and numerous children's activities. An on-site café and, of course, a bookshop, ensure that all the participants' needs are met.

For further **information**, contact the Scottish Book Centre, 137 Dundee St, EH11 1BG (⊤ 0131/228 5444, ⓦ www.edbookfest.co.uk).

EDINBURGH INTERNATIONAL TELEVISION FESTIVAL

A packed schedule of lectures, seminars and parties over the peak Festival Bank Holiday weekend, the **Guardian Edinburgh International Television Festival** is essentially a closed conference, providing the British TV industry with the opportunity to do an annual stocktake. A formal agenda is set by the prestigious McTaggart Lecture, delivered each year by a senior personality in the television world; however, the real business is done in the bar of the *George Hotel*, as producers, schedulers, performers and Fringe participants who want to get in on the act network and hustle like crazy. The Television Festival's presence in Edinburgh at this time adds focus and urgency to the Fringe's sub-plot as an employment showcase – in fact the event has such a direct bearing on subsequent viewing schedules that it has been said that if a bomb dropped on George Street over the Television Festival weekend, all the TV screens in Britain would probably go dark within a few weeks.

For **further details** contact the Guardian Edinburgh International Television Festival, 2nd Floor, 24 Neal St, London WC2 9PS (℡0207/379 4519, ⓦwww.geitf.co.uk).

EDINBURGH INTERNATIONAL JAZZ AND BLUES FESTIVAL

The **Edinburgh International Jazz and Blues Festival**, which used to run concurrently with the other festivals, is now staged immediately prior to the Fringe in the first week in August, easing the city into the festival spirit with a full programme of gigs in many different locations. Just like all the other festivals, this one has grown over the years from a concentrated international summer camp to a bigger, more modern affair, reflecting the panoply of generations and styles which appear under the banner of jazz and blues. Scotland's own varied and vibrant jazz scene is always fully represented, and late-night clubs with atmosphere complement major concerts given by international stars. Past visitors have included B.B. King, Bill Wyman, Dizzy Gillespie, Dave Brubeck, Van Morrison, Carol Kidd and the Blues Band. Highlights include **Jazz On A Summer's Day**, a musical extravaganza in Princes Street Gardens; and a colourful New Orleans-style **street parade**.

The **programme** is available at the end of May from the office at 29 St Stephen's St, EH3 5AN (℡0131/225 2202, ⓦwww.jazzmusic.co.uk).

THE MILITARY TATTOO

Staged in the spectacular stadium setting of the Edinburgh Castle Esplanade, the **Military Tattoo** is the Festival showpiece most instantly recognized by tourists. An unashamed display of pomp and military pride, the Tattoo's programme of choreographed drills, massed pipe bands, historical tableaux, energetic battle re-enactments, national dancing and pyrotechnics has held audiences spellbound every year since it began over fifty years ago. The emotional climax is provided by a lone piper on the Castle battlements. Followed by a quick firework display (longer and more splendid on Sat), it's a successful formula that's barely been tampered with over the years.

Tickets, which cost between £10 and £30 depending on seat location and performance time, need to be booked well in advance, and it's advisable to take a cushion and protective rainwear. Tickets and information are available from The Tattoo Office, 32 Market St, EH1 1QB (☎0131/225 1188, ⊛www.edintattoo.co.uk).

THE EDINBURGH MELA

A festival within a festival, the **Edinburgh Mela** is an itinerant gathering held over the first weekend in September, right at the end of the Festival. Truly a people's event, it was introduced to Edinburgh in the mid-1990s by the capital's Southeast Asian community. The word "Mela" is a Sanskrit term meaning "gathering", and is used to describe many different community events and festivals on the Asian subcontinent. In Edinburgh, the Mela is about cultural diversity, and the family-oriented programme is designed to celebrate the many different cultures resident in the city. Music, dance, foods, carnivals, fashion shows, sports, children's events, crafts and a two-day careers fair for school-leavers combine in a hectic programme of events designed to see the festival season out with a bang rather than a whimper. Further **details** from The Edinburgh Mela, 14 Forth St (☎0131/557 1400, ⊛www.edinburgh-mela.co.uk).

Calendar of events

T hough the Edinburgh Festival is a cultural binge of massive proportions, it doesn't quite leave the city spent for the other eleven months of the year. In addition to the regular diet of arts and entertainment, there are a variety of special annual events, including a famously riotous Hogmanay (New Year's Eve) party and international sporting fixtures, as well as festivals of folk music, science and beer-drinking.

JANUARY

Turner Watercolours

January (when the light is weakest) is the only month of the year when you can see the splendid collection of Turner watercolours owned by the National Gallery on the Mound (see p.89). Entrance is free.

Burns' Night

25 January is the date of birth of Scotland's national bard, Robert Burns. Suppers involving haggis, whisky, speeches and poetry recitations are traditionally held on or around this date; if you haven't secured an invitation, a handful of restaurants put on a special Burns' Night menu.

FEBRUARY/MARCH

Six Nations Rugby Internationals

Scotland's rugby union team plays in the annual Six Nations competition against England, France, Ireland, Italy and Wales. In any given year, matches against at least two of these countries are held at Murrayfield Stadium (Map 2, E5) in the west of the city. The ground holds around 65,000 spectators, and has a terrific atmosphere when full. Tickets for all games sell out extremely quickly; contact the Scottish Rugby Union, 7–9 Roseburn Street (☎0131/346 5000, ⓦ www.sru.org.uk).

Puppet and Animation Festival

Mainly targeted at children, this festival attracts puppet theatres from all over Europe, with shows and films put on across central Scotland in March. The main venue in Edinburgh is the Netherbow Theatre (Map 3, G8; ☎0131/ 556 9579, ⓦ www.story tellingcentre.org.uk).

APRIL

Edinburgh International Science Festival

Edinburgh has important connections with the world of science: the city is the home of John Napier, inventor of logarithms, James Clerk Maxwell, the "father of electronics", and James Hutton, founder of modern geology, as well as being the birthplace of Alexander Graham Bell, inventor of the telephone. These links helped inspire the establishment, in the mid-1980s, of the increasingly respected Edinburgh International Science Festival (☎0131/530 2001), which incorporates serious lectures on ground-breaking topics with hands-on children's events.

MAY

Beltane Fire Festival

Beltane is the name of the old Celtic Festival at the beginning of May, celebrating the arrival of spring. Held on

Calton Hill (Map 2, I4) on the night of April 30 and May 1, there's a New Agey feel to Beltane, the dominant images being fire-lighting and faces covered in woad and other colourful dyes. More conventionally, the traditional ritual for locals is to wash their faces in the dew on Arthur's Seat at dawn on May Day.

Scottish International Children's Festival

The Children's Festival (☎ 0131/225 8050) is a sort of mini-Edinburgh Festival for mini folk, with a lively line-up of book readings, magic shows, mime and puppetry in venues across the city.

JUNE

Beer Festival

The Beer Festival is held at the Caledonian Brewery, 42 Slateford Road (Map 2, F6), one of Scotland's finest independent beer-makers. Look out for their excellent 80 Shilling and award-winning

IPA (India Pale Ale), pitted against a leg-wobbling line-up of real ales from around Britain.

Gay Film Festival

Celebration of gay cinema from around the world at the Filmhouse (Map 2, G5; ☎ 0131/228 2688).

Royal Highland Show

Vast **agricultural fair** held at Ingliston, near the airport (Map 1, C3). Prize livestock and all sorts of agricultural machinery are on show, alongside displays of everything from butter-making to show-jumping. There are green wellies and Range Rovers galore, but also flat caps and shepherds' crooks (☎ 0131/335 6200).

AUGUST

The Edinburgh Festival

See the previous chapter for details of Edinburgh's world-famous, month-long series of festivals.

SEPTEMBER

Open Doors Day

A great opportunity to visit a number of historically and architecturally interesting buildings, most of which are otherwise closed to the public. In recent years, these have included private homes in the New Town, disused churches, the Central Mosque and the marvellous Signet Library. The event is normally held over one of the last two weekends in September – look out for leaflets in public buildings, or contact the Cockburn Association (☎0131/557 8686) for details.

NOVEMBER

French Film Festival

A choice selection of old favourites and new work from French cinema, held at the Filmhouse (Map 2, G5; ☎0131/228 2688).

Autumn Rugby Internationals

After the Six Nations tournament (see "February"), Scotland's rugby team plays a second batch of international matches, often taking on tourists such as Australia, South Africa and New Zealand. Tickets for the games, all played at Murrayfield, are available from the Scottish Rugby Union, 7–9 Roseburn Street (☎0131/346 5000; ⓦwww.sru.org.uk).

St Andrews Day

30 November is St Andrew's Day, commemorating Scotland's patron saint. Controversially, it isn't a public holiday, although it is the one day of the year when you can get free entrance to Edinburgh Castle to view the Honours of Scotland and the Stone of Destiny (see p.28).

DECEMBER

Capital Christmas

Edinburgh prepares for Christmas with the installation of an outdoor ice rink in Princes Street Gardens, a large ferris wheel beside the

Scott Monument, a fun–fair on Waterloo Place, a ton of bright lights stacked onto the trees along Princes Street and various Yuletide events including carol singing and a German-style craft market.

HOGMANAY

Hogmanay is the name Scots give to New Year's Eve, a celebration they have made all their own with a unique mix of tradition, hedonism, sentimentality and enthusiasm. The roots of Hogmanay are in ancient pagan festivities based around the winter solstice, which in most places gradually merged with Christmas. When hardline Scottish Protestant clerics in the sixteenth century abolished Christmas for being a Catholic mass, the Scots, not wanting to miss out on a mid-winter knees-up, instead put their energy into greeting the New Year.

Houses were cleaned from top to bottom, debts were paid and quarrels made up, and, after the bells of midnight were rung, great store was laid by welcoming good luck into your house. This still takes the form of the tradition of "first-footing" – visiting your neighbours and bearing gifts. The ideal first-foot is a tall dark-haired male carrying a bottle of whisky; women or redheads, on the other hand, bring bad luck – though no one carrying a bottle of whisky tends to be turned away these days, whatever the colour of their hair. All this neighbourly greeting meant that a fair bit of partying went on, of course, and after a while no one was expected to go to work the next day, or, if the party was that good, the day after that either. Even today, January 1 is a public holiday in the rest of the UK, but only in Scotland does the holiday extend to the next day too. In fact, right up to the 1950s Christmas was a normal working day for many people in Scotland, and Hogmanay was widely regarded as by far the more important celebration.

Edinburgh's Hogmanay

Edinburgh is one of *the* places around the world to see in the New Year, with a week-long series of events including a torch-lit procession along Princes Street and numerous late-night gigs and ceilidhs culminating in a massive street party on the evening of 31st December. These days, things are a bit more civilized than in the mid-1990s, when 300,000 people attended the celebrations leading to seriously dangerous overcrowding. This resulted in the introduction of a pass system for the street party, limiting numbers to a still busy 100,000. While this was a sensible and necessary step, it has gone hand-in-hand with a growing commercialization of the event, which rather jars with the spontaneity of the origins of the celebration. Most of the city-centre streets are closed to traffic on New Year's Eve, as big-name bands entertain the crowds from various stages and the revels build up to a massive midnight climax, when a huge fireworks display is set off above the Castle and seven other hills around the city. You can get street passes, tickets and information from The Hub (Map 3, C8; ℡ 0131/473 2000), or visit ⓦ www.edinburghshogmanay.org.

Directory

Airlines British Airways
(☎ 0845/773 3377, ⓦ www
.british-airways.com); British
European (☎ 0870/567 6676,
ⓦ www.british-european.com);
British Midland (☎ 0870/607
0555, ⓦ www.flybmi.com);
EasyJet (☎ 0870/600 0000,
ⓦ www.easyjet.com); Go (☎ 0870
/607 6543, ⓦ www.go-fly.com).

American Express 139 Princes
St (Mon–Fri 9am–5.30pm, Sat
9am–4pm; ☎ 0131/718 2501).

Banks Bank of Scotland, The
Mound (head office), 38 St
Andrew Square; Barclays, 1 St
Andrew Square; Clydesdale, 20
Hanover St; HSBC, 76 Hanover
St; Lloyds TSB, 120 George St;
NatWest, 80 George St; Royal
Bank of Scotland, 42 St Andrew
Square.

Consulates Australia, 69
George St (☎ 0131/624 3333);
Canada, 30 Lothian Rd
(☎ 0131/220 4333); Denmark,
215 Balgreen Rd (☎ 0131/337
6352); France, 11 Randolph
Crescent (☎ 0131/225 7954);
Germany, 16 Eglington Crescent
(☎ 0131/337 2323); Italy, 32
Melville St (☎ 0131/226 3631);
Netherlands, 53 George St
(☎ 0131/220 3226); Norway, 86
George St (☎ 0131/226 5701);
Poland, 2 Kinnear Rd
(☎ 0131/552 0301); Spain, 63
North Castle St (☎ 0131/220
1843); Sweden, 22 Hanover St
(☎ 0131/220 6050); Switzerland,
66 Hanover Place (☎ 0131/226
5660); USA, 3 Regent Terrace
(☎ 0131/556 8315).

Dentist The National Health
Service Line (☎ 0800/224488)

will tell you where your nearest surgery is. For emergencies go to Edinburgh Dental Institute, Lauriston Place (☎ 0131/536 4920) or the Western General Hospital, Crewe Rd South (☎ 0131/537 1338).

Football Edinburgh has two Scottish Premier Division teams, who normally play at home on alternate weekends. Heart of Midlothian (known as Hearts) play at Tynecastle Stadium, Gorgie Rd (☎ 0131/200 7201), a couple of miles west of the centre; Hibernian (or Hibs) play at Easter Road Stadium (☎ 0131/661 1895), a similar distance northeast of the centre. Between them, the two clubs dominated Scottish football in the 1950s, but neither has won more than the odd trophy since, though one or the other periodically threatens to make a major breakthrough. Tickets from £12.

Genealogical Research Scottish Genealogy Society, 15 Victoria Terrace (☎ 0131/220 3677); Scottish Roots, 16 Forth St (☎ 0131/477 8214).

Golf Edinburgh is awash with fine golf courses, but most of them are private. The best public courses (all 18-hole) are the two on the Braid Hills (☎ 0131/447 6666); others are Carrick Knowe (☎ 0131/337 1096), Craigentinny (☎ 0131/554 7501) and Silverknowes (☎ 0131/336 3843).

Hospital The Royal Infirmary, 1 Lauriston Place (☎ 0131/536 1000), has a 24hr casualty department. The Infirmary is moving, in stages, to a new location to the southeast of the centre, but the casualty department will be the last to move, some time in 2003; the above phone number will remain the same. There are also casualty departments at the Western Infirmary, Crewe Road North (☎ 0131/537 1000), and for children at the Sick Kid's hospital, Sciennes Road (☎ 0131/536 0000).

Internet The Cottage, 136 Nicolson St (daily 24hr; ☎ 0131/ 662 9216, Ⓦ www.cottagecopies .com; £1 per half hour); easyEverything, 58 Rose St (daily 24hr; ☎ 0131/220 3580; rates vary but the average is £1 per

DIRECTORY

hour); Web 13, 13 Bread St (Mon–Fri 9am–5.30pm, Thurs 9am–7pm, Sat 9am–6pm, Sun 11am–5pm; ☎0131/229 8883, ⒲www.web13.co.uk; £1 per half hour).

Laundry Capital Launderette, 208 Dalkeith Rd, Newington (☎0131/667 0825); Sundial Launderette at 7–9 East London St, Broughton (☎0131/556 2743); Tarvit Launderette, 7–9 Tarvit St, Tollcross (☎0131/229 6382).

Libraries The Central Library is on George IV Bridge (Mon–Thurs 10am–8pm, Fri 10am–5pm, Sat 9am–1pm; ☎0131/225 5584). In addition to the usual departments, there's a separate Scottish section, plus an Edinburgh Room which is a mine of information on the city. The National Library of Scotland, George IV Bridge (Mon–Fri 9.30am–8.30pm, Sat 9.30am–1pm; ☎0131/226 4531), a magnificent copyright library, is for research purposes only, although accreditation is necessary to use the facilities. There is freer access to an annex at 33 Salisbury Place

which contains the Map Room (Mon–Fri 9.30am–5pm, Sat 9.30am–1pm).

Lost property Edinburgh Airport (☎0131/333 1000); Edinburgh Police HQ (☎0131/ 311 3141); Lothian Regional Transport (☎0131/554 4494); Scotrail (☎0141/335 3276).

Opening hours and holidays
The standard **shopping hours** are Mon–Sat 9am–5.30pm, with many city-centre stores opening the same or slightly shorter hours on Sunday, and staying open till 7pm/7.30pm on Thursday evenings. Public (bank) holidays are much the same as in the rest of the UK; the exceptions are that in Scotland the August bank holiday is held on the first rather than last Monday of that month, and January 2 is a holiday whereas Easter Monday is not. In addition, the third Monday in May is a local Edinburgh holiday.

Pharmacy Boots, 48 Shandwick Place (Mon–Fri 8am–9pm, Sat 8am–7pm, Sun 10am–5pm; ☎0131/225 6757) has the longest opening hours.

Police In an emergency call 999. Otherwise contact Lothian and Borders Police HQ, Fettes Ave (℡ 0131/311 3131); or the local police stations at Gayfield Square, Broughton (℡ 0131/556 9270); Queen Charlotte St, Leith (℡ 0131/554 9350); St Leonard's St, Southside (℡ 0131/662 5000); or Torphichen Place, West End (℡ 0131/229 2323).

Post office 8–10 St James Centre (Mon 9am–5.30pm, Tues–Fri 8.30am–5.30pm, Sat 8.30am–6pm; ℡ 0845/722 3344).

Rape Crisis Centre ℡ 0131/556 9437.

Rugby Scotland's international fixtures are played at Murrayfield Stadium, a couple of miles west of the city centre. Phone the stadium on ℡ 0131/346 5000 or visit ⓦ www.sru.org.uk for advice on ticket sales, but be warned that seats can be very hard to come by for the big games.

Sports Stadium Meadowbank Sports Centre and Stadium, 139 London Rd (℡ 0131/661 5351),

is Edinburgh's main venue for most spectator and participatory sports. Facilities include an athletics track, a velodrome and indoor halls.

Swimming pools The city has one Olympic-standard modern pool, the Royal Commonwealth, 21 Dalkeith Rd (℡ 0131/667 7211), and a number of considerably older pools: Dalry Swim Centre, 29 Caledonian Crescent (℡ 0131/313 3964); Glenogle Swim Centre, 3 Glenogle Road (℡ 0131/343 6376); Portobello Swim Centre, 57 Promenade, Portobello (℡ 0131/669 6888); and Warrender Swim Centre, 6 Thirlestane Rd (℡ 0131/447 0052).

Travel agents Edinburgh Travel Centre (student and youth specialist) 3 Bristo Square (℡ 0131/668 2221); STA, 27 Forest Rd (℡ 0131/226 7747). For three- and six-day coach trips to the Highlands, try Haggis Backpackers, 11 Blackfriars St (℡ 0131/557 9393) or MacBackpackers, 105 High St (℡ 0131/558 9900).

CONTEXTS

History

Early settlement and the Middle Ages

The site of today's Edinburgh has been inhabited since the
Stone Age, with hunters and fishermen arriving in the
area around 5000 BC, followed two millennia later by
farmers and shepherds. They in turn were succeeded by
immigrant **Beaker** people from the continent, who introduced metalworking. When tribal warfare broke out in
later periods, Edinburgh's extinct volcanic hills proved useful strategic points, principal among them **Castle Rock**,
which quickly proved central to the subsequent rise of the
city. The one occupying force which chose not to make full
use of it were, strangely, the **Romans**, whose Imperial
frontier lay just to the north – they chose to build their fort
close to the seashore at Cramond.

The name of Edinburgh – in its early forms of Dunedin
or Din Eidyn ("Fort of Edin") – seems to have originated
with the local tribes of the sixth century, rather than, as was
long supposed, King Edwin of Northumbria, whose reign
predated the **Northumbrian conquest** of the Lothians in
638 AD. Edinburgh subsequently remained under the control of English-speaking Anglo-Saxons until the middle of

the tenth century, when it was abandoned to the army of King Indulf of Scotland.

Castle Rock served as the nation's **southernmost border post** until 1018, when King Malcolm I's victory over the Northumbrians established the River Tweed as the permanent frontier with England. Half a century later, under King Malcolm III and his queen Margaret, who replaced the indigenous Celtic church with Roman Catholicism, the castle became one of the main seats of the Scottish court. It was probably also around this time that a town, which was immediately given the privileged status of a **royal burgh**, first began to grow up on the sloping ridge immediately to the east of the castle.

Edinburgh's standing grew further during the reign of Malcolm's and Margaret's son, David I, who established Holyrood Abbey at the foot of the slope in 1128, and shortly afterwards granted its monks permission to found a separate burgh, known as **Canongate**. David also founded a church in honour of St Giles on the present site of the High Kirk of St Giles, and built a chapel dedicated to his mother at the highest point of Castle Rock – where it stands to this day.

Edinburgh as Scotland's capital

The **Wars of Independence** (1286–1371) were a turbulent time for Edinburgh, with the castle a prime target for any army invading from the south. During this period, it was captured in turn by the armies of English kings Henry II, Edward I, Edward II and Edward III, and each time either relinquished as part of a treaty or retaken by the Scots. King Robert the Bruce's **victory at Bannockburn** in 1314, however, won Scotland a degree of security it had seldom enjoyed before, and trade with the continent began to prosper. Bruce granted Edinburgh a new **charter** in

1329, whereby the entire municipality, rather than its individual burgesses, was regarded as a vassal of the crown. He also gave the city jurisdiction over the port of **Leith**, which was developed to take the place of the strategically vulnerable burgh of Berwick-upon-Tweed: the latter fell under English control four years later, and thereafter regularly passed backwards and forwards between the two countries. During the following century, the prosperity brought by **foreign trade** enabled the newly fortified Edinburgh to establish itself as the undisputed capital of Scotland, with a fixed royal residence, central administration and law courts replacing the previous peripatetic setup.

Renaissance and Reformation

Under King James IV, the city enjoyed a short but brilliant **Renaissance era**. This saw not only the construction of a new residential palace alongside Holyrood Abbey, but also the granting of a royal charter to the College of Surgeons (the first of the city's long line of academic and professional bodies), and the establishment of the first printing press, which presaged an equally distinguished literary and publishing tradition.

This golden period came to an abrupt end in 1513 with the calamitous defeat of the Scots by the English at the **Battle of Flodden**, which led to several decades of political instability. Panicked by the prospect of the English army marching north from Flodden, the citizens of Edinburgh hurriedly began building a defensive wall around the town. The English didn't advance, however, and their barricade was only completed in 1560, but this "**Flodden Wall**" was to serve as the city boundary for the next two centuries, in which time the population rose from 10,000 to 30,000, so forcing the tenement houses higher and higher.

The reign of Mary, Queen of Scots

In 1542, the Scots suffered another punishing defeat at the hands of the English at the battle of **Solway Moss**. News of the defeat crushed the dying king, James V, and even the news of the birth of a daughter could not revive his spirit. He died on December 14, 1542, leaving his three-week-old daughter **Mary** as **Queen of Scots**. Quick to see an opportunity, King Henry VIII of England attempted to force a royal union (the so-called "Rough Wooing") by having his son Edward pledged in marriage to the infant Mary, which prompted the Scots to turn to France for help: French troops arrived to defend the city, while the young queen was despatched to Paris as the promised bride of the Dauphin.

Although the French occupiers succeeded in removing the English threat, they themselves antagonized the local citizenry, which had increasingly become sympathetic to the ideals of the **Reformation**. When the great preacher **John Knox** was allowed to return from exile in 1555, he became minister of Edinburgh's parish church, the High Kirk of St Giles, and quickly won the city over to his radical Calvinist message. A Protestant league, the Lords of the Congregation, appealed to Queen Elizabeth I of England for help, and in 1560, the French were driven out and Scotland proclaimed a Protestant nation.

The unions with England

Mary, Queen of Scots returned from France in 1561, but her fervent Catholicism was instrumental in dooming her reign to the status of a melodramatic interlude, and she was deposed in 1567 in favour of her son, **James VI**. His rule saw the foundation of the University of Edinburgh in 1582 – giving Scotland its fourth institution of higher learning, a total England didn't match until well into the nineteenth century. However, James's dynastic ambitions, resulting in his nomination as heir to the English throne, were to prove fateful for the city. Following the **Union of the Crowns** in 1603, when James succeeded Elizabeth to become James I of England, Edinburgh found itself totally upstaged by London: although the king promised to visit his northern capital every three years, it was not until 1617 that he made his one and only return trip.

Kings and Covenanters

In 1633, James I's son Charles I came to Edinburgh to be crowned, but soon afterwards precipitated a crisis by introducing episcopacy to the Church of Scotland, in the process making Edinburgh a bishopric for the first time in its history, with St Giles as its cathedral. This prompted a number of leading figures in Scotland to draw up a **National Covenant** in support of Presbyterianism. It was signed by thousands of townsfolk as well as important nobles in Greyfriars churchyard in 1638, and an **army** dedicated to upholding the Covenant was sent to fight on the royalist side in the English Civil War. Cromwell's army arrived in Edinburgh in 1650, laying waste to many buildings, including Holyroodhouse, the High School and Greyfriars. Following the **restoration of the monarchy**, the brother of Charles II, James, Duke of York, moved into the rebuilt Holyroodhouse, but when he succeeded to the English throne as James II of England (and James VII of Scotland), his overt Catholicism proved too much even for the Scots' loyalty to a Stewart monarch, and the English-nominated Dutch Protestant **William III** was reluctantly accepted as king north of the border as well as south, as James fled to France in 1689.

The Union of the Parliaments

Despite these vicissitudes, Edinburgh expanded throughout the seventeenth century, with a virtual tripling of its popu-

THE UNIONS WITH ENGLAND

lation to 57,000 and the capital proving itself an important catalyst for significant developments in many fields. In 1674, the Advocates' Library in Parliament Square was founded as a focal point for the legal profession, to be followed in 1681 by Lord Stair's *Institutions of the Law of Scotland*, a tome still regarded as the definitive bedrock of Scots law. In the same year the Royal College of Physicians was established in Edinburgh, while in 1695, William Paterson, who had founded the Bank of England the previous year, set up the Bank of Scotland, thus making the first major step in Edinburgh's development as an international financial centre.

However, the much-debated **Union of the Parliaments** of 1707 dealt a further blow to Edinburgh's political prestige, though the guaranteed preservation of the national church, the distinctive legal and educational systems, and the special status of the royal burghs, ensured that it was never relegated to a purely provincial role.

The Enlightenment

Paradoxical as it may seem following the internal struggles within Scotland and the loss of political power to London, it was in the second half of the eighteenth century that Edinburgh achieved the height of its influence, becoming a leading centre of the European **Enlightenment**. Internationally celebrated as, in the words of eighteenth-century novelist Tobias Smollett, "a hotbed of genius", Edinburgh was home to a host of intellectual luminaries, including the philosopher and historian David Hume, the scientist James Hutton (founder of modern geology), and Adam Smith, father figure of the new discipline of political economy. Inspired by the ideals of the Age of Reason, and under the leadership of dynamic Lord Provost, George Drummond, the city belatedly began to expand beyond its cramped medieval boundaries. Following a public competition, a plan by James Craig was accepted in 1766 as the basis for the laying out of a **New Town** on a gridiron plan to the north of Castle Ridge. The result, one of the masterpieces of the European Neoclassical style, was so successful that separate northern, western and eastern extensions were made in the early nineteenth century.

Edinburgh's lofty intellectual reputation was maintained until well into the new century, and the city's greatest artist, Sir Henry Raeburn, immortalized the features of most of its leading figures in a magnificent series of portraits. The dominant figure of the era's last phase was the novelist and poet **Sir Walter Scott**, whose influence is almost impossible to exaggerate: his highly individual, extremely romantic vision of Scotland and its history inspired many of the greatest European writers, artists and composers of the nineteenth century, and (for good or ill) became implanted on popular imagination throughout the world.

The expansion of the city

Nineteenth-century **industrialization** affected Edinburgh less than any other major city in the British Isles, and it never lost its predominantly professional character. The industries which took a hold, such as brewing, distilling, confectionery and glass manufacturing, caused relatively little damage to the environment, and even the railway lines were concealed by the city's topography. By the early part of the nineteenth century, though, Edinburgh had lost its longstanding position as Scotland's largest city to **Glasgow**, which mushroomed into one of the industrial strongholds of the British Empire. Ever since then an intense rivalry has characterized relations between these two geographically close and mutually dependent (yet quite different) cities. Edinburgh's status as capital was never threatened, though, and it became the automatic choice as headquarters for the national institutions which were founded in the course of the century.

The city underwent an enormous **urban expansion** in the second half of the nineteenth century. The old burghs of Canongate, Calton and Portsburgh were incorporated into Edinburgh in 1856; the seaside resort of Portobello was added forty years later, and various new residential suburbs sprang up. In the meantime, the Old Town, which had become notorious for its overcrowding and disease, was revitalized through the initiatives of the crusading conservationist and town planner, Patrick Geddes.

In 1920, the city boundaries were extended once again, reaching to Cramond in the west and the Pentland Hills in the south. Despite considerable local opposition, the port of Leith – which just over a century before had gained full municipal independence, and thereafter developed into one of Scotland's largest towns – was annexed as well. Another important development was the **administrative devolution** granted just before World War II, whereby the Scottish Office was established in Edinburgh, replacing several UK ministries in the day-to-day running of the nation's internal affairs.

The postwar city

Edinburgh came through the war unscathed, and received another major fillip in 1947 when it was chosen as the permanent home for the great **International Festival** of music and drama, which was established as a symbol of the new peaceful European order. Despite some hiccups, this has flourished ever since, in the process helping to make tourism one of the mainstays of the local economy. Originally set up as an adjunct to the main Festival, the **Fringe** now ranks as the world's largest arts event in its own right, and specialist festivals of cinema, literature and jazz, which run concurrently, have likewise become established annual fixtures.

Edinburgh has also been fortunate enough to escape the worst effects of the postwar **planning policies** which blighted so many British cities. There have been some unfortunate losses, notably much of George Square, which was torn down to make way for the tower blocks required by the fast-expanding University, and many fine shop fronts on the north side of Princes Street which were sacrificed to chain-store uniformity. By the 1990s, new construction was dominating many parts of the fringe of the city centre: over half-a-dozen huge but fairly uniform beige-and-glass office complexes have transformed the Lothian Road and Fountainbridge area on the western outskirts, while out towards the airport, a massive office and shopping park has been erected at the **Gyle**. The same period has, however, seen the erection of a number of prominent and architecturally significant public buildings such as the new **conference centre** to the west of the city centre and the impressive **National Museum of Scotland** on Chambers Street, a stylish but unquestionably contemporary addition to the Old Town. New buildings notwithstanding, the city centre's unique architectural and cultural heritage has been largely protected, something recognised in 1995 when the Old and New Towns were jointly declared a **UNESCO World Heritage Site**.

Elsewhere, **Leith**, whose seedy underworld was highlighted in the 1996 hit movie *Trainspotting*, has also been undergoing a rapid, if not always aesthetically successful, transformation. Alongside the conversion of old warehouses into yuppie flats, the old docklands have seen the construction of the vast Scottish Executive building and the Terence Conran-designed Ocean Terminal, as well as the arrival of the former Royal Yacht, *Britannia*, as a permanent tourist attraction.

Devolution and the new political order

A good deal of Edinburgh's development in recent decades has gone hand-in-hand with the transformation of the political scene. **Devolution**, whereby the activities of the Scottish Office would be subject to an elected assembly in Edinburgh, rose to prominence in the late 1970s as Scottish Nationalism established itself as a significant political force. Though it was quashed in a referendum in 1979, and implacably opposed by the Conservative government which took power in the same year, some form of home-rule for Scotland had become inevitable by the early 1990s, as the Tories' support in Scotland dwindled despite the fact that they kept winning election after election in England. In May 1997, the Labour Party swept to power and Tony Blair – who had attended Fettes College boarding school in Edinburgh – became Prime Minister; Edinburgh, along with the rest of Scotland, voted out its remaining Conservative MPs. In the **referendum** held in September of the same year, a large majority voted in favour of the government's proposal to establish a separate **Scottish Parliament** in Edinburgh.

Elections to this were held in May 1999, with Edinburgh voting in, among its representatives, David Steel, a former leader of the British Liberal Party who was subsequently chosen as Presiding Officer (or Speaker) of the Parliament, and Robin Harper, the first Green Party candidate to be elected to a national parliament in Britain. On July 1 of the same year, a day which saw crowds lining the streets of Edinburgh and fireworks bursting above the Castle after a night of city-centre parties, the Queen officially opened the Parliament, Scotland's first in nearly three hundred years. Once it got down to work, however, the assembly had a troubled beginning, losing one First Minister when respected statesman **Donald Dewar** died in 2000, and another a year later when his successor, **Henry McLeish**, stood down following a fairly minor financial irregularity. Now led by the comparatively youthful **Jack McConnell**, the Labour/Liberal Democrat coalition government has the task of promoting the benefits of devolution against criticism from both central government uncertain of the Scots' ability to implement policy effectively, and, on the other side, the Scottish Nationalists who argue that effective government can only be achieved by complete separation from England.

In its first term (fresh elections are due in 2003), the Parliament has created waves in a number of fields, notably education, care for the elderly and land and countryside reform, displaying an enthusiastic work ethic despite the barbs of many media commentators. However, the most prominent controversy has been over the **home** for the Parliament: initially it has met in the General Assembly Hall of the Church of Scotland, just off the Lawnmarket, while the construction of a purpose-built parliamentary chamber and offices takes place at **Holyrood** at the foot of the Royal Mile. Though interrupted by the death of both its champion, Donald Dewar, and its architect, Enric Miralles, and dogged by criticism that the cost of the project has spiralled from a misleading initial estimate of £30 million to over £250 million, the **new Parliament building** is still eagerly awaited, not simply for the importance it will have as the heart of political life in Scotland, but also in the anticipation that its design and presence will define the look and feel of Edinburgh at the start of the twenty-first century. In recent years, the city's profile has already been enhanced by the prominence of its **financial institutions**, including the Royal Bank of Scotland and the Bank of Scotland (now merged with the Halifax), two of the UK's most important high street banks, and its groundbreaking **scientific research**, headlined by the work of the Roslin

Institute, just to the south of the city, where the cloned sheep Dolly was born. Meanwhile, the presence of Scotland's decision-makers on the streets of the capital, together with the media attention they inevitably draw, the continued success of the Festival and the high profile being enjoyed by a number of actors, authors and politicians with Edinburgh connections, all combine to give the city a vitality and sense of importance it has arguably not seen since the days of Sir Walter Scott.

Film

I n spite of its photogenic qualities, surprisingly few **films** have been made entirely in Edinburgh. The city has been used more often to provide an elegant setting for isolated scenes: the Café Royal and Arthur's Seat were used in the Oscar-winning *Chariots of Fire*; the 1995 film *Jude* featured Parliament Square, used in place of the too-modern-looking Oxford; and the Royal Mile appeared in *Mary Reilly*, a disastrous 1996 version of Jekyll and Hyde starring John Malkovich and Julia Roberts. The huge success of *Trainspotting*, however, has led to a rack of Edinburgh-made films in recent years, including *Complicity*, based on an Iain Banks novel, and *The Acid House*, a rather less successful adaptation of another Irvine Welsh novel. The following are the pick of the movies with an Edinburgh setting.

Waverley Steps (John Eldridge, 1947). A hangover from World War II propaganda, this "Lets-all-get-on-together" documentary shows postwar life in the capital, social differences and all, through the eyes of a visiting Danish sailor.

Happy Go Lovely (Bruce Humberstone, 1950). Millionaire David Niven and chorus girl Vera Ellen get together during the Edinburgh Festival.

Battle of the Sexes (Charles Crichton, 1959). Ealing-style comedy, based on a short story by James Thurber, in which a mild-mannered Peter Sellers seeks to disrupt an efficiency drive at an Edinburgh tweed factory led by Constance Cummings.

Greyfriars Bobby (Don Chaffey, 1960). No prizes for guessing which American company, well-known for classic anthropomor-phic cartoons, made this ver-sion of Edinburgh's most senti-mental tale, previously filmed in 1949 as *Challenge to Lassie*. Although there were too many TV aerials in the environs of Greyfriars Kirk to allow filming, local actors were used, includ-ing Donald Crisp as the dog's owner and Andrew Cruickshank as the city's Lord Provost.

The Prime of Miss Jean Brodie (Ronald Neame, 1969). Maggie Smith won an Oscar for her portrayal of the eccentric teacher in this well-regarded version of Muriel Spark's classic tale of life in an Edinburgh girls' school.

My Childhood, My Ain Folk and My Way Home (Bill Douglas, 1972–78). Powerful, moving and unremittingly bleak

trilogy of films on growing up in the mining town of Newcraighall, on the eastern tip of the city. Sadly, Douglas died in 1991 never having filmed his screenplay of James Hogg's *Confessions of a Justified Sinner*.

Restless Natives (Michael Hoffman, 1985). Comic tale of a couple of young lads from an Edinburgh housing scheme who hold up American tourists and become celebrities.

Tickets to the Zoo (Brian Crumlish, 1994). A look at the problems caused by youth unemployment in the 1980s, set in Costorphine and Leith.

Shallow Grave (Danny Boyle, 1995). Three Edinburgh yuppies get lucky then squabble over the proceeds in a patchy film noir. The exciting opening sequence shows a car racing through the New Town.

Trainspotting (Danny Boyle, 1996). This hugely successful film version of Irvine Welsh's best-selling novel of Edinburgh lowlife kicks off with a great chase along Princes Street.

FILM

Complicity (Gavin Millar, 1999). A thriller based on one of the novels of South Queensferry's Iain Banks, starring Jonny Lee Miller as a journalist on an Edinburgh newspaper.

Women Talking Dirty (Coky Giedroyc, 2000). An under-achieving movie, set in Edinburgh suburbia, about two women who become fast friends over a bottle of vodka and detailed post-match analysis. Financially (and musically) backed by Elton John, it stars Helena Bonham Carter.

FILM

Books

Edinburgh is full of literary connections and landmarks. You'll quickly become aware of its two giants of literature, Robert Louis Stevenson and Sir Walter Scott, not least for the fact that the Gothic Scott Monument (see p.88), the largest memorial to a literary figure anywhere in the world, stands prominently in the centre of the city. In Lady Stair's House (see p.38), just off the Royal Mile, there's a museum dedicated to Scott, Stevenson and Robert Burns, a native of Ayrshire who spent plenty of time in Edinburgh. The more determined literary sleuth can uncover the grave of Thomas de Quincey (*Confessions of an English Opium Eater*), the convalescent home where Wilfred Owen collaborated with Siegfried Sassoon, or even the café (now a restaurant) where J.K. Rowling penned the first Harry Potter book. You can familiarize yourself with the works of – and the pubs frequented by – Scott, Stevenson and Burns on the Edinburgh Literary Pub Tour (see p.11), while Andrew Lownie's *Literary Companion to Edinburgh* (Methuen) takes a thorough look at the huge number of residents of and visitors to the city who have left their mark on literature.

Many of the **books** listed below are in print and in paperback – those that are out of print (o/p) should be easy to track down in secondhand bookshops. Publishers follow each title; first the UK publisher, then the US if applicable. Only one publisher is listed if the UK and US publishers are the same. Where books are published in only one of these countries, UK or US comes after the publisher's name, separated by semi-colon.

Classic Fiction

James Hogg, *Confessions of a Justified Sinner* (Penguin; Broadview). First published in 1824, this is a scary tale of the inner torments of the human psyche that's best seen as a penetrating critique of dour Scottish Calvinism. Much of the story is set in Edinburgh, including a memorable fight on the misty slopes of Arthur's Seat.

Eric Linklater, *Magnus Merriman* (Canongate). Vivid descriptions of Edinburgh landmarks in this humorous satire of the Scottish literary and political world of the 1930s.

Sir Walter Scott, *The Waverley Novels* (Penguin). The books that did much to create the romanticized version of Scottish life and history. The most famous of the novels, *Waverley*, the first in the series, includes some passages describing Edinburgh at the time of Bonnie Prince Charlie's uprising, but *The Heart of Midlothian* and *Guy Mannering* do a better job of recreating the capital known by Scott.

Muriel Spark, *The Prime of Miss Jean Brodie* (Penguin; Perennial Classics). One of the most famous Edinburgh novels of the twentieth century, superbly evoking the world of middle-class Edinburgh as inhabited by strict school-teacher Jean Brodie.

Robert Louis Stevenson, *The Scottish Stories and Essays* (Edinburgh University Press); *Dr Jekyll and Mr Hyde* (Penguin). The former Includes *The Misadventures of John Nicholson*, an entertaining account of an innocent's escapades, and the grisly tale of *The Body Snatchers*. Though

CLASSIC FICTION

nominally set in London, Stevenson's classic, and still resonant, horror story of *Jekyll and Hyde* is generally considered to be based on the author's misspent youth in the bowels of Edinburgh's Old Town. Longer novels with good descriptions of Edinburgh include *Catriona* (Harvill; Koenemann) and *Weir of Hermiston* (Penguin).

Contemporary Fiction

Iain Banks, *Complicity* (Abacus; Bantam). Typically lurid tale by Scotland's best contemporary author, dealing with a journalist on *The Caledonian* (a barely disguised *Scotsman*) caught up in paranoia and misdeeds. Also look out for *The Bridge* (Abacus; HarperPrism), centring on the Forth Rail Bridge and Banks' home town, South Queensferry. Essentially well-written thrillers, Banks' books are characterised by tense plots, complex characters and a dark, almost Gothic sense of place.

Pat Barker, *Regeneration* (Penguin; Plume). First part of the prize-winning trilogy based on the real-life meeting of Siegfried Sassoon and Wilfred Owen in Edinburgh's Craiglockhart Hospital, where the two try to come to terms with the horrors they have witnessed in the trenches.

Christopher Brookmyre, *Quite Ugly One Morning* (Abacus; Grove Atlantic). Cynical investigative journalist Jack Parlabane sorts out skulduggery in an Edinburgh NHS trust hospital – a hard-boiled post-Irvine Welsh novel that's a well-judged and readable mix of humour, politics and crime. Also successful is *Boiling a Frog* (Warner, UK), an enjoyable sex-and-crime page-turner set during the early days of the Scottish parliament.

Isla Dewar, *Women Talking Dirty* (Headline Review; Trafalgar Square). Two women – both recognizable Edinburgh stereotypes but unlikely friends – indulge in some gently amusing reflections on their lives, loves and relationships.

CONTEMPORARY FICTION

Laura Hird, *Born Free* (Canongate). From the Rebel Inc. group of writers from which Irvine Welsh first emerged, this impressive debut novel is a tale of a dysfunctional family living in a poor Edinburgh housing estate.

Paul Johnston, *Body Politic* (New English Library; St Martin's Press). Blues fanatic and private investigator Quentin Dalrymple handles a series of grisly murders in the brave new world of 2020 AD, when Edinburgh – the only stable city in the British Isles – exists largely to serve a massive tourist industry.

Ian Rankin, *Knots and Crosses*, *Hide and Seek* (both Orion; St Martin's Press). Rankin's jazz-loving copper John Rebus has developed into Britain's best-loved literary cop in recent years. The Rebus series, which includes the popular *Hanging Garden* (Orion; Minotaur) among many others, trawls through Edinburgh lowlife and can be intensely evocative of the city, albeit parts few tourists normally encounter. Recently filmed for TV starring John Hannah as Rebus.

James Robertson, *The Fanatic* (Fourth Estate, UK). An impressive debut novel which sees the leader of one of Edinburgh's popular ghost tours delve into the haunting and often disturbing complexities of Scotland's past.

Alan Warner, *The Sopranos* (Jonathan Cape; Harvest). Riotous account of the arrival of a group of girls from a convent school in the West Highlands for a choir competition in Edinburgh, and their determined efforts to find out what the big city has to offer in the way of sex, drugs, rock'n'roll and shopping.

Irvine Welsh, *Trainspotting* (Minerva; Heinemann). No-holds-barred account of 1990s Edinburgh lowlife; sordid and guttural. *Marabou Stork Nightmares* (Vintage; Norton) is similarly gross but has more of a plot. Of a mixed bag of more recent books, *Filth* (Vintage; W.W. Norton & Co) was the best received by the critics; with an Edinburgh policeman as its central character, it's typically amusing, disturbing and violent.

CONTEMPORARY FICTION

History and biography

Robert Chambers, *Traditions of Edinburgh 1824* (Chambers). Penned by a 20-year-old struggling bookseller who went on to establish a world-famous publishing house, this is an extraordinary collection of lively tales, many of which would today count as urban myths, about the Old Town streets and closes.

David Daiches, *Two Worlds* (Canongate; University of Alabama Press); *Edinburgh* (Constable; David & Charles). The first is a very dry account of growing up in Edinburgh in the 1920s as the son of the city's chief rabbi, but provides glimpses of a lost world with its own hybrid (and now long-vanished) Scottish Yiddish language. A single-volume history full of entertaining material, *Edinburgh* is especially strong on the city's literary history.

Jan Andrew Henderson, *The Town Below the Ground* (Mainstream). Fascinating exploration of the subterranean streets and closes beneath the Royal Mile, telling stories from the days when these cata-combs were inhabited, as well as the legends which perpetuate about entombed streets and ghostly encounters.

Charles McKean, *Edinburgh: Portrait of a City* (Century, o/p, UK). A short, elegantly written account of the city's history.

Eileen Miller, *The Edinburgh International Festival 1947–1996*. (Scolar Press). Dry account of the history of the Festival; includes cast lists for every major production over the period.

Sandy Mullay, *The Edinburgh Encyclopedia* (Mainstream). For the completist, this contains a huge amount of detail about every corner of Edinburgh's history, from the colours of school rugby shirts to listings of all the city's MPs.

Tim Niel and Allan Campbell (eds), *A Life in Pieces – Reflections on Alexander Trocchi* (Canongate; Rebel Inc). Biographical essays, interviews and stories about Edinburgh's controversial, drug-fuelled Beat writer of the 1960s.

Sir Walter Scott, *Journal* (Canongate). A hefty but incredibly eloquent and honest diary set mainly in Edinburgh and the Borders, covering the years from the height of the great novelist's success through to his debt- and illness-ridden final years.

Art and architecture

John Gifford, Colin McWilliam and David Walker, *The Buildings of Scotland: Edinburgh* (Penguin, UK). Scholarly architectural account of the city's buildings. Critical where necessary, but full of praise for the great monuments of the Old and New Towns.

Duncan Macmillan, *Scottish Art 1460–1990* (Mainstream). Authoritative and up-to-date guide through the history of Scottish art, with all the big names receiving due attention.

Charles McKean, *Edinburgh: An Illustrated Architectural Guide* (Scottish Academic Press, US). A beautifully produced, slim guide to Edinburgh's buildings, full of pertinent and judicious comments and quotations.

Robert Louis Stevenson, *Edinburgh: Picturesque Notes* (o/p, UK & US). This collection of beautifully crafted vignettes couched in hyper-refined prose is considered by most experts to be the finest book ever written about Edinburgh.

Michael and Elspeth Wills, *Walks in Edinburgh's New Town* (Mercat Press, UK). Handy pocket-sized book describing various jaunts around the New Town, with insightful detail on the buildings and the stories behind them. An equivalent volume describing Old Town walks is also available.

A.J. Youngson, *The Making of Classical Edinburgh* (Edinburgh University Press; Colorado University Press). Full account, with wonderful illustrations, of the creation of the New Town.

ART AND ARCHITECTURE

Food and drink

Stuart McHardy, *Edinburgh and Leith Pub Guide* (Luath Press). A lifetime's dedicated research has gone into this entertaining guide to over 200 Edinburgh pubs. Rating system awards between one and five "wee dugs" (Scots dogs) for overall atmosphere, hospitality and decent beer.

Ferrier Richardson, *Edinburgh on a Plate* (B&W Publishing, UK). Glossy food book containing favourite recipes from twenty or so of Edinburgh's smartest places to eat, along with interesting background on the chefs and their restaurants.

INDEX

O

P

Q

R

100 Essential CDs

Eight titles, one name

ROUGH GUIDES

around the world

in twenty years

also look out for our maps, phrasebooks, music guides and reference books

LIFE'S A BEACH...

There's a flipside to tourism

Concern

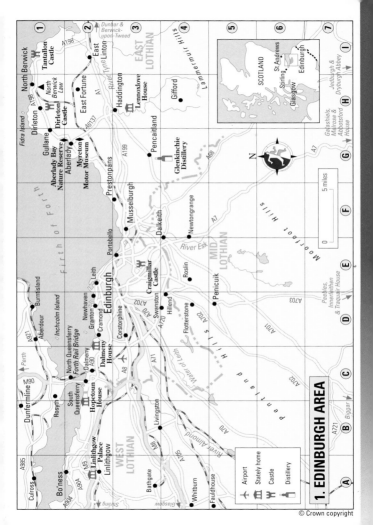

1. EDINBURGH AREA

© Crown copyright

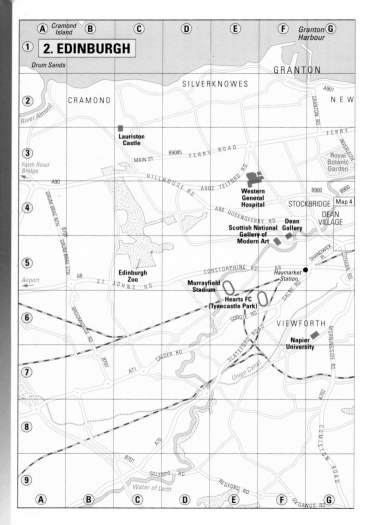

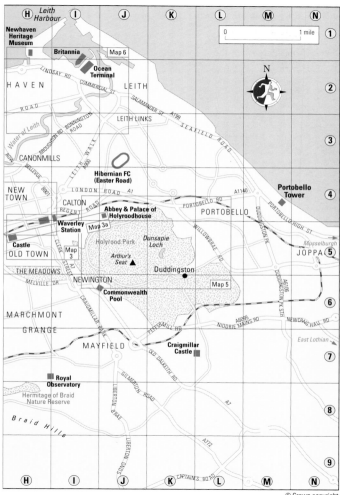

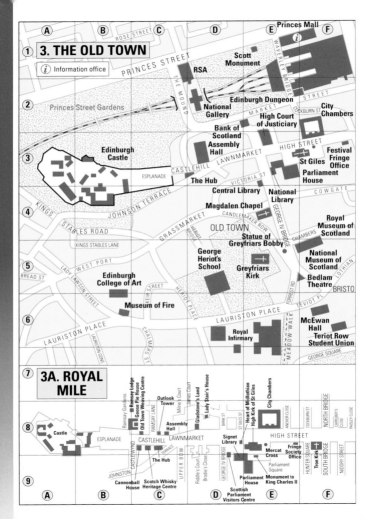

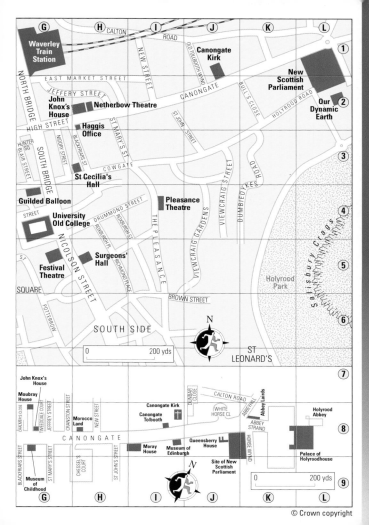

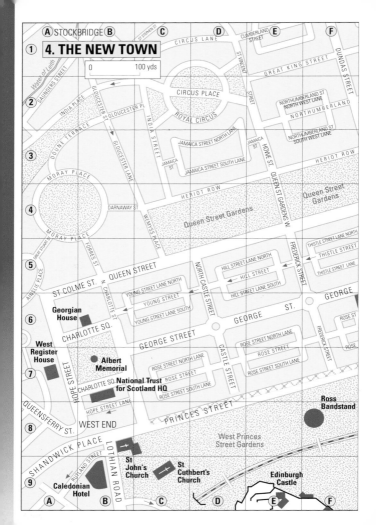

4. THE NEW TOWN

0   100 yds

Map labels:

ST STEPHEN'S CT
CIRCUS LANE
CUMBERLAND STREET
DUNDAS STREET
GREAT KING STREET
ST VINCENT ST
CIRCUS PLACE
ROYAL CIRCUS
NORTHUMBERLAND ST NORTH WEST LANE
NORTHUMBERLAND
NORTHUMBERLAND ST SOUTH WEST LANE
Water of Leith
SAUNDERS STREET
INDIA PLACE
GLOUCESTER STREET
GLOUCESTER PL
GLOUCESTER ST
GLOUCESTER LANE
INDIA STREET
JAMAICA STREET NORTH LANE
JAMAICA ST
JAMAICA STREET SOUTH LANE
JAMAICA ST
HOWE ST
HERIOT ROW
DOUNE TERRACE
MORAY PLACE
DARNAWAY ST
HERIOT ROW
QUEEN ST GARDENS W
Queen Street Gardens
Queen Street Gardens
MORAY PLACE
WEMYSS PLACE
FORRES ST
FREDERICK STREET
THISTLE STREET LANE NTH
THISTLE STREET
THISTLE STREET LANE
GREAT STUART ST
AINSLIE PLACE
ST COLME ST.
QUEEN STREET
N CHARLOTTE ST
YOUNG STREET LANE NORTH
YOUNG STREET
YOUNG STREET LANE SOUTH
NORTH CASTLE STREET
HILL STREET LANE NORTH
HILL STREET
HILL STREET LANE SOUTH
GEORGE ST.
GEORGE
ROSE ST
Georgian House
CHARLOTTE SQ.
GEORGE STREET
GEORGE STREET
CASTLE STREET
ROSE STREET NORTH LANE
ROSE STREET
ROSE STREET SOUTH LANE
FREDERICK STREET
ROSE ST
ROSE
West Register House
HOPE STREET
● **Albert Memorial**
National Trust for Scotland HQ
CHARLOTTE SQ
ROSE STREET NORTH LANE
ROSE STREET
ROSE STREET SOUTH LANE
QUEENSFERRY ST.
HOPE STREET LANE
PRINCES STREET
Ross Bandstand
WEST END
SHANDWICK PLACE
West Princes Street Gardens
St John's Church
St Cuthbert's Church
Edinburgh Castle
Caledonian Hotel
BUTLAND STREET
LOTHIAN ROAD

Grid references:

(A) (B) (C) (D) (E) (F)

1 2 3 4 5 6 7 8 9

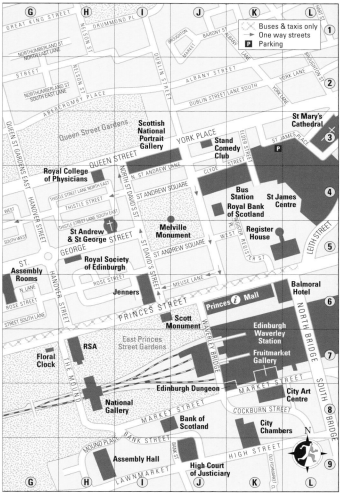

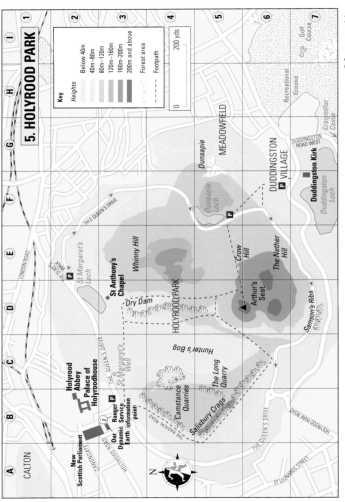

5. HOLYROOD PARK

Key

Heights
- Below 40m
- 40m–80m
- 80m–120m
- 120m–160m
- 160m–200m
- 200m and above

Forest area

Footpath

0   200 yds

CALTON

LONDON ROAD

New Scottish Parliament

Holyrood Abbey

Palace of Holyroodhouse

Ranger Service

Our Dynamic Earth

information point

CANONGATE

HOLYROOD ROAD

THE QUEEN'S DRIVE

St Margaret's Well

THE RADICAL ROAD

Camstance Quarries

Salisbury Crags

Hunter's Bog

The Long Quarry

Dry Dam

St Margaret's Loch

St Anthony's Chapel

THE DUKE'S WALK

Whinny Hill

HOLYROOD PARK

Arthur's Seat

Samson's Ribs

THE QUEEN'S DRIVE

ST LEONARDS STREET

HOLYROOD PARK ROAD

Dunsapie

Dunsapie Loch

MEADOWFIELD

Crow Hill

The Nether Hill

DUDDINGSTON VILLAGE

DUDDINGSTON ROAD WEST

Duddingston Kirk

Duddingston Loch

Craigmillar Castle

Recreational Ground

Golf Course

N

© Crown copyright

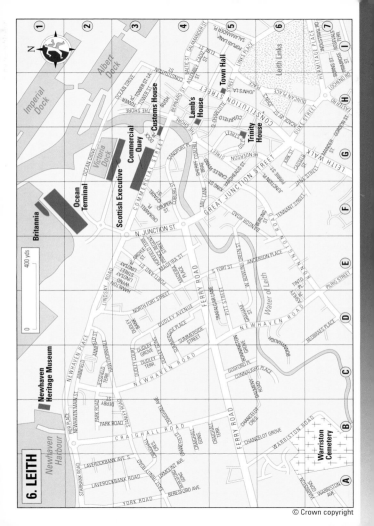

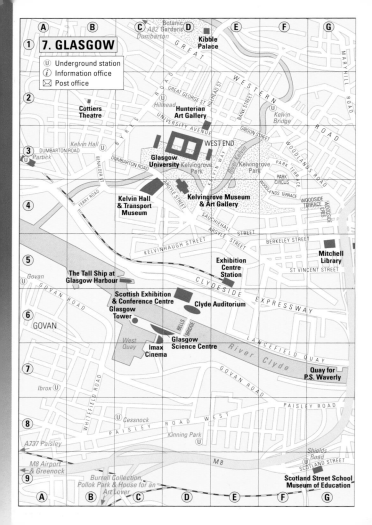

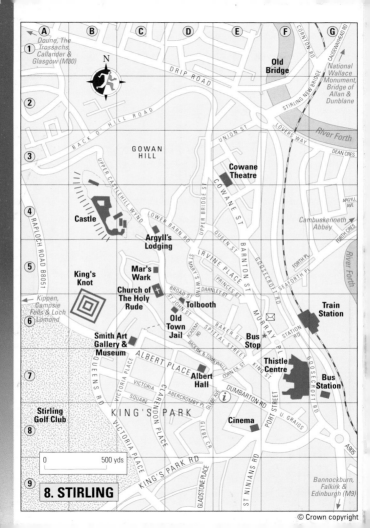

8. STIRLING

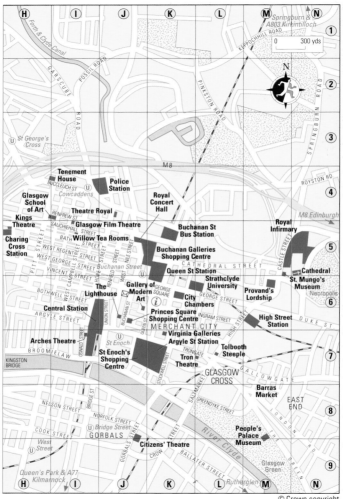

Springburn &
A803 Kirkintilloch

300 yds

N

M8

M8 Edinburgh

M8

Forth & Clyde Canal

GARSCUBE ROAD

POSSIL ROAD

RENFREW STREET

SAUCHIEHALL STREET

BATH STREET

WEST REGENT STREET

WEST GEORGE STREET

VINCENT STREET

BOTHWELL STREET

ARGYLE STREET

BROOMIELAW

KINGSTON BRIDGE

KEPPOCHHILL ROAD

PINKSTON ROAD

SPRINGBURN ROAD

ROYSTON RD

CATHEDRAL STREET

GEORGE STREET

INGRAM STREET

TRONGATE

GALLOWGATE

DUKE ST

RENFIELD STREET

HOPE STREET

BUCHANAN STREET

QUEEN STREET

St George's Cross

Tenement House

BUCCLEUCH ST

Cowcaddens

Police Station

Glasgow School of Art

Theatre Royal

Kings Theatre

Glasgow Film Theatre

Charing Cross Station

Willow Tea Rooms

Royal Concert Hall

Buchanan St Bus Station

Royal Infirmary

PITT STREET

WEST CAMPBELL STREET

UNION STREET

Buchanan Galleries Shopping Centre

Queen St Station

Strathclyde University

Provand's Lordship

CASTLE STREET

Cathedral

St. Mungo's Museum

Necropolis

The Lighthouse

Gallery of Modern Art

GEORGE SQUARE

City Chambers

Central Station

Princes Square Shopping Centre

MERCHANT CITY

HIGH STREET

High Street Station

Arches Theatre

St Enoch

St Enoch's Shopping Centre

Virginia Galleries

Argyle St Station

Tron Theatre

Tolbooth Steeple

GLASGOW CROSS

SALTMARKET

STOCKWELL STREET

Barras Market

EAST END

BRIDGE ST

St Enoch

OSWALD STREET

NELSON STREET

NORFOLK STREET

COOK STREET

West Street

Bridge Street

GORBALS

GORBALS ST

BRIDGE ST

Citizens' Theatre

CROWN STREET

River Clyde

GREENDYKE STREET

BALLATER STREET

People's Palace Museum

Glasgow Green

LONDON RD

THE

Queen's Park & A77 Kilmarnock

Rutherglen

© Crown copyright